'Elena Barabantseva's fascinating book changes the way we think about identity and politics in China. By examining how groups at the margins – overseas Chinese and ethnic minorities – are invoked in Beijing's nation-building and state-building policies, she shows how nationalism and modernization take shape in China. The book is important beyond Chinese studies: by treating nationalism, modernization, overseas Chinese and ethnic minorities as contingent concepts – rather than stable entities – it challenges the view that globalization undermines the nation-state by showing how subnational, national and transnational groups can also support each other in various ways.'

William A. Callahan,
Professor of International Politics and China Studies,
University of Manchester

'To anyone who wants to understand just what China is and is not as a nation, I would recommend turning first to Elena Barabantseva's *Overseas Chinese, Ethnic Minorities and Nationalism*. In clear language and with a fine feel for nuance, Barabantseva shows just how complex are the ideology and the policies of Chinese nationalism. Through examining the ways that successive regimes have tried to include the problematic peripheries of Chineseness – Han Chinese living outside China and non-Han living within China – Barabantseva gives us the clearest explanation yet of what the Chinese state would like people to think China is, and of the contradictions inherent in this view of the relationship between state, territory, race, and nation.'

Stevan Harrell,
Professor of Anthropology, University of Washington

'Chinese nationalism became such a potent political force during the last half century that the relative novelty of its construction is largely overlooked. The overseas Chinese and the country's other ethnic groups counter-intuitively play a central role in that process, as Elena Barabantseva demonstrates. A book that will be of interest to all those concerned with the impact of Chinese nationalism, as well as the dynamics of its construction.'

David S. G. Goodman,
Professor of Chinese Politics, University of Sydney

Overseas Chinese, Ethnic Minorities and Nationalism

Elena Barabantseva looks at the close relationship between state-led nationalism and modernisation, with specific reference to discourses on the overseas Chinese and minority nationalities.

The interplay between modernisation programmes and nationalist discourses has shaped China's national project, whose membership criteria have evolved historically. By looking specifically at the ascribed roles of China's ethnic minorities and overseas Chinese in successive state-led modernisation efforts, this book offers new perspectives on the changing boundaries of the Chinese nation. It places domestic nation-building and transnational identity politics in a single analytical framework, and examines how they interact to frame the national project of the Chinese state. By exploring the processes taking place at the ethnic and territorial margins of the Chinese nation-state, the author provides a new perspective on China's national modernisation project, clarifying the processes occurring across national boundaries and illustrating how China has negotiated the basis for belonging to its national project under the challenge to modernise amid both domestic and global transformations.

This book will be of interest to students and scholars of Asian politics, Chinese politics, nationalism, transnationalism and regionalism.

Elena Barabantseva is a Research Fellow and Lecturer in Chinese politics, University of Manchester, UK.

Asia's Transformations

Edited by Mark Selden, *Cornell University, USA*

The books in this series explore the political, social, economic and cultural consequences of Asia's transformations in the twentieth and twenty-first centuries. The series emphasizes the tumultuous interplay of local, national, regional and global forces as Asia bids to become the hub of the world economy. While focusing on the contemporary, it also looks back to analyse the antecedents of Asia's contested rise.

This series comprises several strands. Titles marked * are available in paperback.

Asia's Transformations
Titles include:

Debating Human Rights*
Critical essays from the United States and Asia
Edited by Peter Van Ness

Hong Kong's History*
State and society under colonial rule
Edited by Tak-Wing Ngo

Japan's Comfort Women*
Sexual slavery and prostitution during World War II and the US occupation
Yuki Tanaka

Opium, Empire and the Global Political Economy*
Carl A. Trocki

Chinese Society*
Change, conflict and resistance
Edited by Elizabeth J. Perry and Mark Selden

Mao's Children in the New China*
Voices from the Red Guard generation
Yarong Jiang and David Ashley

Remaking the Chinese State*
Strategies, society and security
Edited by Chien-min Chao and Bruce J. Dickson

Korean Society*
Civil society, democracy and the state
Edited by Charles K. Armstrong

The Making of Modern Korea*
Adrian Buzo

The Resurgence of East Asia*
500, 150 and 50 Year perspectives
Edited by Giovanni Arrighi, Takeshi Hamashita and Mark Selden

Chinese Society, second edition*
Change, conflict and resistance
Edited by Elizabeth J. Perry and Mark Selden

Ethnicity in Asia*
Edited by Colin Mackerras

The Battle for Asia*
From decolonization to globalization
Mark T. Berger

State and Society in 21st Century China*
Edited by Peter Hays Gries and Stanley Rosen

Japan's Quiet Transformation*
Social change and civil society in the 21st century
Jeff Kingston

Confronting the Bush Doctrine*
Critical views from the Asia-Pacific
Edited by Mel Gurtov and Peter Van Ness

China in War and Revolution, 1895–1949*
Peter Zarrow

The Future of US–Korean Relations*
The imbalance of power
Edited by John Feffer

Working in China*
Ethnographies of labor and workplace transformations
Edited by Ching Kwan Lee

Korean Society, second edition*
Civil society, democracy and the state
Edited by Charles K. Armstrong

Singapore*
The State and the Culture of Excess
Souchou Yao

Pan-Asianism in Modern Japanese History*
Colonialism, regionalism and borders
Edited by Sven Saaler and J. Victor Koschmann

The Making of Modern Korea, 2nd Edition*
Adrian Buzo

Re-writing Culture in Taiwan
Edited by Fang-long Shih, Stuart Thompson, and Paul-François Tremlett

Reclaiming Chinese Society*
The New Social Activism
Edited by You-tien Hsing and Ching Kwan Lee

Girl Reading Girl in Japan
Edited by Tomoko Aoyama and Barbara Hartley

Chinese Politics*
State, society and the market
Edited by Peter Hays Gries and Stanley Rosen

Chinese Society, third edition*
Change, conflict and resistance
Edited by Elizabeth J. Perry and Mark Selden

Mapping Modernity in Shanghai
Space, gender, and visual culture in the Sojourners' City, 1853–98
Samuel Y. Liang

Minorities and Multiculturalism in Japanese Education
An interactive perspective
Edited by Ryoko Tsuneyoshi, Kaori H. Okano and Sarane Boocock

Japan's Wartime Medical Atrocities
Comparative inquiries in science, history, and ethics
Edited by Jing-Bao Nie, Nanyan Guo, Mark Selden and Arthur Kleinman

State and Society in Modern Rangoon
Donald M. Seekins

Asia's Great Cities

Each volume aims to capture the heartbeat of the contemporary city from multiple perspectives emblematic of the authors own deep familiarity with the distinctive faces of the city, its history, society, culture, politics and economics, and its evolving position in national, regional and global frameworks. While most volumes emphasize urban developments since the Second World War, some pay close attention to the legacy of the longue durée in shaping the contemporary Thematic and comparative volumes address such themes as urbanization, economic and financial linkages, architecture and space, wealth and power, gendered relationships, planning and anarchy, and ethnographies in national and regional perspective. Titles include:

Bangkok*
Place, practice and representation
Marc Askew

Representing Calcutta*
Modernity, nationalism and the colonial uncanny
Swati Chattopadhyay

Singapore*
Wealth, power and the culture of control
Carl A. Trocki

The City in South Asia
James Heitzman

Global Shanghai, 1850–2010*
A history in fragments
Jeffrey N. Wasserstrom

Hong Kong*
Becoming a global city
Stephen Chiu and Tai-Lok Lui

Asia.com

This series focuses on the ways in which new information and communication technologies are influencing politics, society and culture in Asia. Titles include:

Japanese Cybercultures*
Edited by Mark McLelland and Nanette Gottlieb

Asia.com*
Asia encounters the Internet
Edited by K. C. Ho, Randolph Kluver and Kenneth C. C. Yang

The Internet in Indonesia's New Democracy*
David T. Hill and Krishna Sen

Chinese Cyberspaces*
Technological changes and political effects
Edited by Jens Damm and Simona Thomas

Mobile Media in the Asia-Pacific
Gender and the art of being mobile
Larissa Hjorth

Literature and Society

Literature and Society is a series that seeks to demonstrate the ways in which Asian Literature is influenced by the politics, society and culture in which it is produced. Titles include:

The Body in Postwar Japanese Fiction
Douglas N. Slaymaker

Chinese Women Writers and the Feminist Imagination, 1905–1948*
Haiping Yan

Routledge Studies in Asia's Transformations

Routledge Studies in Asia's Transformations is a forum for innovative new research intended for a high-level specialist readership. Titles include:

The American Occupation of Japan and Okinawa*
Literature and memory
Michael Molasky

Koreans in Japan*
Critical voices from the margin
Edited by Sonia Ryang

Internationalizing the Pacific
The United States, Japan and the Institute of Pacific Relations in war and peace, 1919–1945
Tomoko Akami

Imperialism in South East Asia*
'A fleeting, passing phase'
Nicholas Tarling

Chinese Media, Global Contexts*
Edited by Chin-Chuan Lee

Remaking Citizenship in Hong Kong*
Community, nation and the global city
Edited by Agnes S. Ku and Ngai Pun

Japanese Industrial Governance
Protectionism and the licensing state
Yul Sohn

Developmental Dilemmas*
Land reform and institutional change in China
Edited by Peter Ho

Genders, Transgenders and Sexualities in Japan*
Edited by Mark McLelland and Romit Dasgupta

Fertility, Family Planning and Population Policy in China*
Edited by Dudley L. Poston, Che-Fu Lee, Chiung-Fang Chang, Sherry L. McKibben and Carol S. Walther

Japanese Diasporas*
Unsung pasts, conflicting presents and uncertain futures
Edited by Nobuko Adachi

How China Works*
Perspectives on the twentieth-century industrial workplace
Edited by Jacob Eyferth

Remolding and Resistance among Writers of the Chinese Prison Camp
Disciplined and published
Edited by Philip F. Williams and Yenna Wu

Popular Culture, Globalization and Japan*
Edited by Matthew Allen and Rumi Sakamoto

medi@sia*
Global media/tion in and out of context
Edited by Todd Joseph Miles Holden and Timothy J. Scrase

Vientiane
Transformations of a Lao landscape
Marc Askew, William S. Logan and Colin Long

State Formation and Radical Democracy in India
Manali Desai

Democracy in Occupied Japan
The U.S. occupation and Japanese politics and society
Edited by Mark E. Caprio and Yoneyuki Sugita

Globalization, Culture and Society in Laos
Boike Rehbein

Transcultural Japan*
At the borderlands of race, gender, and identity
Edited by David Blake Willis and Stephen Murphy-Shigematsu

Post-Conflict Heritage, Post-Colonial Tourism
Culture, politics and development at Angkor
Tim Winter

Education and Reform in China*
Emily Hannum and Albert Park

Writing Okinawa: Narrative Acts of Identity and Resistance
Davinder L. Bhowmik

Maid in China
Media, mobility, and a new semiotic of power
Wanning Sun

Northern Territories, Asia-Pacific Regional Conflicts and the Åland Experience
Untying the Kurillian knot
Edited by Kimie Hara and Geoffrey Jukes

Reconciling Indonesia
Grassroots agency for peace
Birgit Bräuchler

Singapore in the Malay World
Building and breaching regional bridges
Lily Zubaidah Rahim

Pirate Modernity
Delhi's media urbanism
Ravi Sundaram

The World Bank and the post-Washington Consensus in Vietnam and Indonesia
Inheritance of loss
Susan Engel

China on Video
Smaller screen realities
Paola Voci

Critical Asian Scholarship

Critical Asian Scholarship is a series intended to showcase the most important individual contributions to scholarship in Asian Studies. Each of the volumes presents a leading Asian scholar addressing themes that are central to his or her most significant and lasting contribution to Asian studies. The series is committed to the rich variety of research and writing on Asia, and is not restricted to any particular discipline, theoretical approach or geographical expertise.

Southeast Asia*
A testament
George McT. Kahin

Women and the Family in Chinese History*
Patricia Buckley Ebrey

China Unbound*
Evolving perspectives on the Chinese past
Paul A. Cohen

China's Past, China's Future*
Energy, food, environment
Vaclav Smil

The Chinese State in Ming Society*
Timothy Brook

China, East Asia and the Global Economy*
Regional and historical perspectives
Takeshi Hamashita
Edited by Mark Selden and Linda Grove

The Global and Regional in China's Nation-Formation*
Prasenjit Duara

Overseas Chinese, Ethnic Minorities and Nationalism
De-centering China

Elena Barabantseva

LONDON AND NEW YORK

First published 2011
by Routledge
2 Park Square, Milton Park, Abingdon, Oxfordshire OX14 4RN

Simultaneously published in the USA and Canada
by Routledge
711 Third Avenue, New York, NY 10017, USA

First issued in paperback 2014

Routledge is an imprint of the Taylor & Francis Group, an informa business

© 2011 Elena Barabantseva

The right of Elena Barabantseva to be identified as author of this work has been asserted by her in accordance with sections 77 and 78 of the Copyright, Designs and Patents Act 1988.

Typeset in Times New Roman by
Book Now Ltd, London

All rights reserved. No part of this book may be reprinted or reproduced or utilised in any form or by any electronic, mechanical, or other means, now known or hereafter invented, including photocopying and recording, or in any information storage or retrieval system, without permission in writing from the publishers.

British Library Cataloguing in Publication Data
A catalogue record for this book is available from the British Library

Library of Congress Cataloging in Publication Data
Barabantseva, Elena.
Overseas Chinese, ethnic minorities, and nationalism: de-centering China / Elena Barabantseva.
 p. cm.
Includes bibliographical references and index.
1. Minorities—China. 2. Nationalism—China. 3. Chinese—Foreign countries—Politics and government. 4. Nation-building—China. 5. China—Ethnic relations—Political aspects. 6. China—Politics and government—2002– 7. Transnationalism—Case studies. I. Title.
JQ1506.M5B37 2010
320.540951—dc22 2010006919

ISBN 13: 978-0-415-57950-6 (hbk)
ISBN 13: 978-0-415-85504-4 (pbk)

Contents

List of illustrations xv
Acknowledgements xvii
List of abbreviations xix

Introduction   1

1   Overseas Chinese and ethnic minorities in imperial and Republican China   18

2   Overseas Chinese and minority nationalities in socialist nation-building   39

3   Post-socialist modernisation and China's national outlook   64

4   Ethnic minorities and overseas Chinese in the post-socialist modernisation discourse   88

5   Transnationalising Chineseness: 'overseas Chinese work' in the reform period   108

6   The politics of localisation: ethnic minorities in post-socialist modernisation   138

Conclusion   160

Notes 168
Bibliography 181
Index 200

Illustrations

Figures

3.1	Yangtze River model	76
3.2	Peace Dove strategy of China's international modernisation	84
6.1	Regional divisions of the People's Republic of China	151

Tables

5.1	Overseas Chinese law and documents	112
5.2	Overseas Chinese remittances to the PRC, 1982–99	115
5.3	Overseas Chinese foreign direct investments in China, 1979–2000	116
6.1	Han and minority populations in the western region, 2000	154
6.2	GDP in central and western provinces, 1999 and 2002	156

Acknowledgements

This book evolved from the PhD thesis which I started at the University of Manchester in the early 2000s. Throughout its lifetime, this research project has benefited from many people who I met in Manchester and beyond.

My first word of gratitude goes to Peter Lawler who agreed to supervise my PhD project and assisted with funding applications. Peter showed great interest in the subject, which is not his area of specialty, and expressed a comforting confidence in the project. I am also grateful to my co-supervisor Susanne Brandstädter for her attentive supervision and words of encouragement.

This book would not have materialised from the PhD thesis without the involvement of two people. I am grateful to my mentor at Manchester, William A. Callahan, for breaking the institutional barriers and existing hierarchies, and becoming a good friend. His advice and support were indispensable for bringing this book project to fruition. I cannot thank Mark Selden enough for his generosity and passion for scholarship, as well as for his attention to detail and meticulous editing.

I am deeply indebted to David Goodman, Frank Pieke, Pál Nyíri, Jim Seymour, Outi Luova, Gunter Schubert, and Shogo Suzuki who all, at different stages, expressed interest in my research and spent their time reading parts of the manuscript. Their insightful comments and criticisms have been extremely useful. Tom Fenton and Tom Wells, two editors who I happened to work with during this project, contributed greatly to making the manuscript read better.

My thanks also go to the funding bodies without whose financial support this project could neither have been started, nor accomplished. I am thankful to the Faculty of Social Science and the Overseas Scholarship Scheme of the University of Manchester for paying the tuition fees, and to the Hulme Hall Trust, which not only gave me an opportunity to find a shelter in the friendly environment of Hulme Hall for three years but also supported me on my two trips to China. I am grateful to the Vice-Chancellor's Fund of the University of Manchester for their generous support on my first trip to China. I would also like to thank the following organizations and funding bodies for sponsoring my contributions to different conferences at national and international levels: the China Universities Committee in London, the British International Studies Association, the Chester Fund, the British Association of Chinese Studies, the Economic and Social Research

Council, and the Universities' Service Centre for China Studies at the Chinese University of Hong Kong.

I would like to thank those who helped me oganise and carry out my fieldwork in China, especially my fellow PhD student at Manchester Wu Guofu, for helping me to make contacts in China and for giving the most useful guidance on doing fieldwork there. I would like to thank Wang Jianmin and Zhang Haiyang of the Central University of Nationalities, and Li Anshan of Beijing University for helping me to arrange interviews.

The circle of my friends worldwide abounds. They all provided me with great support through their friendship. Even when we have not been in touch for months or even years, there is always a strong sense of their support present. The list is far too long to be included here, but I hope you all know who you are.

My deepest debt of gratitude is reserved for my family in Belarus, Canada, and Spain. They were first forced to engage in the PhD process and then manuscript writing – despite their geographical distance – and stoically provided their emotional support throughout.

Parts of the book have been published as journal articles. I thank the journals for giving their permission to reproduce earlier arguments in this book. Parts of Chapter 3 appeared in 'From the Language of Class to the Rhetoric of Development: Discourse of "Nationality" and "Ethnicity" in China', *Journal of Contemporary China* 17(56): 565–589. Chapter 5 is a revised and updated version of 'Trans-nationalising Chineseness: Overseas Chinese Policies of the PRC's Central Government', *ASIEN* 96 (July 2005): 7–28. The argument presented in Chapter 6 is revised from 'Development as Localization: Ethnic Minorities in China's Official Discourse on the Western Development Project', *Critical Asian Studies* 41(2), 2009: 225–254.

Most of all I would like to thank Eduardo and Sofia for entering my life at the speed of light, and making it so much more fulfilling and complete.

Abbreviations

ACFROC	All-China's Federation of Returned Overseas Chinese
CCP	Chinese Communist Party
CCTV	China Central Television
CPPCC	Chinese People's Political Consultative Conference
FBIS	Foreign Broadcast Information Service
FDI	Foreign direct investments
GMD	Guomindang
LRNA	Law on Regional and National Autonomy
NAC	Nationalities Affairs Commission
NPC	National People's Congress
NPCOCC	Overseas Chinese Commission of the National People's Congress
OCAC	Overseas Chinese Affairs Commission
OCAO	Overseas Chinese Affairs Office
PLA	People's Liberation Army
PRC	People's Republic of China
SC	State Council
UFWD	United Front Work Department
WDP	Western Development Project

Introduction

'But there is no relation between the overseas Chinese and ethnic minorities! They are so different and distant. So, what's the point of examining their roles in China's national project?' This was one of the most common responses I confronted during my field research in China. The lack of an apparent link between overseas Chinese and ethnic minorities seemed to baffle my interlocutors.

But analysing the margins of a concept can provide valuable insight into how it is constituted. Geographers, historians and anthropologists have long observed the importance of analysing frontiers and borders for gaining a better understanding of how geographical space and communities are constructed. In political science, which is preoccupied with the study of ideologies, political institutions, political processes and political concepts, it is less common to place peripheries and margins at the centre of one's analysis of a concept. Yet margins and the marginalised often become the centre of social movements and, under certain circumstances, they can become the center of scholarly discourse. They not only have the capacity to draw attention to themselves, but also reveal the complexities and problems at the core of major political concepts, such as the nation and nation-state.

Two intertwined events of March–April 2008 that were played out on the global stage brought key marginal groups to international attention. Tibetan uprisings across the Tibetan areas of China, and then abroad, sparked heated discussions and public outcry around the world over PRC interactions with ethnic minority cultures. Overseas Chinese students abroad – a growing body of young Chinese who are one of the targets of the Chinese state's overseas Chinese work (*qiaowu gongzuo*) – protested the anti-Chinese sentiments that they discerned in Western media coverage of the Tibetan events. Both Tibetans and overseas Chinese became subjects of media attention and worldwide public discussion of growing Chinese nationalism and the position of ethnic minorities in Chinese society. While many in the Western world sympathised with the Tibetans' plight and criticised the government for oppressing minority populations, Chinese students abroad organised protests on university campuses and the Internet was abuzz with criticisms of the 'biases' of the Western media's coverage of the Tibetan riots. They accused Western media of propagating the cultural superiority of the West and looking down on China, its achievements and its government.

They particularly criticised the 'bigotry' of the Western media's coverage of the Tibetan riots, which many overseas Chinese students argued were organised by groups of Tibetan 'hooligans' and 'vandals' who primarily targeted the Han populations of Tibetan areas. Chinese students overseas produced numerous YouTube videos and leaflets stressing positive transformations that had taken place in Tibet since its incorporation in the People's Republic in the 1950s. The overseas Chinese students' main message was that the Tibetan rioters were ungrateful for the improvements that the Chinese government had brought to the region since its liberation and were acting under the influence of the Dalai Lamas' clique. They argued that Tibet had always been part of China and that most Tibetans welcomed the transformations which had taken place under Chinese rule.[1] The overseas Chinese students' backing of CCP-led transformations in China grew to such an extent that even a Chinese Internet blogger who called on his compatriots to rethink their relationships with the West and ethnic minorities as well as their brand of nationalism was accused of betraying China.[2]

The events brought the overseas Chinese students and Tibetans, who are an officially designated ethnic minority (*shaoshu minzu*), to the centre of public discussions on what constitutes the Chinese nation. The debates on the status of ethnic minorities in China and the overseas Chinese students revolved around the following issues: What do these groups have to do with the Chinese nation as celebrated by the Party-state? What in the formulation of the Chinese nation unites the diverse groups of Chinese around the world to support the Chinese nation led by the CCP? Why might some representatives of ethnic minorities who have enjoyed improvements in the quality of their material lives express dissatisfaction with government policies? And what is it about the Chinese nation that leads overseas Chinese students to feel embraced by it, while at least some Tibetans feel alienated? This book attempts to answer these questions and others about ethnic minorities in China and overseas Chinese. It examines how these two diverse social groups have been constructed and how they have related to China's pursuit of nationhood since the late nineteenth century. These elusive and contested constructs have both taken prominent, although seemingly marginal, positions in formulations of the Chinese nation and make it possible to conceptualise the nation-shaping dynamics at its conceptual margins. The book explores how the different ideological and political agendas of national survival, anti-imperialism, class struggle, and market socialism – unified by the twin goals of modernisation and prosperity – have reoriented the approach of the Chinese nation towards ethnic minorities and overseas Chinese. By examining changes in the official discourse and policies towards these two groups, who in territorial and ethnic terms are loosely linked to the construct of the Chinese nation-state, along with changes in their statuses, we can gain important insights into the twists and turns of the Chinese nation-crafting. For example, we can see how the Chinese state adjusts internal territorial and ethnic boundaries in response to particular demands, and how state sovereignty takes different, seemingly conflicting, forms. We can also trace domestic transformations in China brought about by historical processes that shape China's articulation of the basis for belonging to its national project.

China's historical, cultural, and geo-political borders have recently become a subject of rigorous scholarly investigation (Tu 1991; Harrell 1995a; Blum and Jensen 2002; Rossabi 2004; Crossley et al. 2006; Larry 2007). The majority of these studies focus on either geographical borders of China or the cultural frontiers of Chinese identity. Studies on China's geographical limits illuminate the historical and contemporary interactions between the centre and its geographical peripheries where the latter are sometimes divided into inner periphery (Tibet, Xinjiang and Mongolia) and outer periphery (Taiwan, Macao and Hong Kong) (Potter 2007). The majority of China periphery studies look to present 'disaggregated views' of China (Blum and Jensen 2003: 3), to undermine the superiority of China's 'eternal civilising centre' (Woodside 2007) or to argue that geographical and conceptual China exists 'at the centre of concentric borderlands' (Potter 2007: 241). Examinations of the varieties of Chinese identities have taken shape in response or in opposition to the terms 'Greater China' or 'Cultural China' coined by Tu Weiming (Tu 1991; Ong 1999; Louie 2004; Zhang W. 2005) and the notions of Chineseness and overseas Chinese popularised by Wang Gungwu (1991a, 1991b). Notably, studies on China's borderlands rarely take into account factors of Cultural China, such as those framed with an eye to the overseas Chinese, while studies on Chinese identities and Greater China largely exclude ethnic minorities from their analyses. There are two exceptions. One is an article by David Wu (1991), who researched the formation of Chinese identities among overseas Chinese in New Guinea and the Bai ethnic minority in the PRC from the point of view of their absorption and negotiation of Chinese attributes. His essay mainly questions the essence of Chinese cultural rather than political identity. Another is Stevan Harrell's chapter on two types of periphery inclusion in Chinese nationalism (Harrell 1999). By 'periphery', Harrell refers to China's ethnic minorities who live within the borders of China and to those people who culturally and genealogically see themselves or are seen as part of China's majority group, the Han, and live outside China on the territories to which the Chinese government makes sovereign claims (Taiwan). In Harrell's analysis Chinese government claims to territory are integral to its policies toward people on the periphery. In contrast, in this book I de-emphasise the primacy of official Beijing's territorial claims and stress its policies towards particular kinds of populations. I look at how the Chinese nation is constructed through the discourses and processes at its conceptual and territorial margins, and how the state-led discourses and practices aimed at ethnic minorities and overseas Chinese shape the core of the Chinese nation.

While marginality can be understood in many ways, I use this term to denote the ambiguous positions of overseas Chinese and ethnic minorities in China's national modernisation project. Overseas Chinese (*huaqiao huaren*) and ethnic minorities (*shaoshu minzu*) are found on the territorial or ethno-cultural edges of what is often assumed to be the Chinese nation. Marginality refers to their statuses as simultaneously insiders and outsiders of the Chinese national project. Although their level of importance to national project has varied through the historical period covered in this book – the late 1890s through to the early 2000s – the state's policies towards these groups have always been articulated to reflect the groups' positions relative to the core of the nation, as well as their extraterritoriality and ethnicity. Analysis of the shifting positions of these groups in China's modernisation efforts illuminates how the state has embraced or withstood historical processes and interpreted its relationship with ethnicity and territoriality in an attempt to preserve and enhance its position both nationally and transnationally.

The book also examines how China has negotiated the basis for national belonging under the challenge to modernise amid both domestic and global transformations. And it highlights how the lines of inclusion and exclusion in the national project have been redrawn by policies designed to attain particular national goals. These policies raise questions about the roles of territoriality and ethnicity in the nation-state's organisation, and how membership in the Chinese national project is defined. At a more general theoretical level, examining the positions of overseas Chinese and ethnic minorities in the sequence of national modernisation efforts provides a new perspective on the contested nature of a nation-state.

Modernisation and nationalism

The book analyses China's relationship with the overseas Chinese and ethnic minorities through the lenses of the dominant Chinese modernisation discourses and practices. Modernisation has been an ongoing goal of the Chinese leadership ever since the word entered the Chinese political vocabulary in the mid-nineteenth century. The nation-salvation projects have been accompanied by a modernising agenda aimed at creating a stronger and independent Chinese state. This preoccupation with the formation of China as a strong and independent state has been a constant component of Chinese state-formulated nationalism. Realisation of this national goal pursued by the Chinese leadership has been informed and guided by a particular vision of China's future and ways of attaining it.

Chinese discourses of modernisation and nationalism deal with articulating and representing the nation and modernity. Modernisation criteria provide powerful yardsticks for perceiving ranking China's citizenry. Nationalism serves as a potent discourse for mobilising people on the grounds of ethnicity, race, religion or language in the name of a common national destiny Nationalism and modernisation are mutually constitutive because, in the context of the official Chinese discourses on modernisation and the Chinese nation, they create parallel linear narratives of the nation. The discourse on the Chinese nation is located in history and looks towards the future of China's development, while the narrative of modernisation presents the present development from the point of view of goals that are set to be attained by a certain period in the future. The future of the Chinese nation is premised on the successful accomplishment of the modernisation process. In other words, modernisation determines the path of national development from the perspective of its goals. The language of modernisation also often serves as legitimising rhetoric, as all transformations are undertaken for the purpose of achieving a strong and modernised Chinese nation. The official discourse on modernisation produces a particular knowledge of what constitutes a modern nation, and designates how the dominant formulation of the Chinese nation is produced, delimiting its contours. This is not to say that the Chinese official formulations of modernisation goals and the mechanisms of attaining them remain constant. In recent years, there has been a dramatic shift from revolutionary modernisation to market-driven modernisation policies in China. Just as the boundaries of the Chinese nation shift, so do the conceptions of modernisation.

This book emphasises the close relationship between state-led nationalism and the idea of modernisation, and describes how this relationship shapes China's national project. I show how the interplay between modernisation and nationalist discourses has influenced the nature of participation in China's national project and the ways the criteria for membership in this project have historically evolved. By looking specifically at the ascribed roles of ethnic minorities and overseas Chinese in the sequence of state-led modernisation projects, I also show how the boundaries of the Chinese nation have been shifting. The analysis underscores the importance of discursive practices in the construction of the Chinese nation. I emphasise that by examining the state policies aimed at the production of a modernised and ideologically coherent Chinese nation, along with the discourses informing and underlying these practices, one can attain greater insight into the reformulation of the Chinese nation. The desire to build a strong state and a prosperous society as the ultimate goal, to overcome the legacies of imperialism and invasion, and to resolve the dilemmas of modernisation have all been underlying themes of state-led nationalism in China. The goal was pursued through different political solutions – racially informed nationalism, anti-imperialism, class struggle and a socialist market economy – in response to divergent historical contexts. This book emphasises how Chinese state-formulated discourse has reacted and adapted to both global changes and domestic challenges in an attempt to build a modern Chinese nation. Simply put, I treat the socio-cultural discourses and practices of modernisation as nation-shaping, with impact extending beyond China's borders to the region and the world.

Beyond territoriality: the nation-state and population

Traditionally, nationalism is understood as a feeling of being bound to the territorial confines of a nation-state and is directed at establishing a categorical construction of the 'people'; it is used to distinguish between the members and outsiders of a political community. The dominant approaches to nationalism treat it as a discursive or policy-oriented tool of the territorial state or as the practices and discourses of a political movement entertaining the goal of achieving statehood. Most of the modernist and primordialist literature stipulates that common territory is a crucial marker of a people's unity and group identity, and that it contributes to a perception of a group as something naturally bounded by shared beliefs and myths and a common destiny (Anderson 1991: 2; Hastings 1997: 3). This literature stresses that common territory promotes a sense of group distinctiveness and separateness and draws a defined inner/outer borderline between the members of the political community and outsiders. This argument raises crucial questions about the nature of nationality and citizenship, exclusion and inclusion, and the ends of the nation-state. The literature emphasises that territorial boundaries are a primary condition for the formulation of the identity of a nation-state (Anderson 1991: 19; Hastings 1997: 30; Guibernau 1996: 47). Grosby (1995: 155), a prominent advocate of the archaic origins of nations, boldly proclaims that territoriality is a feature of all societies, modern and ancient.

While the role of territory in nationalist discourses has always been and remains important in shaping the outlook of a particular national project pursued by a state or a community aspiring to statehood, the nonterritorial aspects of discourse also influence the national project at certain points in history. The scope and content of a national project, as well as the status of those who are incorporated in it, cannot be restricted by the territorial limits within which it is pursued. Whereas territorial components play a fundamental role in how a national project is formulated at one point in history, other aspects take precedence at other points. Many scholarly writings in recent years point to the multifarious character of nationalism, which can be subnational, national, as well as transnational (Ben-Ami 2000; Maybury-Lewis 1997; Meyer and Geschiere 1999; Guibernau 1996). The distinctions drawn between different types of nationalism suggest that the role of territory, whether acquired or sought land, and the attributes associated with it, are often presumed. That is even truer when the focus is on established nation-states, which are organised around the idea of territoriality. But to appreciate the complex and often contradictory character of a national project, it is not sufficient to take into account only the territorially-based components. It is important to explore not only how these components are employed to achieve particular goals, but how in a particular historical context they intersect with nonterritorial factors, such as class, gender or ethnicity, to shape a national project. While the nation-state is actively engaged in formulating policies that draw the lines of inclusion and exclusion, the role of territoriality (and cultural factors associated with it) in erecting these lines is more ambiguous, with diferent meanings at different points in history. At the same time, nonterritorial factors take precedence in delimiting the outlook of the nation as conceived and implemented by the state elite. With the expanding process of globalisation affecting the economic, social and political dimensions of life, the meaning of territory and the nation-state is undergoing transformation. By focusing on how people at the conceptual margins of the Chinese nation figure in the nation-building practices of the Chinese state, this book shifts the analytic gaze from national territory to population. This is not to say that I disregard the validity of national territory as a feature of nationalism. Particular attention is paid to an interplay between the territorial and non-territorial factors, and how this interplay evolves over time and relates to the boundaries of the nation.

Shapiro (2004) observes that the character of national idea expressed by a particular political regime is defined by how it formulates the future of the nation as much as by how it reconstructs the past and interprets the present. When it comes to the national goals of a particular political regime in an established nation-state, one should also account for the ideological outlook informing the rationalities of the regime, in addition to how the factors of language, religion, kinship, race and territory are employed. Examining how different systems of values adopted by the ruling elite affect the outlook of the nation at particular periods might help one go beyond treatment of state-led nationalism as a system of tools for synchronising the state with the nation.

This book broadens the debates on the nature of the nation-state by considering both subnational and transnational levels of the state and its discourses as well as popular discourses. I suggest that a territorial approach for making sense of the Chinese state-formulated national identity is limited, because it does not take into account China's transnational initiatives to invoke a common modernising identity, nor the historically problematic role of ethnic minorities in the national project. Through focusing on the statuses of overseas Chinese and ethnic minorities in the evolving Chinese nation-state, I offer an alternative to analyses that separate the internal/international and national/transnational realms, and show how the Chinese state crafts its national identity in opposition to or through incorporation of groups that are not easily accommodated by its nation-building efforts.

Beyond issues of territorial sovereignty, the Chinese nation is constituted through subjectivisation of the group identities of the ethnic minorities and overseas Chinese. Historically, these two marginal populations have been produced as carriers of certain identities in relation to the Chinese nation, and through discourses and other mechanisms they become subjects of it. Foucault's notion of the 'subject' is useful here. In a Foucauldian sense, subjectification works through either the exertion of control and dependence, or through identity and conscience. In both cases, power works to construct, recognize and shape subjects (Foucault 2002: 331). The preoccupation with the population of all Chinese leaders and the centrality of this issue in Chinese politics have been emphasised by a number of scholars of modern and contemporary China (Solinger 1999; Anagnost 1997, 2004; Greenhalgh and Winckler 2005). They have considered the Chinese population as a governance, social-political and bio-political issue, where optimiszation of human life is part of the work of the government. But in this book I look at how the state's preoccupation with particular segments of the population is related to how the Chinese nation is formulated, and how those segments feature in the identity politics propagated by the state. In other words, I examine how the identities of overseas Chinese and ethnic minorities have been constituted historically and what they reveal about the Chinese nation.

The Chinese nation: its domestic and transnational character

The bulk of research to date on globalisation's effects on the nation-state has concentrated on the ways globalisation both questions and undermines the very essence of the nation-state. A considerable number of studies have recommended abandoning the nation-state as a framework for social analysis altogether, as 'multiple belongings' minimize 'the relevance of nation-states and political entities' (Shambaugh 1993: 655) or shatter 'the monopoly of autonomous nation-states over the project of modernisation' (Appadurai 1997: 10). Cross-border solidarities of transnational migrants have been portrayed by this scholarship as a challenge to national projects and sometimes as an alternative to the project of building and sustaining nation-states (Harvey 1989; Appadurai 1997; Mittelman 1996; Guarnizo and Smith 1998; Meyer and Geschiere 1999). The nation-state notably falls out of this analytical framework as a factor conditioning the formulation of cultural identities.

The undermining effects of globalisation on the governing power of the Chinese state have been studied from the perspective of the role of transnational capital and networks of the overseas Chinese. The vital role of overseas Chinese in China's economic take-off in the late 1970s to early 1980s, and continuing to today, has led many scholars to rethink the underpinnings of the Chinese national project. There are numerous studies on the Chinese diaspora and on the emerging 'glow of Chinese fraternity' that are relevant to transnational views of the Chinese community (Ong and Nonini 1997; Ong 1999; Wang Gungwu 2000). These works look at Chinese transnationalism as a phenomenon that arose with a global shift from mass industrial production to globalised regimes of flexible accumulation, which was identified by David Harvey and others in the late 1980s. These studies speak of the 'momentary' and 'flexible modernities' of overseas Chinese (Ong and Nonini 1997; Ong 1999). Transborder ties between mainland and overseas Chinese, and between Chinese socialism and foreign capitalism, this literature claims, help to disrupt the political borders of the nation and weaken a sense of national integrity, promoting what Kahn (1998: 22) calls new kinds of 'post-national' identity. According to this argument, a sense of ethnicity and nationality tied to a particular history and place is undermined. Importantly, most analyses of China's transnational relations are framed without reference to the Chinese state.

However, transnational forces, which allegedly undermine the authority of the Chinese nation-state, operate alongside the centrally-formulated policy of opening up China and encouraging such transnational links.[3] Indeed, these forces contribute to a particular re-articulation of China's socio-political transformations characterised by Harvey (2005) as 'neoliberalism with Chinese characteristics'. Therefore, the developments which seem to undermine the project of the Chinese nation-state are also a product of processes taking place within the state as much as a by-product of transnational and local capitalism. Put differently, the state's production of national identities and transnational subjectivities affects its own contours.

The increasing effects of global mobility and fluidity do not leave the workings of the nation-state unaffected. However, these effects do not necessarily erode the boundaries of the nation-state. Basch *et al.* (1994: 269) demonstrate that with increased human mobility, the nation-state does not relax its powers over the thinking of its transnational subjects, but rather seeks to extend its control over them. Similarly, Duara (2005) underscores the importance of de-territorialised activities of the nation-state in reshaping the cultural and symbolic confines of the nation. While the project of the nation-state is organised around the idea of

Introduction 9

territoriality, its nationalist ideology and political reach exceed territorial confines, facilitated by processes associated with globalisation.Territory and territory-related issues, such as autonomy, self-determination, nationality, and citizenship remain relevant and important components of nationalist rhetoric promoting political legitimacy (Calhoun 1997: 123). But nationalist discourses and practices often go beyond the territorial boundedness of nation-states.

Rather than dismissing the concept of a nation-state as a tool for analysis, this book explores how the nation-state can change and adapt its national identity policies to the evolving historical context. Here a nation-state is treated as a socio-political formation that adapts to and engages the processes taking place at different levels and at different points in history; it is also shaped by these processes. By accommodating the transformations brought about by historical processes, the nation-state can influence national identities and shift their contours in an attempt to strengthen its relevance and primacy. Instead of downplaying the framework of the nation-state as less relevant in the era of globalisation, this book analyses how the nation-state adapts to the changes caused by globalisation, is shaped by them, and refines its assumed postulates. It shows that, in the case of China, both ethnic minorities and overseas Chinese are critical to this redefinition. The analytical perspective proposed here delineates the dynamics of designating subjects of the Chinese nation across its territorial boundaries, and allows us to trace how those dynamics have been shifting along with the political, socio-cultural and economic contexts, both domestic and global.

In addition to the role of overseas Chinese in the Chinese nation, this book traces how the roles of ethnic minorities are produced as both subjects of the Chinese nation and carriers of particular identities. There have been numerous important scholarly publications on China's historical and present relationships with its ethnic minorities. The majority of the previous studies are concerned with what China's policies towards ethnic minorities reveal about the nature of the Chinese state (Harrell 1995a, 1995b; Safran 1998; Shih 2007), the role and cultural composition of its Han majority group (Gladney 1994; Schein 1997, 2000; Sautman 1998; Shih 2002), and the role of market and global capitalism in influencing ethnic politics (McCarthy 2004, 2009; Brown 2002). Many of these works emphasise the crucial role of China's ethnic policies for upholding the regime legitimacy and control over the territory of the PRC (especially Sautman 1998; Shih 2002).

This book's focus on the state's projects and dominant discourse is not premised on the notion that territoriality is essential for understanding the functioning of the nation-state, because the scope of those projects can exceed or not match the territorial boundaries of the political construct of the state. This perspective allows one to explore how the officially popularised category of 'nationality' and linear views of progress influence the projects of the Chinese state, and how certain groups are included or excluded from the development of these projects. It also highlights how the racial component of the interpretation of ethnicity complements scientific-rational formulations of the developmental path of the Chinese nation. Further, this approach allows us to explore how the policies of

10 *Introduction*

rigid territoriality, pursued by the Chinese state ever since it mapped out its national borders, converge with non-territorial ideologies (racial or class based), and what place ethnic minorities take in these political, cultural and economic aspirations. So, rather than confining the analysis to the congruity of the state and its national boundaries, I look at how the Chinese state has been preoccupied historically with certain population groups, and how it has produced them as the ethnic minority members of the Chinese nation.

This book calls into question the supposedly determined and fixed nature of the Chinese nation-state. Here I follow, among others, Basch *et al.* (1994), Duara (1999), Nyíri (2001), and Callahan (2006), who propose that a nation-state, by accommodating the new conditions created by historical processes and by pursuing the politics of transnationalism, can reinforce rather than undermine its authority. These authors show that nationalist rhetoric on 'relevant people' can go beyond a nation-state and its territoriality, and, more importantly, that post-national overseas communities can actively participate in nationalist politics and echo the state (Glick Schiller *et al.* 1992; Callahan 2006; Liu Hong 2005). Overseas Chinese, for example, are actively engaged in not only cosmopolitan practices, but the production of nationalism and a particular national identity: in Callahan's expression, they constitute 'an important cosmopolitan part of nationalism' (Callahan 2006: 150). The case of China, where nation-building and transnational projects occur in parallel, raises the question of how previous theories of nation-building and transnational projects relate to each other. If these projects occur concurrently, then transnational theories cannot simply be set against previous understandings of the nation-state and nationalism. On the contrary, they complement each other in addressing the issue of the changing nature of a nation-state in the context of globalisation, and in explaining the inclusion or exclusion of particular groups in the national project. The analysis in this book integrates Chinese identity policies towards national minorities with analysis of the PRC's internal discourses and policy strategies toward the nonterritorial pan-Chinese community in an attempt to examine the shifting bases of belonging to the Chinese nation. It treats the PRC's transnational attempts to invoke the sentiments of overseas Chinese toward China and domestic ethnic accommodation as two sides of one project aimed at refining the power of the Chinese nation-state.

Ethnic minorities, overseas Chinese and the link between them

Over the time span covered in this book (the late 1890s through to the early 2000s), the application of the concepts of 'overseas Chinese' and 'ethnic minorities' changed significantly. Throughout the book I make explicit the connotations of these key terms at different periods while following the major shifts in the official discourse. Some notions, such as 'minority nationalities'(*shaoshu minzu*), attained their present meaning after the establishment of the PRC in the mid-1950s during the minority identification project (*minzu shibie*). However, unlike during the pre-reform era, *shaoshu minzu* is now often translated into English as 'ethnic minorities' rather than 'minority nationalities'. This signifies a shift in the connotations of the term in official ideology and its relationship to broader issues of China's modernisation and nation-building (Barabantseva 2008). The earlier class-based interpretations of ethnic relations which dominated China's Maoist period are now replaced by the developmental approaches to ethnicity. Chapter 6 discusses how in the reform period the Party organs and the state pay close attention to the application of the *shaoshu minzu* concept and revise it to fit their political interests.

When I deal with the notion of the overseas Chinese (*huaqiao huaren*), I also try to follow changing official usage during particular historical periods. The concept of overseas Chinese can be traced back to pre-modern times, but those who fall within this category and the attitudes toward them of the Chinese state have changed many times. There is confusion in the West over how the Chinese terms *huaqiao*, *huaren*, and *huayi* should be translated into English. While there are important differences in how at present the Chinese state defines the status of each of these groups and their relationship to China – *huaqiao* denotes citizens of China living abroad, while *huaren* and *huayi* refer to foreign nationals of Chinese descent – in the PRC's policy-making realm these distinctions have not always been drawn. Much of the official position and policies toward overseas Chinese from the late imperial period to the early PRC period were informed by the principle of *jus sanguinis*, according to which membership in the Chinese political and cultural community was identified through descent. During the Maoist period the government rejected the *jus sanguinis* principle in favour of the territorial and class-based understanding of Chinese citizenship. However, most of the Chinese official publications of the post-1978 period use the generic term *huaqiao huaren*, signifying that both Chinese citizens abroad and foreign nationals of Chinese descent fall within the scope of the PRC government's current policies toward overseas Chinese. Thus, the principles of territory and descent have become fused in the articulation of membership in the Chinese nation. The book traces what the official conceptualisations and applications of the term 'overseas Chinese' and policies which they inform reveal about the boundaries of the Chinese nation.

One can observe a number of ways of thinking about how ethnic minorities and overseas Chinese relate to the Chinese nation. For example, looking at historical discourses on Chinese orders reveals one way they relate to it. Prior to the Republican period (1911–49), to be Chinese was a matter of accepting Confucian principles. In the eyes of China's rulers, every person was either Chinese or in need of conversion to Confucian principles, after which they would be Chinese (*huaren*). In fact, those who were not Chinese in this sense were not even considered fully people. China was conceived of not as a territory but as All-under-Heaven (*Tianxia*). In Shih's (2002) terminology, this China is the celestial order of China. As such, the individuals coming from different traditions, such as the Manchu royal court, could be part of the Chinese people as soon as they ruled according to the principles accepted in the celestial order – that is, the one prescribed by Confucianism. The modern sovereign order of China developed in response to Western imperialism in the late nineteenth century, when China had to conform to the dominant Western vision of modernity that was synonymous with sovereignty and territoriality. The two principles distinguishing these two notions of China are the principle of sovereignty through territoriality and the ethno-cultural principle of membership in the Chinese nation. Whether or not ethnic minorities and overseas Chinese are part of China depends on which conception of China one employs. In the pre-modern celestial nonterritorial order, both overseas Chinese and ethnic minorities would be seen as part of China as soon as the minorities subscribed to the Chinese mode of governance. However, in the sovereign order, which is limited by political and territorial confines, only ethnic minorities fall within the domain of China; overseas Chinese would be members of the state they are citizens of. This book shows how the basis for membership in the Chinese nation has historically been informed by interplay between territorial and ethno-cultural principles, and remains so today.

Another way of connecting ethnic minorities and overseas Chinese to the idea of the Chinese nation, rarely observed in the non-Chinese discourse, is found in the official rhetoric from revolutionary days. Chinese leaders utilised the concept of a United Front to appeal to forces within and outside China to unite around the idea of a world revolution in the pre-reform period, and to unite around the project of modernisation in the post-1978 era. The notion of United Front is built around the focal role of the CCP and the central government but reaches out to generic groups, such as overseas Chinese and ethnic minorities, who have been included in official formulations of the United Front. Mao Zedong always mentioned overseas Chinese and minority nationalities next to each other in his speeches on the United Front directed towards revolutionary struggle. For example, in his declaration at the First Plenary Session of the Chinese People's Political Consultative Conference entitled 'Long live the great unity of the Chinese people' delivered on 30th of September 1949 (the day before the official foundation of the PRC), Mao referred to both overseas Chinese and ethnic minorities as representatives of 'the will of the people' (Mao Zedong 1949). The post-Mao leadership of China has also been referring to these groups together when talking about the need to unite forces behind the modernisation drive. For example, President Hu Jintao, in his speech to the 17th CCP Congress in October 2007, stressed the need to 'consolidate the great unity of the ethnic peoples of the whole country, strengthen the great unity of the sons and daughters of the Chinese nation at home and overseas ... to provide the immense power to overcome all difficulties and obstructions and propel the cause of the Party and people towards new and even greater triumphs'.[4] Perhaps most telling, in Reading Room 1 of the National Library in Beijing, the book holdings on ethnic minorities are kept next to the literature on the overseas Chinese. In other words, there is a certain discursive field bringing the two groups together, implicitly reiterating the link between them. This dominant discursive regime becomes further apparent when one pays attention to the common rhetoric of many Chinese people, who refer to both overseas Chinese and ethnic minorities as 'privileged' (*you tequan*) members of the Chinese nation. Both groups qualify for certain special rights and benefits, like university quotas, exemption from China's one-child policy and other priviliged

Introduction   13

treatments, for which nonholders of overseas Chinese or ethnic minority status are not qualified.

Methods and sources

The book is based on analysis of Chinese primary sources on the roles of ethnic minorities and overseas Chinese in China's national modernisation project. These sources include national legislative and policy papers issued by the Central government during the twentieth century, statistical yearbooks on ethnic and overseas Chinese policies, news digests released by the national news agencies, and other official published accounts on the topic. The book is also based on in-depth reading of Chinese secondary materials and Western primary and secondary sources that discuss historical discourses on China's national project. These materials were supplemented by interviews I conducted with central government officials and informal discussions that I had with Chinese scholars. The interviews were conducted in the principal state institutions that deal with the issues of ethnic minorities and overseas Chinese, namely the Nationalities' Affairs Commission of the State Council, the Overseas Chinese Affairs Office of the State Council, the All-China Federation of the Returned Overseas Chinese and the Central University for Nationalities in Beijing. The information collected in the interviews can be divided into three levels: the official level (obtained from interviews with representatives of the Office for Overseas Chinese and the Commission for Ethnic Minorities), the public level (obtained from interviews with representatives of the All-China Federation for Returned Overseas Chinese),[5] and the academic level (obtained from discussions with Chinese scholars). The interview data served to qualify findings from other sources. I employed the qualitative technique of discourse analysis to interpret the officially-generated discourse on the Chinese nation and modernisation. By 'discourse' I mean a force which, through the powerful means of language and practices, produces certain meanings that are taken for reality or truth in particular socio-historical contexts. I predominantly deal with the official dominant discourse as expressed in official documents, policy papers, law and speeches, and in their extensions in the practices initiated by the PRC's central government. In examining the official discourse on modernisation and the Chinese nation, I am concerned with how the identities of overseas Chinese and ethnic minorities have been constituted through a variety of discursive mechanisms and practices.[6]

Structure of the book

Chapter 1 traces the emergence and development of the discourse on the modern nation in China. The discussion argues that modernisation and nationalism are inseparable; they both shaped the early conceptions of the Chinese nation. The positions which overseas Chinese and ethnic minority groups occupied in the evolving national discourse, and the political strategies associated with it, are the main concerns of this chapter. The concepts 'overseas Chinese' and 'minority nationalities' acquired institutional and political formulations during this time.

The conceptual shaping of these two groups was a product of how their roles were viewed. On the one hand, overseas Chinese were identified and targeted by the politically-conscious elite as the group which could assist China in overcoming China's dependence on the West, and in regaining its independence and respect in the eyes of the rest of the world. On the other hand, the positioning of the competing political elites towards numerous ethnic populations in the Qing Empire was shaped by heightening grievances towards the Manchus. The conceptual formulation of both groups coincided with, and in many ways resulted from, China's encounter with the modern world, and is directly related to China's emergence as a modern nation-state. The formulation of their statuses and links to and within China was part of the process of negotiating what constituted China and who the Chinese people were.

This chapter examines the debates on the roles of overseas Chinese and ethnic minorities in the Chinese nation, and on the competing interpretations of the concept *minzu*. The discussion explores the spaces which ethnic minorities and overseas Chinese occupied in the formulations of the idea of the Chinese nation-state. Through analysing how the statuses of ethnic minorities and overseas Chinese were articulated in the competing debates on the nature of the Chinese nation-state, I also consider the role of ethnicity and territoriality in the production of the modern idea of the Chinese nation. Although the study focuses on official (i.e. state) discourses and practices, the late nineteenth century was marked by the presence of an array of competing political trends and debates. The Qing Empire was in decline, and there were many candidates to take over in China and abroad. Instead of discussing only one politico-ideological trend, the chapter considers the standpoints of competing groups and their leaders.

Chapter 2 analyses socialist nation-building strategies in the People's Republic and the roles of minority nationalities and overseas Chinese in them. From the moment of the creation of the CCP, followed by the power struggle with the Guomindang (GMD) and the PRC's establishment in 1949, the communist leadership embarked on the socialist project by 'uniting' a broad range of revolutionary forces in the United Front. The unifying concept employed by the communists was the amorphous class-defined concept of 'the people', which united the revolutionary elements and referred to a human collectivity with a common goal. The implementation of the shared goal of constructing socialism received priority over other unifying elements, such as territory and political identity and ethnic identity. This chapter looks at how the CCP managed its policies towards overseas Chinese and minority nationalities in the period of socialist construction. The chapter examines how the regime sought to imbricate ethnic minorities, sometimes by force, into the project of nation-building. It also explores how identity politics played out in relation to the overseas Chinese, who were regarded as an extension of China – that is, as its transterritorial nationals – from the adoption of the Law of Nationality in 1909 until the repudiation of the *jus sanguinis* principle in the mid-1950s. In addition, I discuss the ways that the idea of a unified Chinese state was propagated among ethnic minorities and overseas Chinese, and the roles these two groups were assigned to play in the process of socialist nation-building.

This chapter describes how nationalist and communist ideologies were both employed by the Chinese communists in their propaganda and their organisation of the nation-building project in the first ten years of their rule in China. The two ideologies were used simultaneously to taget different groups who were involved, or who were asked to be involved, in the project. While communist slogans were used to create 'socialist Chinese' out of 'backward' ethnic minorities, ethno-nationalist rhetoric was employed to attract overseas Chinese to the socialist-building project. Whereas both groups were seen as participants in the same United Front and socialist project, the strategies used to draw them into the project were different. To capture the divergent nature of the PRC's policies towards ethnic minorities and overseas Chinese, the terms 'domestic cosmopolitanism' and 'ethnic internationalism' are introduced.

Chapter 3 discusses modernisation as the PRC's current central nation-shaping principle and developmentalism as its ideological denominator. The recently assumed course of economic reforms and modernisation was preceded by revolutionary ambitions and class struggle. Today, China officially adheres to the principles of a market economy and the ideology of Marxism as its guiding principles for modernisation. Its developmental agenda has not completely replaced the socialist rhetoric of the state; instead, the socialist rhetoric and the modernisation agenda are synthesised. The persistent presence of the United Front slogan in the post-Mao period, which now calls for all-out modernisation, testifies to this trend.

This chapter illuminates the perplexities of Chinese nation-making by examining the officially-endorsed concept of modernisation in China. It explores the dominant discussions on modernisation and how they compare to those of their Western predecessors as well as to official policy directions. It looks at what aspects of human life receive priority in the formulation of the Chinese modernisation project and how this prioritisation might be reflected in the roles played by groups that do not neatly fit into the framework of the Chinese nation-state. These groups include both overseas Chinese and ethnic minorities.

Chapter 4 considers the roles and images of overseas Chinese and ethnic minorities in the dominant modernisation rhetoric in China during the reform period started in the late 1970s. It looks at modernisation as a nation-shaping project and draws implications for the groups that do not easily fit into the construct of the Chinese nation-state. Discursive portraits of overseas Chinese and ethnic minorities in the modernisation project are painted through analysis of Chinese scholarly articles linking modernisation debates with these two groups; I also examine official statements by state leaders. To obtain relevant academic publications, I used the journal database of the Beijing National Library and searched for the keywords 'modernisation', 'overseas Chinese', and 'ethnic minorities'. Most of the articles examined were published in the 1990s and early 2000s in leading national and provincial academic journals. I found the positions of ethnic minorities and overseas Chinese in the scholarly narratives to be diametrically opposite, though both groups have been crucial participants in the modernisation project. Overseas Chinese represent modern values in line with

China's modernisation goals, while ethnic minorities are associated with backwardness, poverty and traditional values. I demonstrate how contemporary modernisation discourse in China reinforces and fixes images of the two groups and reduces understanding of their roles: they are presented as a simple dichotomy of holders of opposing values associated with modernisation. My portraits of these two groups are not exhaustive, but they arguably convey the prevailing thinking in official and scholarly realms. They reflect a widespread view on the relationship between these two groups and modernisation in China.

Chapter 5 examines how the Chinese nation-state exercises its policies toward overseas Chinese in the context of modernisation and globalisation. It considers the mechanisms of incorporating the overseas Chinese into the Chinese modernisation strategy, which is built into the organisation of 'overseas Chinese work' (*qiaowu gongzuo*) and the practices of the relevant government institutions. This chapter aims to show how the Chinese nation-state travels outside its national space to operate within contemporary global processes to preserve its power over the identity of Chinese transnationals and to legitimise and reinforce itself outside its territory. The discussion demonstrates how Chinese leadership appeals to ethnicity and culture as potential bases for community-building across borders in an attempt to unify the diverse and dispersed overseas Chinese communities for the goal of integrating the PRC into the global economy under the leadership of the CCP.

This chapter builds upon themes elaborated in earlier chapters on Chinese modernisation discourse and the place of the overseas Chinese in the vision of modernity. It looks at the policies and tactics of the Chinese government towards the overseas Chinese and how they potentially shape the subjective identity of these Chinese transnationals. The success of those policies is beyond the scope of this study. Instead, I seek to demonstrate that the strategies of the Chinese authorities are directed at nourishing and maintaining a particular kind of Chinese identity beneficial for the PRC's economic, political and social transformations. I consider dominant discourses and policies as mutually reinforcing and constitutive in producing a mode in which a nation-state operates.

Chapter 6 considers the roles of ethnic minorities in the post-socialist modernisation project through analysing endeavours to advance the economic, cultural and political positions of ethnic minorities in Chinese society. This discussion centres on how the 'ethnic question' (*minzu wenti*) and 'ethnic work' (*minzu gongzuo*) have changed in the reform period, and on the positions of ethnic minorities in the official formulation of the Western Development Project (*xibu da kaifa*) (WDP). I argue that the PRC's leadership, through its developmental strategies and policies towards ethnic minorities, essentially demarcates them as localised elements of the Chinese nation-state. Localisation, however, does not mean inclusion in the national modernisation project, at least not on equal terms. The type of localisation practiced by the Chinese state distances ethnic minorities from the celebrated modern practices of flexibility, mobility and openness, albeit understood more in a physical than a political or ideological sense. Dictated by the demands of the market economy, these practices are commonly perceived by many officials in China as an inalienable part of the socio-economic transformations initiated with the start of reforms. Although the Chinese government asks all its people to adapt to modernisation demands of the reform period, the portrayals of ethnic minorities in the official discourse do not allow for their active inclusion in the formulation of China's modernisation practices even if ethnic minorities are following the government-formulated principles. As such, bearers of an ethnic minority identity represent territorial and cultural spaces assigned to them by the state.

Through the discussion and analysis of the events that brought overseas Chinese and ethnic minorities to the forefront of China's domestic and international news in spring–autumn 2009, the Conclusion summarises the findings of the book. I show that, by looking at how the conceptual margins of the Chinese nation figure in these events, we can better understand what the Chinese nation is and what it is not, and where it starts and where it ends. I discuss how these events reveal China's leadership's attempts to conceal the ambiguous premises of China's national project through legal, conceptual and policy tools. I conclude that the changing statuses of overseas Chinese and ethnic minorities in the Chinese state's practices point to contingent and incoherent premises of the Chinese nation allowing simultaneously for its flexible and rigid interpretations.

1 Overseas Chinese and ethnic minorities in imperial and Republican China

The processes of dealing with ethnic and cultural difference and managing Chinese migration overseas have been closely intertwined with the history of China. The expansion of China was in many ways the result of the policies towards populations outside its core and its orientations towards overseas trade and migration. The way China's leaders viewed these policies and acted them out shaped the development of China as a national and regional power. In other words, the history of the conceptual formation of the overseas Chinese and ethnic minorities is closely related to the processes of China's transformation from the empire to the nation-state. And so, a historical overview of China's conceptual formulation of overseas Chinese and ethnic minorities and of policies toward them sheds light on the dynamics of China's formation as a multinational state.

Chinese society had been ethnically diverse long before its encounter with the Western powers. The legacy of the dynastical rule over ethnically-diverse populations influenced the institutional codification of this diversity during the period of China's decline as a dynastical power in the second half of the nineteenth century. Similarly, China's stance towards its subjects abroad in the last years of dynastic rule presented the next generations of China's leaders with a lesson to learn from. At the turn of the twentieth century, identity politics associated with securing the population's loyalty were made a priority. Overseas Chinese and ethnic minorities played crucial roles in this process as, through assuring their support and loyalty, Chinese leaders essentially guaranteed the security of the territorial border and unity of the multinational entity. The themes of territory and ethnicity in nation-state building were intimately intertwined.

The conceptualisation of overseas Chinese and ethnic minorities coincided with, and in many ways was a product of, China's encounter with the modern world in the era of imperialism. Their conceptualisation was part of the process of negotiating what constituted China and who the Chinese people were. Elites debated how to establish links among these groups and the emerging structure of the new state, and how to include them in China's nation-building process. At the turn of the twentieth century, overseas Chinese were identified by the politically conscious Chinese elite as a group that could help China overcome its dependence on the West, and regain independence and respect internationally. The issue of ethnic minorities emerged as the contested site of heated discussions on the origins and character of the Chinese nation among the predominantly Han revolutionaries. They resorted to discussions of *minzu* in their plans to unite with other minorities in the struggle against the Manchu rule.

This chapter examines the positions that overseas Chinese and ethnic minorities occupied in the evolution of the national discourse, and political strategies associated with it in the Late Imperial and Republican China. The Chinese rulers had been dealing with both groups long before their encounter with the Western powers, but the concepts of overseas Chinese and ethnic minorities were conceptualised and institutionalised during the turbulent years of China's transition from the empire to the nation-state. The discussion in the chapter traces the roles of ethnic minorities and overseas Chinese in the debates on modernisation and nationalism which shaped evolving conceptions of Chinese nationhood since the mid-nineteenth century. It also examines their statuses in relation to the concept *minzu*, which featured prominently in the debates on the nature of the Chinese nation-state, and discusses the stances of the competing groups, in particular nationalists and communists, on the role of the overseas Chinese and ethnic minorities in their conceptions of the Chinese nation.

Pre-Republican China's relations with ethnic diversity and transnational subjects

The Chinese empire's relationship with 'otherness' has been a longstanding subject of scholarly enquiry. It became a common wisdom that the earliest rulers of the unified China referred to their domains as central state (*zhongguo*), and distinguished between people who inhabited central state's territories and those who dwelled outside them. It is widely acknowledged that in their governing practices the Chinese followed a distinction between *xia* (civilisation) of the Empire's core and *yi* (barbarism) of the borderlands – this distinction is captured in the imperial ruling principle *yixia zhibie* (distinction between barbarism and civilisation). The populations outside the territory of the central state were called *man, yi, rong* and *di*. For a long time the dominant academic interpretations of the Chinese central state's dealings with outsiders were divided between those who characterised these interactions as assimilation and those who adhered to the argument of accommodation, the debate which Shin cogently summarises in his recent study (Shin 2006: 2). This binary interpretation of imperial China's relations with ethnic diversity has been recently questioned for its unproblematic treatment of the Chinese cultural core, *xia*, and its policies. It has been argued that a lot of policies of the Chinese central state towards outside populations cannot be characterised as either accommodation or assimilation, as their policies varied over time and included demarcation, categorisation and differentiation (Gladney 2004; Crossley *et al.*, 2006; Shin 2006).

The Empire's diverse approaches to dealing with its ethnic others gained prominence during the Ming and Qing dynasties, whose reign essentially shaped the contemporary territorial boundaries and ethnic composition of the PRC. The southern border of the contemporary China was shaped by the imperial conquests of the Ming dynasty, while China's northern border was finalised during the rule of the Qing dynasty. For example, during the expansion of the imperial rule to the south in the Ming period (1368–1644), when Yunnan was incorporated into the central dominion and Guizhou established as a province, the minority categories appeared in the historical chronicles, and ethnographic demarcations of the borderland populations were made (Shin 2006: 13). Shin finds in his study of the Ming's expansion to the south that the Ming rulers distinguished the people who belonged to the Empire and those who were outside it along the categories of the subject of the Empire *min* (citizen) or *hua* (civilised) and *man*, *yi* or *man yi* (beyond the pale). He documents that the Ming developed very elaborate policies of 'culture of demarcation' towards the 'beyond the pale' people who were classified according to their level of difference from the people inhabiting the core of the Empire.

With the Manchu conquest of the Ming in 1644, the new rulers of China had to tackle the dual problem of establishing its legitimate authority as the non-Han rulers of the Empire and to guarantee the unity of the growing multiethnic polity. They dealt with these challenges through a combination of policies of assimilation, often violently enforced, adaptation, and recognition and inclusion of ethnic difference. Elliott (2001: 3) credits their abilities to rely on existing Chinese political and cultural tradition of Confucianism and to maintain their distinct Manchu identity, manifested in the success of the banner system (*baqi zhidu*), for their prolonged rule of the Chinese Empire.

The Manchu origins as barbarians of the Empire played a central role in their organisation of rule. After taking over the empire, the Qing, whose Manchu origins were opposed by the Ming loyalists, adopted the language of the earlier dynasties. For example, Lydia Liu's study shows that the Qing did not prohibit the use of character *yi* (barbarian), which was used by the Han dissidents in their opposition to the Manchu rule (Liu, L. 2006: 72). Instead the Qing used the Confucian language of *yi* to consolidate their empire. The Manchu Emperor Yongzheng undermined the *hua/yi* distinction as a valid basis for legitimacy, emphasising instead the Confucian value of virtue as the criterion for legitimate rule. In contrast to the earlier governing principle of *yixia zhibie* the Qing popularised the idea of *zhongwai yijia* (the Center and the Outer are one family) to emphasise the universalism and multiethnic character of their empire. The Manchu adaptation tactics extended even further. They referred to their expanded Empire as both *Da Qing Guo* (Qing Empire) and *Zhongguo* (Central State) calling all subjects of the Empire recently and previously conquered as 'Chinese' (*Zhongguo zhimin, Zhongguo zhiren*, and later *Zhongguoren* or *Zhonghuaren*) (Zhao Gang 2006: 6–7; Leibold 2007: 10–11). The Qing used the earlier imperial language in their dealings with the ethnically diverse subjects of the Empire, but had to apply this language in new ways to address the issue of their non-Han origins. *Hanren, huaren, huaxia, xiaren* referred to the core of the Empire, and *waifang* (exterior), *xiyu* (western regions) or *bianqu* (borderlands) were used to refer to the newly incorporated territories (Leibold 2007: 9). The multiethnic view of the empire was endorsed in state and private schools, where students of geography were required to study one of the four 'dialects of China': Tibetan, Manchu, Mongol or Uyghur (Zhao Gang 2006: 13).

Although the Qing talked of the Empire in the language of multiculturalism and equality of all subjects, the Manchu enjoyed a privileged status in the imperial political hierarchy and society. Manchu hairstyle and dress were made compulsory for all Chinese males to display their loyalty to the Manchu regime. Those who were resentful and did not obey were severely punished. The intermarriage between the Manchu and Han, and the Han migration to Manchuria were banned. The tensions between Manchu and Han officials were observed by Lord Macartney during his mission to China: 'The predominance of the Tartars [Manchu] and the Emperor's partiality to them are the common subject of conversation among the Chinese whenever they meet together in private, and the constant theme of their discourse' (cited in Elliott 2001: 218).

In addition to addressing the task of securing the legitimacy of its rule, the Qing had to guarantee unity and stability of the expanded multiethnic empire.The Qing dynasty had significantly enlarged the territory of the empire through conquest that secured its position in Xinjiang, southwest China, Tibet, Mongolia and Taiwan. This expansion brought with it myriad ethnic groups. In this system, the state appointed officials to administer the distant regions, gradually transforming the mode of governing these regions; the state treated them as the interior part of the empire (Hostetler 2000: 626). The Qing ethnic policies in the newly-incorporated northern parts of the Empire were more accommodating than the tactics towards 'southern' peoples in Guangxi, Yunnan and Guizhou (Elliott 2001: 456, note 11). The Qing loosely reigned (*ji mi*) many of these territories, restricting their role to internal supervision and allowing most regions to maintain their own institutions and styles of governing (Hamashita 2008; Leibold 2007).

The territorial conquest and encounter with ethnic populations in the newly-dominated regions, which previously had not been directly ruled from the imperial centre, gave impetus to numerous ethnographic studies of the frontier people commissioned by the imperial court. Hostetler (2000, 2001) demonstrates how the emerging ethnographic studies of the populations on the empire's frontier showed the imperial character of the rule of the Qing Empire.[1] The fascination with the newly-encountered populations and cultures produced numerous detailed records of their customs, modes of dress and traditions, formalising the apparent cultural differences with the imperial centre. Tellingly, the writing of the history of the diverse populations inhabiting the empire and their relations and statuses within it became the prerogative of state officials.[2] The state was preoccupied with 'scientific' representations of the people inhabiting the empire through cartography and ethnography, which were employed for precise designation and demarcation of the Chinese territories.

The process of cultural identification and classification of diverse populations comprising the Qing Empire went hand in hand with the creation of its fixed territorial borders, long before the empire's break-up. The negotiation and signing of the border treaties, most notably the treaty of Nerchinsk with the Russian Empire in 1689, initiated what one can characterise as the beginning of the conversion of the land into the national territory (Kaiser 2004: 231). The border agreement signed by the Qing court and Tsarist Russia was the first attempt to draw a permanent territorial dividing line with another empire. Perdue (2005b: 191) illustrates how the fixation of the territorial borders closed off the intermediate space, with its multiple identities, and transformed it into national territories with assigned identities, laying the ground for the future nation-state before the expansion of the ideology of nationalism in the late 1800s. Importantly, the enclosed territory of the empire was not, strictly speaking, organised around one culture. Zhao Gang (2006: 12) points to the fact that one year after the treaty with Russia was signed, the memorial stone was inscribed in Latin and Russian on one side and in Chinese, Manchu and Mongol on the other. This signifies that there was an attempt to publicly endorse the official view that the Chinese empire was a multiethnic entity.

The administrative division, ethnographic categorisation, promotion of the idea of a multiethnic entity and territorial demarcation prior to the Western and Japanese imperialist incursions into China in the nineteenth century suggest that the processes associated with nation-crafting were part of the imperial ruling structure. The concepts of ethnicity and territorial fixity, albeit not in the contemporary senses, were applied to the ruling mode of the Chinese empire. [3] With the collapse of the Qing Empire these concepts were further formalised and reorganised to fit the model of the nation-state imported from the West. The formulation and institutionalisation of these concepts in relation to the ethnically diverse populations of the territories included in the empire contributed to the process of transformation of the imperial space into a nation-state.

Before the Qing Empire, the policies towards overseas Chinese was an aspect of China's foreign trade policies. Chinese maritime expeditions in search of new markets and tributaries were accompanied by the movement of Chinese subjects overseas. The first wave of emigration from China is attributed to the seventh- to eighth-century emigration to the Penghu islands andTaiwan where Chinese served as middlemen between their homeland and their host communities (Hamashita 2008: 33). The second wave of Chinese migration coincided with the travels of Admiral Zheng He in the fifteenth century under the auspices of the Yongle emperor. The Ming (1368–1644), with the exception of the reign of the Yongle emperor, were antagonistic to private maritime commerce and restricted it until 1567. Zheng He's journeys to 'the West', the area which we now call Southeast Asia, resulted in the establishment of seventy Chinese missions in tributary states. These relations stimulated trade with many Southeast Asian communities and boosted Chinese emigration to Southeast Asia. Notwithstanding the lift of the ban on migration, the prejudice against emigration continued into the Qing dynasty who, between 1656 and 1717, issued a series of imperial decrees which made overseas travel a capital crime and prohibited the Empire's subjects from leaving and re-entering China (Zhuang 2006: 98). The Chinese abroad were condemned for refuting the Confucian value of filial piety and engaging in trade, an activity deemed corrupting by Confucianists (Yen 1981: 264). The nature of overseas Chinese as mobile subjects did not correspond with the sedentary agricultural values emphasised in Confucianism. They were seen as traitors, rebels, opium smugglers and conspirators. The emperor referred to them as 'undesirable subjects' or vagabonds who were suspected for their involvement in 'secret societies' and conspiracies against the imperial rule (Zhuang 2006: 98). These first two waves of migration laid the foundation for Chinese traders' (*hua shang*) migration pattern, which was dominant until the mid-nineteenth century when the coolie trade established another channel for Chinese migration (Wang Gungwu 1989).

A new wave of Chinese migration was the result of China's early relationship with the West in the aftermath of the two Opium wars. Foreign trade was replaced by war, rebellions and China's growing population as the push factors for migration from China. With China's defeat in the Opium Wars, the treaties of Tianjin and Beijing included clauses on overseas travel by Chinese workers, who were needed by the victorious states as a substitute for the slave labour from Africa made unavailable with the abolition of the slave trade. The 1866 Chinese Labour Immigration Agreement signed by China with Britain and France established the framework for the Chinese coolie trade (Hamashita 2008: 33). The impact which these historical developments had on the conditions of Chinese coolies around the world changed the overall view of the overseas Chinese by the Qing in the last decades of their rule. After 1860, knowledge of the working conditions of Chinese in British colonies significantly increased among Qing officials, since China was forced to allow its subjects to work in those colonies. In 1874 the first systematic investigation of the conditions of overseas Chinese in Cuba was undertaken by Chen Lanpin who would become China's first ambassador to the United States, Spain and Peru. Chen's investigation report detailed the forcible nature of transportation, disastrous working conditions and atrocities committed on the Chinese workers (Godley 1981: 65–66). This investigation dramatically changed the image of overseas Chinese in the eyes of the Qing government. Chen's Cuban mission laid the foundations for establishing China's first consulates in the territories with a substantial presence of overseas Chinese. These diplomatic missions provided first-hand information on the conditions of Chinese workers in ports across Asia, and later in gold mines in America. Overseas Chinese were now seen as victims of coolie brokers, ill treated and discriminated at their workplaces abroad. Rather than being made to feel guilty for abandoning Confucian values and culture, they were pitied and considered in need of governmental protection. In the eyes of the Qing, their image changed from traitors of the empire (*han jian*) and servants of the imperialists, to coolies or Chinese labour force (*hua gong*) who were deceived into performing heavy labour abroad and suffered at the hands of imperialists; they became well-regarded members of the Chinese stock (Yen 1981: 266).

Besides protection of the Chinese coolies, there was a growing recognition among the Qing officials of the potential service of the overseas Chinese merchants in Southeast Asia in the cause of China's early modernisation. By the second half of the nineteenth century it was estimated that hundreds of thousands of overseas Chinese pursued fortunes in Southeast Asia. Speaking of the Singapore and Malaya communities of the late nineteenth and early twentieth century, Wang Gungwu, for example, noted that they could be seen along the two societal divisions of 'merchants and those who aspired to be merchants' (cited in Godley 1981: 33). Despite their business-orientated nature, many overseas Chinese valued the prestige of a high official standing in the Qing bureaucracy and the virtue of traditional education. Awareness of the economic potential of the overseas Chinese led some Qing officials to believe that overseas Chinese capital could create an alternative to China's dependence on foreign capital. In the 1860s the Qing started sending special envoys to the ports around Southeast Asia with large concentration of overseas Chinese. The officials working abroad were instructed to 'seek among the emigrant Chinese, those who have particular skills such as the ability to make machines, to steer steamships, to handle foreign firearms, and to send them back to China with paid passage so that these men will be useful' (in Godley 1981: 67). Similarly, with the hope to recruit talented overseas Chinese youth, the Qing court initiated establishment of overseas Chinese schools throughout Southeast Asia. In 1877 the Qing court officially approved a policy of soliciting overseas Chinese capital. The Qing court commissioned inspection tours around Southeast Asia for the purpose of persuading overseas Chinese to invest in China. In return for their investments, the overseas Chinese were ofered honours and titles. Godley's research shows that 51 different Qing titles, ranks and degrees were offered to overseas Chinese for purchase (Godley 1981: 41).

From the mid-1870s, Qing officials increasingly referred to overseas Chinese as *huamin*, *huaren*, *zhongguo renmin* or *zhongguo shangmin* in contrast to the earlier offensive term *yumin*, unproductive vagabonds, coined during the reign of the Ming dynasty (the *yumin* term is used in Godley 1981: 60). In addition, the term *huaqiao* gradually entered the diplomatic vocabulary; later, in the years of Republican China, it became a common term for overseas Chinese, irrespective of which migration pattern they followed. This shift in language signified that overseas Chinese were recognised as Chinese subjects despite their displacement from China. They were no longer suspected of treason, persecuted for desertion or pitied for their ill treatment as coolies. Rather, they were recognised as culturally Chinese and politically loyal to the regime in China, ready to support their ancestral homeland if provided enough protection. The introduction of the all-embracing *huaqiao* term was the strategic move of the late Qing government to demonstrate its willingness to offer help and protection to all its subjects abroad, as well as a way of reaching out to the wealthy overseas Chinese (especially in Southeast Asia) to invest in China's modernisation projects (Wang Gungwu 1989). Through this discursive move and political socialisation, through the establishment of Chinese schools, associations, and newspapers, all overseas Chinese became part of China's modernising mission and targets for achieving its national goal. *Huaqiao* was used to appeal to the national sentiments of overseas Chinese and to galvanise their affinity with the idea of the Chinese nation.

The abolition of the prohibitive emigration policy in 1893 marked the end of the transition to a positive image of overseas Chinese and the adoption of a new approach to them. The imperial decree of September 1893 stated that 'all Chinese merchants irrespective of how long they have been abroad whether married or with children may return home to practice their trade upon receiving a pass from the Chinese minister or consul. If the situation requires it, they may go abroad again to carry out their business and must not as in the past be subjected to extortion' (Godley 1981: 78). It was the beginning of a campaign to attract the support of overseas Chinese merchants. As a result of this campaign, millions of dollars were raised for investment in mining, railway construction, manufacturing and banking projects in China, with the biggest achievement being the system of railways constructed with the help of overseas Chinese funds (Godley 1981: 149–72). Overall, overseas Chinese capital failed to replace Western capital in the Chinese economy and ultimately did not prevent the end of the rule of Qing. The Qing laid the foundations for the overseas Chinese policies which were later embraced and further developed by the subsequent leaders of China.

Prior to China's collision with the Western powers in the mid-nineteenth century, Chinese rulers had formulated policies and attitudes towards ethnic populations on the empire's frontiers that departed from the earlier strategy of indirect rule. They also revised policies and attitudes toward the overseas Chinese and their relationship with the imperial court. Although these developments demonstrate that later nationalist debates were not solely a response to the Western incursion and were rooted in earlier processes, they were nonetheless shaped by the imperial structure, which came under pressure and underwent significant transformations in subsequent years. Therefore, even though the notions of overseas Chinese and ethnic diversity had already been present during the dynastic rule, they acquired new political meanings later during the period of heightening political debates on the future political order and national character of China. Competing political factions defined how ethnic populations and overseas Chinese should be included in the new entity of modern China. But rather than identifying their place in the imperial structure, these factions helped define the relationship between the emerging Chinese nation-state and its people both within and outside its territory.

Modernisation and nationalism in shaping the Chinese nation

Since the last half of the nineteenth century, China has pursued a succession of national and regional projects to modernise and build a politically-, economically- and culturally-distinctive nation. China's debates on modernisation paths were sparked by the challenges posed by Western and Japanese imperialism in the mid-nineteenth century. The debates on development and the nature and composition of the Chinese polity were integral to the process of becoming a modern nation-state. The idea of modernisation was closely linked with liberating China from foreign rule and imperialism. These goals stimulated the emergence of the modern Chinese nationalist discourse and the formation of associated concepts, most prominently *minzu*.[4] Modernisation (*xiandaihua*) and *minzu* were interpreted in many different ways, and remain contested terms in contemporary Chinese political and scholarly vocabulary. While both have been indispensable to China's national project, the meanings of modernisation and *minzu* changed with the shifts and turns of China's modern history and national priorities. The goals of modernisation and building an independent and strong Chinese nation have been two sides of one grand process of national development, complementing and reinforcing each other. The conception of the unified Chinese nation-state that was to emerge, however, has been constantly revised under *historical-political* pressures and the clash of conflicting ideological currents.

The new formulation of China's organisational order in relation to its inhabitants and the outside world was a product of China's attempt to withstand the expanding influence of Western imperialism at the end of the nineteenth century. In this period the idea of a clearly defined territorial Chinese state, distinguished from other states by an established regulatory bond between the government and its citizens, came into existence. China's defeats in a series of confrontations with the West challenged the superiority of Chinese civilisation over Western 'barbarians' in what was coined a 'system-to-system' skirmish and 'a mismatch between Western nationalism and Chinese culturalism' (Kim and Dittmer 1993: 249). China proved unable to counter the Western challenge, bringing nearer the collapse of the traditional Chinese world order. This marked the transition from the pre-modern to the modern era. Immediately before and during the years of Republican China (1911–49), China was adapting to the dominant Western visions of modernity synonymous with sovereignty and territoriality. Its modern sovereign order developed in response to the Western challenge. In a sense, China's pre-modern view of the world was brought down to the level of a nation-state and territoriality, whereas its ambitions to excel and exhibit a certain code of values were preserved from imperial times.

In the late Qing period, after the defeat in the Opium wars, a range of ways to improve China's economic performance and political prestige was suggested, along with nation-salvation projects. The so-called Yangwu movement (*yangwu yundong*), led by Zeng Guofan, Li Hongzhang, Zhang Zhidong and others, called for army reform, the abolition of the old examination system, and the introduction of Western-style schools and technology. Advocates of all-out reforms under the slogan 'Science and Democracy', including Kang Youwei, Liang Qichao and their followers, were active at the end of the nineteenth century. These early reform efforts drew on the idea of *ti-yong*, which is usually translated into English as 'essence' and 'function'. [5] The full phrase is 'Chinese studies as essence, Western studies as function' (*zhong xue wei ti, xi xue wei yong*). The phrase calls for the use of Western knowledge and technology to strengthen Chinese identity. It is rooted in the reification of China's cultural and philosophical traditions at a time when Western military superiority called Chinese traditions into question. *Ti-yong* provided a conceptual tool for Chinese intellectuals who held that new technologies would pave the way for a type of modernisation that would leave intact core Chinese values and institutions.

There were growing debates on possible paths of Chinese development. Liang Qichao, among others, contended that 'Chinese learning is the *ti*, and Western learning the *yong*; they depend on each other and neither can be preserved at the cost of the other ' (Tong Shijun 2000: 137). Yan Fu, a famous liberal and anti-traditionalist at the turn of the twentieth century criticised that idea: 'Chinese learning has both its *ti* and its *yong*, and it is the same with Western learning' (Tong Shijun 2000: 145). Rather than seeing the *ti–yong* relationship as dichotomous, Yan Fu characterised it as syncretistic – that is, composed of unstable elements that could not be attributed to a single source.

The search for particular modes of modernising the country was inseparable from discussions on the national outlook and the composition of the modern Chinese nation-state. In this way, the interdependence of the *ti–yong* learning mode is reminiscent of the relationship between nationalism and modernisation, the parallel and complementary elements of the project aimed at establishing China as a modern and independent nation-state. The nationalist ideology and theories of the Chinese nation became integral to China's search for a modernisation path. In China's attempt to come to terms with its own distinct form of political community immune to foreign subversion and dominance, the process of entering the modern world was closely associated with the emergence and formulation of the concepts *minzu* and *guomin*. The former involved outlining the national composition and outlook of the Chinese state, while the latter referred to the state as the public property of the people.

Amid the turmoil of the late imperial period, reform-oriented journals and newspapers published by new study societies became arenas for nationalist debate. Much of this debate took place in the newly-born overseas Chinese press. The main theme was the search for ways to respond to the Western challenge and prevent a decline of imperial China. In an attempt to ensure China's national survival, Chinese intellectuals manipulated and fused foreign evolutionary theories with traditional Chinese schools of thought; Frank Dikötter (1992, 1997) presents a rich account of their efforts. Liang Qichao, Sun Yatsen, Zhang Binglin, Zhang Taiyan, Kang Youwei, Wang Tao and others ignited a fervent intellectual debate on the nature of the Chinese nation.

The overseas Chinese were central to the vision of many of the advocates of a modern and independent China. Many were part of the overseas Chinese community themselves as, after the failure of the coup in 1898, the leaders of the reforms in China had to seek asylum abroad. Thus, the idea of a modern China propagated by Chinese intellectuals first found supporters outside China's territory. Liang Qichao and Sun Yatsen, albeit from opposing perspectives, actively promoted the idea of an independent, modern Chinese state among overseas Chinese; Liang was the spokesman of the reformers between 1898 and 1911, Sun the leader of revolutionaries. National elite appealed to the overseas Chinese on grounds not only of territorial nationalism – addressing the stability and security of the vast territory of the Republic, which had suffered at the hands of the Japanese (1895) – but on the basis of older pre-modern and non-territorial discourses of common culture and descent. As Duara (1999) shows in his study of Chinese transnational communities, different nationalist groups within China recognised quite early the significance of the Chinese abroad for the nation-building project, and made extensive efforts to raise contributions and investments among them for projects. Constrained by the emerging territorial concept of a nation-state, which excluded overseas Chinese from the political community, this discourse appealed to a symbolic 'biological' attachment to a 'native home', and emphasised the common ancestral and cultural roots of all Chinese.

Both revolutionary and reformist Chinese intellectuals linked overseas Chinese to China through an imaginary group consciousness (*qun*) or blood relations (*xie tong*), and saw them playing the missionary role of rescuing China from outside domination. In the late 1890s, Liang Qichao, whose thinking on nationalism developed in response to Western imperialism, invoked the concept of *qun* in his calls to overseas Chinese to form a cohesive community (Hao Chang 1971: 150–55). For him *qun* involved strengthening group consciousness and promoting a collective oneness. His view contrasted with the anti-Manchu orientation of the revolutionaries. The essence of Liang Qichao's nationalism was comprised of civic ideas with elements of social Darwinism, which he applied at the level of nations. *Qun* was critical to his conceptualisation of public morality, which China, in his opinion, historically lacked (in contrast to private morality). Collective consciousness was fundamental to creating the cohesive political structure of a state. Liang fused the notions of nation, *qun* and democratic institutions into a new notion of civic solidarity, and reconceptualised the role of the people as *guomin* (participating citizenry). He emphasised the need for a 'corporate feeling of oneness' among all Chinese to resist the encroachment of Western powers. He also advocated promoting solidarity among overseas Chinese through appealing to their civic feelings rather than their blood relatedness to Chinese in China (Hao Chang 1971: 154–55).[6]

Sun Yatsen's definition of 'nation', on the other hand, narrowly focused on the 'Han descendants of the Yellow Emperor' (*xiao minzu zhuyi*). The founding father of the Nationalist Party and the Communist Party, Sun Yatsen famously first blamed the Manchus for China's misfortunes, saying that these foreign rulers had sacrificed Chinese territory and rights in order to preserve their dynastic rule. His views found fertile ground in China: dissatisfaction with the rule of the alien Manchus had been aggravated by the defeat of China by Japan in the Sino–Japanese War in 1895, the failure of the Hundred Days Reform of 1898, and the debacle of the Boxer Uprising in 1900. According to Sun, the notion of a 'race war', which originated in the theories of social Darwinism and was employed by Liang and other reformers against foreign encroachment, was not adequate to mobilise a new political struggle against the Manchu government because the idea of 'yellow race' encompassed Manchus. The revolutionary movement led by Sun Yatsen was the first to champion Chinese nationalism based upon the invoked notions of blood lineage and common race. These ideas were first expressed in his *Principle of the Nation* (1924) and later formed part of his *Three Principles of the People* (1932).[7]

In the run-up to the 1911 revolution, Sun Yatsen referred to overseas Chinese as the mother of the revolution (*huaqiao shi geming zhi mu*), as with their organised financial support the revolution was possible (Lin Jinzhi, Li Guoliang *et al.* 1993: 77; Yen 1976: xviii-xix). Overseas Chinese communities were at the centre of the leaders' revolutionary activities. In the period from 1902 to 1905, support groups for dissemination of revolutionary ideas were set up throughout Southeast Asia as well as in America and Europe. Much effort and many resources were devoted to nurturing a revolutionary spirit and support for an independent China among overseas Chinese with strong attachments to their places of origin in China (Lin Jinzhi, Li Guoliang et al. 1993: 100). According to Duara (1999: 63), promotion of the new image of Chineseness among the overseas Chinese communities was based on the newly-discovered virtues of successful Chinese entrepreneurs and the deemed racial superiority of the Han over other peoples. The Chinese communities overseas were first mobilised by the GMD and the new Republic of China in support of the anti-Manchu struggle and were later granted representation in Republican national assemblies. In the late Qing period, adoption of the *jus sanguinis* principle, confirmed in the Nationality Law of 1909, established a basis for citizenship of the Chinese overseas and allowed a 'dual citizenship' for Chinese nationals living in other countries.[8] The Republican government of China considered itself the defender of the overseas Chinese and established its consulates throughout Southeast Asia. In 1917, the government attempted to register all Chinese abroad. These policies and the nationalist slogan of 'where there are Chinese, there is China', which informed much of the nationalist practices, would subsequently cause friction between China and governments across Southeast Asia (Purcell 1965: xi).

The propagation of the idea of China's territorial sovereignty and reinvention of the nation's past went hand in hand with the revival of the transnational links of the overseas Chinese and their reattachment to the nation through biological lineages or civic feelings. The work of the Chinese leaders among overseas Chinese has prompted Rebecca Karl to argue that 'Chinese-ness first emerged as a global topos and only after [that] became a reified culturalist-ethnic one' (Karl 2002: 53). According to Duara (1999: 53), the strategy of 'domesticating' transnational overseas Chinese engendered a new symbolic bond among all Chinese, which overcame the territoriality of the political community and generated a debate over the emergence of 'de-territorialised nations' (Duara 1999: 48). Nationalist ideology, aimed at recovering China's territorial independence and sovereignty on a par with other modern states, coincided with the activities of revolutionary-minded people who mobilised transnational forces for the formation of the Chinese nation-state. Rescuing China's territory was the priority, but the means of doing so were essentially transnational. The national members of the emerging political community viewed by the Chinese leaders as an extension of blood and race played key roles in designating who belonged to that community and who was excluded. Their efforts were theoretically directed at securing China's independence.

The transnational extension of the Chinese nation to embrace the overseas Chinese occurred alongside discussions tackling the ethnically diverse populations within China. Ethnic diversity was a legacy of the imperial period that had to be dealt with for China to become a modern nation-state with one homogeneous culture and identity. The integration of the ethnic groups situated at the territorial and ethno-cultural margins into a uniform political whole became critical for China's formation as a nation-state. The views of the leaders were initially diverse, but they were gradually overshadowed by the dominant nationalist stance most prominently expressed in the writings of Sun Yatsen and later Chiang Kaishek. The racial nationalist interpretations were the foundations of subsequent formulations of the Chinese nation-state.

The nationalist discourses on *minzu*

Although it is generally accepted in Chinese scholarly circles that the concept *minzu*, which was introduced as part of modern nationalism, was initially borrowed from the Japanese term for people or nation, *minzoku*, in the late nineteenth century, there have recently been attempts to ascertain its indigenous origins. According to one scholar, the first mention of *minzu* was in a source dated back to the Tang dynasty (Zhou Chuanbin 2004: 3). There are also traces of the concept in a publication dated 1837 that are related to the work of Western missionaries and their Biblical stories of the Jewish nation (Zhou Chuanbin 2004: 3). Whatever the roots of the term, at the end of the nineteenth century it attained new significance with the challenge posed by Western imperialism. The concept *minzu* was deftly utilised by competing groups to propagate new kinds of political and nationalist sentiments among the Chinese. It served the purpose of strengthening internal borders in order to confront outside threats, and later it served the ruling regime of China. This evolving concept was related to the emergence of the idea of a Chinese nation free of aliens and independent from foreign influences. *Minzu* also marked the start of development of the theory of the nation, providing China and its people a rooted history and culture.

At that time, a mystical Yellow Emperor was purported to be the ancestor of all Chinese. A traditional folk notion of patrilineal descent was reconfigured into a racial discourse which called all inhabitants of China 'yellow species', 'lineages of Yellow Emperor' and a 'yellow race'. The term *minzu* integrated the notion of people (*min*) and the fiction of descent (*zu*) from the Yellow Emperor. 'Nation' meant a lineage that shared territory and an ancestor, or 'both an organic and a corporate unit', in Dikötter's words (1992: 92). The distinction between different ethnic groups was overcome by use of the terms *zu* (lineage) and *zhong* (species): 'one original *zhong* had engendered several unequally endowed *zu*', as Dikötter puts it (Dikötter 1992: 75). Thus, numerous ethnic groups within the Chinese empire, such as Mongols, Hui and Manchus, fell within the 'yellow race'.

For Sun Yatsen, *minzu* was related primarily to 'common blood'. He famously wrote in *Three Principles of the People* that blood overrode language, customs and religion as a basis for integrating the nation's citizens into a powerful community:

> The greatest force is common blood. The Chinese belong to the yellow race because they come from the blood stock of the yellow race. The blood of ancestors is transmitted by heredity down through the race, making blood kinship a powerful force.
>
> (Sun Yatsen 1932: 9)

In other words, Sun used *minzu* to promote the symbolic boundaries of blood and descent: 'nations' as political units were equated with 'races' (*zhong*) as biological units.⁹ *Minzuzhuyi*, or 'the doctrine of *minzu*', was the first principle of Sun Yatsen's *Three Principles of the People*; it was later adopted by both the GMD and the CCP. *Minzuzhuyi* was used to translate the ideology of nationalism into Chinese, indicating the overlap envisaged between nation and race.

In 1907 a famous political propagandist and revolutionary, Zhang Binglin, introduced the concept of the 'Chinese people-state' (*Zhonghua minguo*) (Chow 1997: 50). This notion further elaborated on the nationalist idea of the Chinese nation-state. It emphasised a 'racial-kinship' bond of the Chinese and their ties to the land. The image of the Yellow Emperor was reconstructed in such a way that he became the first ancestor of the Han Chinese rather than a pro-father of the 'yellow race'. The long-standing principle of culturalism, according to which people from different groups could become Chinese by adopting Chinese culture, was refuted. Instead, the concepts *hanzu* (Han race-lineage) and *zhonghua minzu* (Chinese nation) were linked by the emphasis placed on the patrilineal line of descent of a kinship group. Surnames were regarded to be reliable for tracing descent and distinguishing between kinship groups. This revision of the nationalist concept was primarily directed against Manchu rule, as expressed by Zhang Binglin in his definition of nationalism: 'The most important point to know is that nationalism does not mean the rejection of people of a different race. It means that no people of a different race are allowed to take away our government' (quoted in Chow 1997: 52).

The Han group was considered to constitute the absolute majority in China, a distinct people with shared physical attributes and a line of blood which could be traced back to the ancient period.¹⁰ Nationalities other than Han were viewed as sub-branches of Han and combined into a broader notion of the Chinese nation dominated by Han.¹¹ Thus, nationalists tried to establish a biological unity between all peoples within the political boundaries of China, and to equate the state and nation.¹² China as a single state, according to this view, naturally developed out of a single race.¹³ While nationalists stressed strengthening the sense of a nation-state (*guomin*) among the Chinese people, the Han were considered the focal group in the Chinese nation. To secure the achievements of the revolution and guarantee a favourable future for the newly-born republic, the leaders of the Chinese republic introduced an extensive programme of innovations to fuel nationalist and civic sentiments among the population under the banner of Sun Yatsen's *Three Principles of the People*. Reforms in the sphere of education and the adoption of Mandarin as the official spoken language as well as the medium of instruction at schools sought to equate the new Chinese state with the new Chinese nation and to unite all Chinese around the new government.

However, the shift from a cultural to a lineage/descent notion of nationhood served to divide the multiethnic population of China rather than to unite it against the Manchus. The demise of the old empire left behind problems stemming from the great variety of non-Han Chinese minorities in the large territory of the newly-born republic. In fact, in the late nineteenth century there were a growing number of nationalist movements at China's borders seeking independence from China (Crossley 1990). Because of the separatist implications of excluding ethnic groups on the territorial periphery from mainstream China, the two concepts of nation and state had to be synchronised and the concept of *minzu* had to be changed. To do so, Sun Yatsen and other leaders of the newly-established republican government coined a new inclusive term, *zhonghua*, by combining the two concepts 'middle kingdom' (*zhong guo*) and 'brilliant *xia*' (*huaxia*). The new republican name *zhonghua mingguo* (Chinese Republic) made the new Chinese state coterminous with the Chinese nation, which now embraced five main nationalities (*minzu*): Han, Manchus, Mongols, Tibetans and Muslims. The boundaries of the new Chinese nation-state thus coincided with the outline of the old Qing Empire. The shift from the narrow interpretation of nationalism against the rule of the Manchus to the integration of different groups within one notion of the Chinese nation was manifested in the adoption of a five-colour national flag. The stripes of red, yellow, blue, white and black symbolised the 'harmonious cohabitation of five ethnic tribes'(*wuzu gonghe*) – the Han, Manchus, Mongolians, Muslims and Tibetans – in one single nation.[14]

Yet the interpretation of *minzu* offered by nationalists had internal contradictions that required resolution. Chiang Kaishek (1887–1975), the effective head of the Nationalist Republic from 1927 to 1949 and the leader of the GMD, wrote in his study *China's Destiny and Chinese Economic Theory* that the five tribes composing China's population belonged to the same stock or family. To counteract the belief that the Chinese nation consisted of five different peoples, he added in a later edition that alien peoples – Manchus in the first place – should be driven out of the country or naturally assimilated (notes 9 and 17 in Chiang Kaishek 1947: 36). He underlined that the Manchus represented a different ethnic group and had to be incorporated into the Chinese nation by the Han. Chiang Kaishek also emphasised the 'common historical destiny of the various clans' in China, which were united and harmonised by the Chinese core, the Han. He claimed that all of the clans inhabiting Chinese territory had a common origin and differed only in religion and lifestyle. He clearly saw the nation as a culturally diverse but racially unified entity:

> Our various clans actually belong to the same nation, as well as to the same racial stock. Therefore, there is an inner factor closely linking the historical destiny of common existence and common sorrow and joy of the whole Chinese nation. That there are five peoples designated in China is not due to differences in race or blood, but to religion and geographical environment. In short, the differentiation among China's five peoples is due to regional and religious factors, and not to race or blood. This fact must be thoroughly understood by all our fellow countrymen.
> (Chiang Kaishek 1947: 39–40)

But the idea of different Chinese tribes united by common descent and blood was weakened when in the early 1920s the principle of 'harmonious cohabitation' (*gonghe*) was discarded for a policy of 'amalgamating' (*ronghe*) all ethnic groups into the Han to form a 'great Chinese nation' (*da zhonghua minzu*) (Chen, L. 1995). According to this policy, the Chinese state was constituted from the Han or had to be turned into a Han state by means of natural assimilation.

One of the most important ways that nationalists planted the seeds of the modern Chinese nation was by drawing a distinction between traditional loyalty to the dynasty and modern loyalty to the nation (Zarrow 1994: 100). They questioned the legitimacy of dynastic rule, accusing the Manchus of bending to the powers of Western imperialism, failing to represent the interests of the Chinese people, and ultimately being racist (Zarrow 1994: 105). Nationalists ascribed these faults of Manchu rule to Manchus' origins outside the core of the Chinese nation-race. They conflated race, culture and nation as they searched for China's distinctness from other nations and its roots as a nation. They reinvented the emperor's subjects as the Chinese nation-race.

Throughout this early period when nationalists were searching for a suitable model of nation-building, the ruling elite and intelligentsia ran the risk of being alienated from their own people as well as from China's past. Nationalists argued that cultural differences between the ruling Manchu and other ethnic groups attributed to racial background could help unify the nation against the foreign rule of the Manchus. However, they fell short of proposing initiatives inclusive of other minorities and therefore risked being estranged from these populations, who might then seek independence from the Chinese state. While attempting to unite the nation against foreign rule and Western dominance by nationalist means, the ruling elite and intelligentsia created a racially exclusive model that alienated not only the ruling Manchus but also a significant body of the population. That is why minorities were more receptive to communist programmes that offered solutions to the disenchanted and estranged sections of the population.

In their nationalist rhetoric, the elite laid out the contours of the Chinese nation through demarcating niches of belonging. The theme of who could be counted as Chinese, and on what grounds, was part of the long process of Chinese nation-building. Inclusion in the nation-building project depended on showing the officially-defined qualities of those who belonged to the nation; there were also corresponding definitions of estrangement. Influenced by politics and the need to unite the territory of the country against foreign rule, the revolutionaries constructed a new sense of identity that narrowly focused on the Han race, pictured as a perennial biological unit descended from a mythological ancestor. By 1911, culture, nation and race had become fused together for many revolutionaries fighting the Qing dynasty. Nationalists used the concept of *minzu* to refer to all the peoples inhabiting the territory of China, which in a sense was close to the Western notion of nation. However, the concept centred on the Han, who were seen as the unifying core of the nation and its key biological element that provided a common blood that flowed (or, through natural assimilation, should flow) in all the people inhabiting the territory.

An important outcome of this debate on the nature and character of the Chinese nation was the marriage of two different concepts, *zhongguo* and *huaxia*. The territorial boundaries of *zhongguo* were conflated with the cultural and racial delimitations of *huaxia*. The vague and ambiguous character of the resulting term, *zhonghua*, whose meaning is not expressed in territorial or political terms, allowed for wide-ranging interpretations of the limits of the Chinese nation. The emergence and popularisation of this term was also beneficial for policymakers, as the notion accorded them a certain amount of flexibility.

The qualitative change in the formulations of people's relations to political power in China was the most significant transformation that took place in the years of nationalist/revolutionary debates of Republican China. These formulations employed the new categories of race and ethnicity and common national territory in outlining the bases for belonging to China. Though they had shaped the contours of the Chinese polity earlier, they gained new impetus and formalisation with the decline and collapse of the Qing Empire. With the adoption of these new formulations of the Chinese polity and nationhood, the roles of the overseas Chinese and ethnic minorities changed, causing tensions that the Chinese leadership had to resolve or conceal. This transformation from apparent practices and formulations of belonging in late imperial China to their formalisation and institutional incorporation into the modern structure of the Chinese state was intimately related to how the protagonists of the political events saw the modern Chinese nation.

Throughout the period of Republican rule, the only slight deviation in the interpretation of the origins of the Chinese nation related to the status of the ethnic minorities. At different points, the ethnic minorities were seen as different races, subgroups of the Han, and people in need of assimilation into the great culture of the Han. These viewpoints dominated most of the discourse over *minzu* in China until the communists took power in 1949. Chinese communist interpretations of *minzu*, rooted in the ideology of Marxism–Leninism, had another aim.

Pre-People's Republic of China communist interpretations of the 'national' and 'overseas Chinese' questions

When the Chinese Communist Party was first formed, it adhered to the general ideas expressed by Sun Yatsen, including his *Three Principles of the People*. However, the CCP's interpretations of Sun Yatsen's principles, especially the principle of nationalism, had different connotations. While, for nationalists, nationalism had primarily an international character – that is, it represented a struggle for China's independence and equal status with other states – communists emphasised the domestic aspects of nationalism. They specifically associated nationalism with the status of minority nationalities in the revolutionary struggle and later in the People's Republic. The communists, who were primarily concerned with the 'class struggle' and peasant revolution, also considered the issue of how to acknowledge the diversity of the Chinese population and find an adequate form of governance for the emerging socialist state. But in contrast to the nationalists' dependence on social Darwinism and Western-born racial theories, the communists' analysis of the national situation and their formation of the national question were influenced by the works of Marx, Lenin and Stalin. Although the CCP and the GMD combined their forces in the United Front to repulse the increasing threat from Japan on two occasions, their views on the nature and form of revolutionary transformation differed significantly, which subsequently turned the two organisations against each other in a fierce struggle for power.

The evolution of the national issue in the CCP went through several stages in accordance with the phases and objectives of the party's revolutionary struggle. The early period, which started with the CCP's establishment in 1921 and lasted until Mao's ascent to power in the early 1930s, was characterised by the fusion of Chinese nationalist and Soviet communist interpretations of nationalism and the national question. At that period of the power struggle, communists assumed that the key Han provinces of a revolutionary nature would rise together with other nationalities of China according to the principle of internationalism in a joint struggle to establish the foundations of a proletarian society (Songben 2003: 7). One objective, and the core of the national question, was seen to be the integration of national minority 'peasants and workers' with the Han revolutionary classes in their struggle against foreign and internal oppression, and in building a single socialist state. The first mention of the national question by the CCP can be found in the CCP's early documents adopted in the 1920s.[15] The Manifesto of the Second National Congress names 'unification of China proper (including Manchuria) into a genuine democratic republic' and 'the achievement of a genuine democratic republic by the liberation of Mongolia, Tibet, and Sinkiang into a free federation' among seven primary CCP objectives (Manifesto 1959:64). While it is not certain what 'free' means here, it is clear that even at that early stage in the formulation of the Chinese communists' position on the national question there was no intention to guarantee the right of self-determination to national minorities. Rather, the emphasis was on building a new united multinational country under the single rule of the Communist Party; national minorities did not need their own communist parties, as 'their interests are abundantly guaranteed by the unique communist party of the country' (Moseley 1966: 7). This interpretation significantly differed from the one formulated by Lenin in Soviet Russia, which was initially developed around the idea of self-determination through the free will of people inhabiting the country; it was later reflected in the 1918 constitution of the Soviet Union. Minority nationalities were referred to in the first years of the CCP's existence as 'heterogeneous, various, weak, and small nationalities' (Jin Binggao 2002: 3). The first formulation of the concept *shaoshu minzu* (minority nationalities) was part of the development of policy strategies in the Red Army. In 1926 a document entitled 'On the Directions of Work of the National Army' stated, 'In relation to Manchu and Hui nationalities we need to respect their minority rights' (Jin Binggao 1988, 2002: 3).

After the communists' break with Chiang Kaishek's GMD in 1927, the tone of their statements on nationalism changed. They became hostile towards nationalists. Thus, the 1931 Constitution of the Soviet Republic stated that the country would 'do its utmost to assist the national minorities in liberating themselves from the yoke of the GMD militarists' (Art. 14, Constitution of the Soviet Republic 1931). The document went further to recognise 'the right of self-determination of the national minorities in China, their right to complete separation from China, and to the formation of an independent state for each national minority' (ibid.). Although self-determination for the minorities was explicitly promised, it was, in reality, no more than propaganda and lip-service to the right of self-determination (Connor 1984: 69). The mention of self-determination can be partly attributed to the attempt of Chinese communists to gain the support of people dissatisfied with Qing rule and Chiang Kaishek's nationality policy, which played down ethnic differences and stressed the unity of all peoples as members of the Chinese race.

Chinese communists quite early realised the strategic significance of areas inhabited by national minorities for the future of the socialist state. Also, at the time of the civil war between nationalists and communists, areas inhabited by nationalities were the only places that could offer outside support to the Long March of the Communist Party.[16] The period of the CCP's Long March, which marked the next stage in the CCP's national policies, was characterised by promotion of equality and friendship with national minorities in order to unite them against Japan and the GMD. The Party's self-determination rhetoric was a means to secure minorities' support and loyalty in a critical period of the power struggle. As soon as the communists gained confidence in their exercise of power, however, this rhetoric was no longer needed, and it gradually disappeared from Mao's public speeches and the Party's official documents. The right to self-determination (*zijue*) was withdrawn from the Party's programme by the mid-1930s, and self-government (*zizhi*) was offered instead.[17]

The CCP's approach to the national question shifted for the third time in the pre-PRC years when Mao Zedong re-united with the GMD in 1937–45. In his speech 'On Coalition Government', Mao Zedong (1945) re-confirmed that the communist understanding of nationalism was fully in line with Sun Yatsen's early principle of nationalism, which advocated the liberation of the Chinese nation and the equality of all the nationalities in China. However, when he discussed the right to self-determination of the nationalities in China, as declared by the GMD, he referred to an earlier statement he had made that the nationalities' 'spoken and written language, their manners and customs and their religious beliefs must be respected' (Mao Zedong 1945). He made no mention of their right to secede, although it was openly recognised as part of the idea of self-determination.[18] The transition from *zijue* to *zizhi* was further endorsed by the *Common Programme of the Chinese People's Political Consultative Conference 1949* (Common Programme 1962), which proclaimed the establishment of the PRC. Articles 50–53 of the Common Programme offered regional autonomy to national minorities in China, with the right to develop or reform their cultures and oppose 'nationalism and chauvinism' (Common Programme 1962: 51–52).Article 10 called on the army 'to defend the … territorial integrity and sovereignty of China' (ibid.: 37).

Having achieved power, the communists ceased emphasising, or indeed even mentioning, the self-determination slogans. 'Liberated' minority areas, which in some instances were liberated by force, were offered the diminished prospect of regional autonomy instead of the right of political independence promised during the propagandist phases of the revolution. After communist rule was secured, the national agenda changed further and was increasingly presented in the language of socialist construction and social class.

Before taking over power, the CCP had not developed an independent position on overseas Chinese policies, and in many ways relied on the earlier practices established by nationalists. The communists' ideological convictions significantly differed from those of nationalists and were reflected in their stance toward overseas Chinese. Their attitudes towards overseas Chinese were based on the communist belief in their revolutionary potential. The fact that the majority of the overseas Chinese were exploited coolies was a promising base for building an international revolutionary front. Moreover, in some cases overseas Chinese workers were politically conscious and outspokenly supported the idea of independent China (Bailey 2006: 65). To consolidate these patriotic sentiments of the overseas Chinese, a branch of the Chinese Communist Youth Party was established in Paris in late 1910s–early 1920s (Benton and Gomez 2008: 235). The communist ideological principle of class solidarity rising above national and ethnic distinctions precluded communists from appealing to the overseas Chinese directly on the basis of common culture and descent. Instead, their overseas Chinese policies were formulated within the anti-imperialist framework of the United Front discussed in Chapter 2. In the run up to the second United Front between the GMD and CCP, the CCP established direct links with the overseas Chinese calling them to contribute to China's war against Japan. During the anti-Japanese war, overseas Chinese were seen as the major source of financial support and were encouraged to form an army of volunteers. It is estimated that between 1937 and 1940 overseas Chinese contributed more than 294 million Chinese dollars to China's war efforts against Japan (Benton and Gomez 2008: 242).

Conclusion

The relationship between the sovereignty and its subjects changed qualitatively during the transition from the imperial to the state form of governance in China. Though the question of who belonged to China, which was a concern throughout China's imperial history, was inherited by the subsequent regimes, China's encounter with Western modernity prompted modern formulations of pre-existing political processes. The overseas Chinese and ethnic minorities featured prominently in this transitional period, when China was coming to terms with the challenges of the Western-dominated modern world. The Chinese intellectuals debated who was a member of the Chinese nation and how China's independence and territorial integrity should be secured. Neither overseas Chinese nor ethnic minorities fitted easily into the new formulations of the Chinese nation-state. The Chinese leadership had to reconcile imperial ambitions to preserve the conquered territories with the new model of state governance based on territoriality and aspired national homogeneity. The desire to include overseas Chinese in the nation on the basis of common descent clashed with the principle of territorial citizenship of modern nation-states. China had to resolve this problem as it transformed itself into a modern nation-state.

With the emergence and early development of national discourse in China, Chinese elites debated the term *minzu*. After entering the vocabulary of the political and intellectual elite, this concept was central to defining the composition and limits of the Chinese nation. The leadership used it to define who belonged to the nation. In the late Qing Empire and Republican China, the limits of belonging were defined by race and common origins. The racial underpinnings of the notion of nationhood propagated by Chinese nationalists were rooted in part in social Darwinism. Their views were also shaped by their aggravation with the ruling Qing regime and their fear – which had been deliberately generated – that China would be extinguished as a nation.

Race-dominated discourse prevailed until the communists took power in 1949. The positions of the Chinese communists on the national issue fluctuated, reflecting ups and downs in their power struggle with nationalists and shifts in the priorities of the revolutionary struggle. Their positions grew more systematic after they secured power. In contrast to nationalists, communists shifted the focus of their nationality work to the domestic level, and in invoking the concept *minzu* they were predominately concerned with the national minorities issue. Because of different priorities in their political rule – national survival for nationalists, consolidation of power for communists – their formulations of the national question diverged. In both interpretations of Chinese nationhood, however, racially-based ethnic factors and territoriality offered different visions of the nation.

Though the idea of a territorially defined China was propagated by the Chinese elite through its transnational activities among overseas Chinese, the nonterritorial aspects of nation-building were prominent in China's national project and part of the struggle to secure an independent and sovereign Chinese state. China submitted to the Western vision of modernity, but its modernisation project involved nonterritorial, ethnically-invoked social mobilisation. The roles of ethnicity in Chinese society and nation-building were important issues during the late Qing and Republican periods. Although the nationalists and communists advocated different interpretations of *minzu*, both saw the so-called Han majority as the core of the nation and its most developed group. *Minzu* in its broad sense referred to the whole Chinese nation – the Han-dominated nation – while *minzu* as a nationality referred to the backward minorities who should be assisted to achieve at least the developmental level of the Han under Party tutelage. In both cases, *minzu* played highly instrumental roles and demonstrated Han dominance over the national discourse. Whatever meaning was ascribed to the term – whether *minzu* was conceptualised in purely racial terms or presupposed a combination of certain 'objective' criteria of belonging – its primary role was to fulfil political aims of the ruling elite. The flexible use of the term by those in power shows China's unstable and pliable national framework, which could be revised to serve particular interests and goals.

2 Overseas Chinese and minority nationalities in socialist nation-building

With the takeover by communists and the founding of the PRC in 1949 came a new state with a new national doctrine. The unity of the country, which encompassed a single 'Chinese nation', was assumed to be achieved through the integration of all revolutionary classes into one United Front of revolutionary struggle. As much as Republicans had used race to promote national unity, communists employed the idea of class to assert the essential unity of the Chinese people in their struggle and consolidation of power. Class struggle, a key principle of Marxism, joined the nationalist discourse of 'citizen' and 'race' in conceiving the nation as a political community (Fitzgerald 1996: 71). Class became a parameter of belonging to the Chinese socialist nation. It served to establish China's place in the world as a distinctive 'class nation' with a mission to resist oppressor nations.

The new communist government under the leadership of Mao Zedong embarked on the socialist-building project by 'uniting' a broad range of revolutionary forces in the United Front. Two immediate participants in the front whose loyalty and allegiance the Communist Party religiously sought to win were the Chinese ethnic populations and the overseas Chinese. Throughout the period of the power struggle with the GMD, the Chinese communists regarded the support of ethnic minorities and overseas Chinese as extremely important for their legitimacy and for building a new socialist China. Ethnic minorities occupied the vast and most strategically important areas of the north and southwest borderlands, which were rich in resources. The mobilisation and physical integration of these areas into the project of socialist construction were among the primary goals of the new government. The overseas Chinese represented a substantial group, and many had accumulated capital, influence and power, especially in Southeast Asian countries. Since the early twentieth century they had customarily been included in the realm of Chinese domination. It was a group that was difficult to define, influence and control, because of its transterritoriality and subjection to the authority of other sovereign territories. Although the CCP did not require the overseas Chinese to legitimise its rule, or to represent and advocate the communist ideals of the Chinese government abroad, their accumulated financial and human capital constituted an important body of resources which the newly-established regime hoped could contribute to Chinese socialist construction. Both groups had exclusive participatory roles in the United Front of revolutionary struggle (later called the United Front of socialist construction), and were often mentioned hand in hand in the Party's propaganda documents and Mao's public speeches. On numerous occasions Mao stressed that a front of 'workers, peasants, soldiers, intellectual and business men, all oppressed classes, all people's organisations, democratic parties, minority nationalities, overseas Chinese and other patriots' should be mobilised to realise the socialist revolution in China (Mao Zedong 1947: 170). Moreover, in many of Mao's speeches 'minority nationalities and overseas Chinese' appeared next to each other as if they occupied similar roles in the socialist project of the Chinese state.

This chapter examines how the PRC managed its policies toward overseas Chinese and minority nationalities in the period of socialist nation-building (1949 to the late 1970s). I discuss the tactics of the Communist government towards minority nationalities and how they were included in the project of socialist nation-building. I also examine how the communist leadership sought to bolster the sentiments of belonging to the newly-established Chinese Communist state among the overseas Chinese. Members of this group had been regarded as China's transterritorial nationals since the adoption of the Nationality Law by the Qing dynasty in 1909. Both nationalist and communist ideologies were employed by the Chinese communists in their propaganda and organisation of the nation-building project in the first ten years of their rule in China. These ideologies were simultaneously used to target different groups involved in the project. While communist slogans were used to create 'socialist Chinese' out of backward minorities, ethno-nationalist rhetoric was employed to reach out to and attract overseas Chinese to the socialist-building project. Thus, whereas both groups were seen as participants in the United Front and the socialist project, the strategies used to draw them into these initiatives were different and somewhat conflicting. The unifying concept employed by the Communists to substitute for the notion of a nation-state was the amorphous class-defined concept of the People, which united the revolutionary elements and served as a denominator of a human collectivity with a common goal. The pursuit of the shared goal of constructing socialism dominated over other unifying elements, though these other elements, such as territory and political and ethnic identity, were not neglected.

The PRC's overseas Chinese and ethnic policies changed throughout the period of socialist nation-building. There were periods of relative pluralism and others of rigid dogmatism. The only consistent continuity throughout the period was the aspiration to build a socialist society, free of class divisions and united by a single proletarian culture. The first period can be designated as lasting from the moment of the CCP's ascent to power in 1949 until 1958, when the Party initiated a country-wide experiment of accelerated socialist building termed the Great Leap Forward. The second period ran from that time until the end of the Cultural Revolution and was characterised by rigidity and dogmatism, which affected all aspects of Chinese society.

The first section of this chapter analyses the ideological and institutional arrangements for the implementation of national socialist construction by the

United Front. The United Front work was directed at the domestic affirmation of power by the CCP and at the internal societal and economic transformations conforming to the communist doctrine rather than at the international revolutionary struggle. To capture the nature of the PRC's policies towards minority nationalities and overseas Chinese during this period of socialist construction, I introduce the terms 'domestic cosmopolitanism' and 'ethnic internationalism' in the second section. Section three examines how the national question was conceptualised by the CCP. Here I point to an important shift in the national discourse from the international to the domestic level and discuss how the Chinese leaders flexibly adapted Stalin's definition of nationality to fit their political interests and agenda for socialist transformation. Section four considers the PRC's early strategies towards minority nationalities. Here I elaborate on the notion of 'domestic cosmopolitanism' and demonstrate that the CCP's strategy towards ethnic minorities aimed to detach them from the localised and fixed allegiances that conflicted with the Party's interpretation of patriotism. The fifth section of this chapter deals with the complexities of socialist China's policies towards the overseas Chinese. I demonstrate that in pursuit of these policies China adhered to the seemingly contradictory principles of ethnic nationalism and internationalism. China had to find a balance between sustaining the communist regime economically – overseas Chinese and their considerable funds provided a partial solution – and being recognised as a legitimate regime internationally. The last section highlights the shattering effects of the radical projects – the Great Leap Forward and Cultural Revolution – on the PRC's policies towards the overseas Chinese and minority nationalities. While all policies of China's socialist period were translated into class terms, the class formulations were based on racially-defined ethnic premises. Class designated who was in and who was out of the revolutionary socialist construction project, while ethnic factors determined the scope of revolutionary activities practiced inside and outside the new Chinese state. The seemingly contradictory policies combining class and race, nationalism and cosmopolitanism, and internationalism and extra-territorialism that characterised China's approach towards overseas Chinese and ethnic minorities during the years of socialist nation-building show the ambiguous and often oppositional foundations upon which the Chinese socialist nation was based.

Socialist nation-building: the United Front of revolutionary struggle

The birth of the idea of the United Front is commonly attributed to Lenin's writings on the popular front of world revolution. On the territory of its origins, the Soviet Union, it was implemented by Stalin during the Second World War, as well as through the activities of the Comintern internationally. However, China's utilisation of the term acquired a wider scope and application. The domestic situation in the 1920s, when China faced a mounting threat from expansionist Japan and was being torn apart by the competing groups within China, contributed to the popularisation of the idea. The United Front emerged as a tactic of the CCP and can be summarised as a strategy of uniting with a lesser enemy in an attempt to defeat a greater common threat. At first the idea of the United Front was a marriage of convenience between the GMD and the CCP in their mutual struggle against the Japanese invasion. However, it later progressed into an ideological formula for improving China's domestic and international performance, and served as a key slogan in the CCP's struggle with the GMD; it was a defining principle of party-building. Hence Armstrong (1977: 19) calls the United Front a 'dual policy of struggle and unity'. The main goal behind this dual strategy was to win over the hearts and minds of the hesitating masses and to undermine the popularity of the GMD. Having started off as a vocal principle, the United Front found its institutional realisation in the communist government's Bureau of United Front Work, which in 1938 progressed into the United Front Work Department (UFWD) (Van Slyke 1970: 129). In practical terms, the United Front of the revolutionary struggle was implemented through a series of policies aimed at the consolidation of power and support by the CCP. The UFWD was also a key player in monitoring the government's overseas Chinese and nationalities policies.

While the United Front was a strategy to win the revolutionary struggle, it did not amount to a strategy of world revolution, which largely remained an overarching ideological principle. Van Slyke (1970: 120) identifies two distinct levels in the structure of the United Front. One was what he dubs 'the United Front from above' which defined the relationship between the GMD and the CCP and their leaders. The other level was the CCP's attempt to gain popular support for its goal of exclusively ruling the country – 'the United Front from below'. At both levels, the tactical line of the United Front was characterised by its domestic orientation. As Van Slyke (1970: 122) observes, at that early period the PRC did not heed the call of the Soviet Union to organise an international United Front policy. Only in the short period from 1958 to 1964, according to Armstrong (1977), did the PRC adhere to the broader principle of the United Front in its foreign policy.

After the CCP seized power in 1949, the function of the United Front primarily concerned gaining more popular support for the ruling party and advancing its legitimacy. Yet the United Front's activities also expanded beyond the political and territorial boundaries of the People's Republic. Internationally, the CCP faced the challenge of winning its battle of legitimacy with Taiwan and being diplomatically recognised as the only viable government of China; it sought to be accepted by the international community and thereby sustain the newly-established government economically and politically. Additionally, the language of the United Front was extensively employed in the PRC's dealings with the overseas Chinese. While the communists called for solidarity of the overseas Chinese with the communist regime in Beijing, this call rested on a largely nationalist postulation of the blood ties between the overseas Chinese and people in mainland China. Furthermore, the efforts and resources of 'overseas Chinese work' were used to promote the overseas Chinese's contributions to the PRC's socialist construction rather than to encourage them to take part in a communist revolution in their host countries.

The PRC's policies towards its ethnic minority populations and overseas Chinese during the period of socialist nation-building must be considered within the framework of the United Front. But these two policy strands were significantly different from each other. While the policies undertaken by the communists to encourage ethnic minorities and overseas Chinese to express their loyalty to the regime could be seen as similar, in fact they were quite divergent tactics of imposing abstract and uniform criteria of who could be part of China's people, a concept which was dependent on the class division of Chinese society. The application of the concept of the People to minority nationalities and the overseas Chinese was carried out in distinctly diferent ways. Toward the overseas Chinese, an ethnic sentiment was emphasised over class stratification, while at the domestic level strategies towards ethnic minorities stressed their class position and loyalty to the communist regime as essential to inclusion in the United Front.

When the Chinese communists came into power, they used nationalist rhetoric extensively and were preoccupied with socialist nation-building, but their national discourse was presented in a new way. They replaced the ideology of nationalism associated with the GMD's independence struggle with the principle of patriotism (*aiguo zhuyi*), which called for the devotion of all citizens to the state, its institutions, its leadership, and the CCP. Nationalism was regarded as a divisive and pejorative sentiment. It was renounced by the PRC's leadership as a subversive and counter-revolutionary doctrine, and associated with the independence-seeking claims of some minority groups or with reactionary Han-chauvinism. Thus, while in the late Qing and early Republican periods Chinese nationalism and the national question served as factors unifying the Chinese people in fighting against foreign imperialism, the same national concerns were used by the Chinese communists to consolidate their power at the domestic level.

The communists manipulated the issue of the national question to earn the support of the minority populations. At this stage they also wanted to satisfy the expectations and secure the support of the forerunners of the revolutionary struggle – the Soviet Union. In a sense, the Chinese communists' formulation of national policies to meet the hopes of minority populations became their trump card in their power struggle with nationalists. Their withdrawal of the right of self-determination after their successful takeover of power is especially illustrative of how the national issue was utilised by the communists to secure their power. In relation to the overseas Chinese, the Chinese communists appealed to their roots in China as well as their internationalism and extraterritorial patriotism. This line of patriotic/nationalist appeal found its expression after 1949 when the overseas Chinese were granted representation in the Chinese People's Political Consultative Conference (CPPCC) and the National People's Congress (NPC).

In contrast to nationalists who saw the Chinese nation in racial terms, the communists conceived it in an essentially 'cosmopolitan' way. For the CCP, Chinese people were part of the world revolutionary front rather than a self-sufficient collectivity of a single race. However, the communists did not discard nationalist rhetoric in their struggle against the GMD. In their attacks against the GMD, the CCP condemned the GMC's detachment from the people (*renmin*) and its betrayal of the Chinese nation by its complicity in Japan's encroachment. This protean character of Chinese communism was manifested in the communists' hyphenated construction of people (*renmin*) and nation (*minzu*) – *minzu-renmin*. *Renmin* here refers to people in an abstract internationalist sense, to the people of the world who, on par with Chinese, participate in revolutionary struggle. All people are united on the grounds of their subjugated position and are destined for a common future. At the same time, people of every nation (*minzu*) were expected to unite in a coherent whole for the common cause of the world's people. It was Levenson who originally suggested that Chinese communists used the idea of socialist transformation of the Chinese nation in a cosmopolitan way. According to him, the Chinese employed a Marxist–Leninist time-scale to 'extend' China's history as a 'modern but not western' proletarian nation (Levenson 1971: 28). By adapting foreign conceptualisations to China's cause, the communists used the trappings of cosmopolitanism to advance the Chinese nation. Or, in Levenson's words, 'the internationalist term *renmin* becomes the vindicator of nationalism' (Levenson 1971: 28).

The obscure and amorphous concept of the people reflected the CCP's categorisation of who belonged and who was excluded from the Chinese revolutionary stock, which was identified with the notion of the Chinese revolutionary nation. Mao stated:

> We must first be clear on what is meant by 'the people' and what is meant by 'the enemy'. The concept of 'the people' varies in content in different countries and in different periods of history in a given country. Take our own country for example. During the War of Resistance against Japan, all those classes, strata and social groups opposing Japanese aggression came within the category of the people, while the Japanese imperialists, their Chinese collaborators and the pro-Japanese elements were all enemies of the people. During the War of Liberation, the US imperialists and their running dogs – the bureaucrat-capitalists, the landlords and the Kuomintang reactionaries who represented these two classes – were the enemies of the people, while the other classes, strata and social groups, which opposed them, all came within the category of the people. At the present stage, the period of building socialism, the classes, strata and social groups which favour, support and work for the cause of socialist construction all come within the category of the people, while the social forces and groups which resist the socialist revolution and are hostile to or sabotage socialist construction are all enemies of the people.
>
> (Mao Zedong 1957)

As Schoenhals (1994) explains, in the Chinese communist interpretation, the concept of the people is different from 'nationals' or citizens, which encompass all persons living in the territory of the PRC, including landlords and bourgeois elements. The people refers only to revolutionary toiling masses. The people were presented by the communist leadership in opposition to the preceding 'imperialist' regimes in China where the people were 'suppressed and exploited'. The new

PRC government was popularised as the first true people's government. The prerogative to represent the people's rights, opinions and even feelings was granted exclusively to the CCP, making it, therefore, the people's platform. Those who did not fall into the category of the people were automatically dismissed as counter-revolutionary or non-people elements, widely referred to as 'ox-monsters' or 'snake-demons' (*niugui sheshen*) during the Cultural Revolution (Schoenhals 1994). The new socialist style of nation-building produced novel notions of the United Front and the people which referred to diferent groups. The United Front reached out broadly to the groups of people – irrespectively of their class – participating or potentially participating in the revolution. The notion of the people, in turn, was ideologically contingent on class and encompassed only revolutionary masses, dismissing the rest of the population as enemies or non-people. Other identity-defining factors, such as territory, ethnicity and kinship allegiances, were relegated to secondary roles as the communists pursued a society free of divisions and united by the common idea of socialism.

'Domestic cosmopolitanism' and 'ethnic internationalism'

Minority nationalities and overseas Chinese were included in the United Front of revolutionary struggle on different terms, and the policies towards them had different principles. To characterise the ways China acted towards these two groups during the period of socialist nation-building, I invoke the concepts of internationalism and cosmopolitanism. It is important to emphasise that these are two distinct terms. Although they are not often contrasted, they are essentially different, and adherence to them results in qualitatively different politics. In interpreting these terms I follow the distinctions drawn by, among others, Yashin (2000) and Humphrey (no date), who maintain that internationalism rests on presupposing and respecting national borders and the sovereignty of other members of the international system. Cosmopolitanism, on the other hand, is a nonterritorial concept based on the absence of socio-political boundaries and nominally does not prioritise any particular cultural system over others.

To illustrate how different ideas, policies and principles were used to coax or force overseas Chinese and minority nationalities to participate in the socialist revolution in the early years of communist rule, I will next introduce the terms 'domestic cosmopolitanism' and 'ethnic internationalism'. The idea of 'domestic cosmopolitanism' may strike one as counterintuitive. The Western perspective on cosmopolitanism derives predominately from the Kantian tradition, which does not recognise territorial limits to cosmopolitan practices and where a human being is an end in itself. Cosmopolitanism in this tradition is perceived in essentially unbounded terms and is often summarised in the literature as to think and act beyond the local. 'Domestic cosmopolitanism', on the other hand, can be understood as denoting Chinese communist strategies to nurture a sense of loyalty among ethnic minorities towards the new communist government; it relies on a cosmopolitan understanding of class rather than on other social or territorial adherences. The Chinese communist use of the idea of class is a cosmopolitan one, as class transcends territorial boundaries, as well as culture and gender, to unite people in one revolutionary-minded collective.

As used here, cosmopolitanism is restricted by China's traditional self-centred image of the world. The ideas of *tianxia*, an all-encompassing realm with ultimate values imposed by the Emperor and the Confucian code of practice, and *huaxia*, a civilized core within this area, are often seen as shaping much of China's modern worldview.[1] The Confucian ideas attributed to the governing principles of the rulers of imperial China have been employed by the Chinese leaders to serve their current political interests. Chinese leaders, including in the socialist period, have always treated China as a civilisation that provided a set of ideals for implementation in *tianxia*. This realm is defined not by territorial limitations, but by the reach of the universal ideals proliferated by the 'civilized' core. As a result of China's confrontation with the imperialist ambitions of the West and Japan at the end of the nineteenth century, China's ambitious vision of its central position in the world was shifted to the national level and pursued in relation to domestic 'others' in China. In a sense, China's world was brought down to the level of a nation-state and territorially restricted, whereas its ambitions to excel and count as a holder of a certain code of values were preserved from the imperial times. With the establishment of the communist regime in China, 'domestic cosmopolitanism' was exercised through the proliferation of the idea of class solidarity, which was promoted as an overarching sentiment necessary for participation in socialist construction on the national level and which undermined localised allegiances. From the outside, the policies towards minorities could be seen as a strategy of homogenising groups in a restricted territory; from an inside perspective (i.e. the Chinese traditional view), the world was encouraged to abandon its internal boundaries.

Overseas Chinese fell essentially within the same conceptual framework of socialist nation-building, albeit on different conditions. The ethnic principle, as defined and followed by the previous Republican leadership, was thoroughly followed by the communists in their designation of who belonged to the overseas Chinese stock. Through a range of policies, termed here 'ethnic internationalism', the PRC discreetly claimed an extraterritorial attachment of the overseas Chinese to communist China on the basis of their blood and ethnic ties. At the same time, in its early period of existence, the PRC was compelled to accommodate to international norms, such as noninterference in the internal affairs of the home countries of the overseas Chinese, in order to secure greater diplomatic recognition and peaceful relations with other states in Southeast Asia. In this international environment, the PRC's survival and strength outweighed its ambition to subvert the 'oppressive' regimes and appeal to the overseas Chinese to take a greater part in socialist construction. In the later years of China's socialist period, the overseas Chinese were referred to as class enemies or non-people and essentially fell out of China's national realm.

China's policies towards ethnic minorities and the overseas Chinese both had the primary purpose of giving prominence and legitimacy to China's young communist government. As such, they were more concerned with domestic socialist nation-building and the international status of the newly-formed government than with the realisation of world revolution.

National question in Maoist China

The trend of reversing China's isolationism and introducing foreign ideas into the Chinese polity started in the late nineteenth century. As discussed in Chapter 1, under the influence of foreign racial and evolutionary theories, China's ethnic minorities were regarded in the late Qing and early Republican periods as sub-branches of the Han nationality rather than distinct ethnic groups. The Chinese state had first been considered a republic of five races, but later racial interpretations of the Chinese state biologically united the Han people and their sub-branches. Although both reformers and nationalists developed theories on the national question, they did not take root due to the inability of the reformers and nationalists to secure power. Therefore, systematic conceptualisations of the national question and its practical realisation did not take place until the communist takeover in 1949. Work aimed at transforming Chinese society reached its apogee in the early years of the PRC's existence.

Chinese communists developed their position on the national issue in line with the positions of Soviet leaders, especially Stalin. These positions significantly differed from the Western Weberian interpretations of an ethnic group or nation. The Weberian approach emphasises self-ascription as a main characteristic of an ethnic group, while Soviet and Chinese communist approaches saw the nation as an objective type of social group which could be measured by a set of criteria. According to Stalin's definition, a nation as 'a historically evolved, stable community of language, territory, economic life, and psychological makeup manifested in a common culture' belonged to the epoch of capitalism and would disappear when capitalism was replaced with communism under pressure of the 'international solidarity of workers' (Stalin 1954: 308). According to this interpretation, the nationality question reflected the class struggle within society and was a manifestation of 'a peasant question'. Stalin saw its solution in the unity of the world proletariat.

Minzu as used by the Chinese communists is reminiscent of the Soviet terms nationality and *narodnost*. *Minzu* was primarily used to refer to different groups within the country rather than to the nation-state as a whole. Direct translation of the Soviet terms was impossible due to differing interpretations and the lack of corresponding Chinese notions. While the Soviet Union differentiated between concepts such as *natsia* (nation), *natsionalnost* (nationality), and *narodnost* (ethnic group), which referred to different rights, privileges and degrees of administrative autonomy, there was only a loose concept of *minzu* in the Chinese language. The Chinese concept of *buzu* was closer in its meaning to Stalin's interpretation of *narodnost*. *Buzu*, as summarised by Wang Lei (1983: 176), 'is merely an unformed nation', and it is transformed into a nation or nationality as a result of a qualitative change in the four factors behind the formation of a nation. In 1962, a special conference was held that examined the use of the terms *minzu* and *buzu*. At the conference the term *buzu* was rejected as inadequate for referring to minority nationalities in China. It was agreed that although *shaoshu minzu* was really *narodnosti* or *buzu*, i.e. temporal formations, they should be referred to as nationalities for convenience (Moseley 1965: 20–21). The aim of the 'nationalities work', or *minzu gongzuo*, was seen in the designation of minority nationalities as immature nationality groups and in the desire to facilitate their transformation into nationalities with the four requirements identified by Stalin. As such *minzu* acquired a minority overtone and was associated with minority nationalities (*shaoshu minzu*) and the nationalities question (*minzu wenti*) in China. The national question became the national minorities question, and it was devoted to the development of policies towards national minorities.

The problems that the Chinese communists had to tackle in order to reconcile Stalin's definition of a nation with China's official view of its history were the level of economic development of the minority populations and the pre-capitalist origins of the Han nationality. Stalin's definition, with its link to the capitalist mode of economic development, was problematic, because of all the groups living in China, according to Chinese scholars, only the Han were approaching the capitalist stage of socio-economic development.[2] For Stalin, no nations existed prior to the rise of the capitalist mode of economic development, and at the moment of the PRC's creation only the Han could qualify for the status of *minzu*. Chinese leaders, however, found it quite problematic to admit that there was no Chinese nation, or at least Han nationality, prior to the spread of capitalism in the mid-nineteenth century. Acceptance of this opinion would have challenged a long-held belief in ancient roots and in the longtime existence of some form of national unity on the territory of China, which in some instances dated back to the Qin and Han dynasties (221 BC–220 AD). With the existence of different categories of minority populations, it was difficult to demonstrate the commitment of the CCP to guaranteeing them equal status in a newly-formed state. And so the leadership decided that, while Stalin's interpretation of a nation was 'completely correct for explaining the formation of nations in Europe', it did not take into consideration all the factors at play in the case of China (Wang Lei 1983: 169). Instead of arguing that capitalism was an essential requirement for the emergence of a nation, and indeed its primary characteristic, Chinese leaders chose to emphasise the role of internal cohesion in a community. It was officially decided that a stable group of people sharing a common territory, no matter how populous or territorially extensive, whether they had a low or high level of social development, or whether the core of this group was located within or outside the territory of the PRC, would be referred to as *minzu* (Wu Xiaohua 2003: 14).

After almost ten years of debates in the Party and academic institutions, it was determined that, while the Han formed a coherent *minzu*, due to the combined forces of imperialism and domestic feudalism, other groups in China were prevented from forming modern nations and remained at feudal or pre-feudal levels of development (Moseley 1966: 15). Furthermore, the groups which had not reached the level of capitalism could progress straight into socialism, bypassing the earlier development stages. Thus, emphasis was put on the different levels of socio-economic and cultural development of the groups, and the role of the Han was to assist other peoples of China to emerge from their backwardness and to get them on their way to building a common good in the form of socialism. Another objective of the Han, who were presented as the chief promoters of communism, was overcoming the alienation of the ethnic minorities from the revolutionary process and its achievements, and integrating them into the revolution.

A loosely-developed term with numerous interpretations, *minzu* is sometimes referred to in the Chinese scholarly literature as a concept with two immediate meanings. According to this view, one of *minzu's* meanings is a broad one (*guang yi*), and the other is a narrow one (*xia yi*). The narrow sense of *minzu* refers to all the nationalities inhabiting China (*zhonghua ge minzu*) and emphasises their distinct characteristics, such as culture, traditions, religion and so on. In the broad sense, *minzu* encompasses the idea of the unity of peoples, hence the unity of the Chinese nation as whole (*zhonghua minzu*). In its narrow sense, *minzu* is nominally regarded as a neutral term which equally refers to all nationalities within China. Policy documents of the socialist period equalised all the nationalities within the territory of the PRC and granted them equal rights. [3] However, all minority nationalities which in the process of the identification project were defined as *shaoshu minzu* were set in opposition to the dominant Han nationality. Apart from the quantitative inequality, the term *shaoshu minzu* also carries associations with primitivism, backwardness and a lack of culture. It is related to the attributes of underdeveloped societies which have not achieved a capitalist mode of production. As Jin Binggao (1988) noted, 'such words as "weak and small nationality" (*ruoxiao minzu*), "small nationality" (*xiao minzu*) and "backward nationality" (*luohou minzu*) ... were used interchangeably to refer to the same or similar status', i.e. national minorities. Therefore, the introduction of the term *shaoshu minzu* at the time of the identification project justified the right of the Han-Chinese, being more advanced economically, socially and culturally, to rule over minorities. The Chinese communists institutionalised a low level of development as a norm for status as a minority nationality, which, in the end, prevented officially-identified *shaoshu minzu* participating equally in socialist construction. Although, as noted by Gladney (1996: 319), the idea of the Chinese nation-state 'has been predicated on the idea, if not the myth, of pluralism', from the very beginning, the Chinese national socialist project was based on the principle that Han people were superior to minorities.

While the narrow sense of *minzu* was extensively revised in the socialist period to reflect the ideological outlook and political position of China's new government, the broad sense of *minzu* did not undergo significant historical and theoretical revisions. The popularisation and general acceptance of the broad sense of *minzu* was related to China's pre-historic vision of itself as a nonterritorial formation centred around the patrilineal ties and deemed unity of the Chinese people. Chinese communists did not refute this nationalist interpretation of the broad sense of *minzu* emphasising common race and descent as unifying factors of the Chinese nation. Overseas Chinese were still viewed in accordance with this nonterritorial vision of China and as a desired part of the Chinese revolutionary socialist experiment. Only when the class affiliations and transterritorial character of overseas Chinese clashed with China's shaky international position, the communist leadership had to limit its ambitions for the overseas Chinese.

In diverging from the Soviet approach to the nationality question, Chinese leaders produced their own way of theorising about it. Approaching *minzu* loosely from two perspectives allowed for flexibility in interpretation. By introducing the concept of *shaoshu minzu*, a hierarchical relationship among national groups in China was established. The Han took the leading role of an 'elder brother' (*da ge*) not only in numerical terms, but in economic and cultural areas. Reference to *minzu* in the broad sense, i.e. to the unified multinational Chinese nation-state (*tongyi de duo minzu de guojia*), did not change the dominant role of the Han either. On the contrary, it pointed to the seeming unity of the dominant nationality in China with the overseas Chinese on the basis of their common ancestral and ethnic origins in pre-historic China. The organisation of the Chinese state and the official name of the PRC never reflected the pre-PRC communist promise that minority nationalities would enjoy equality with the Han. The official name stated that a country of Chinese people, not *peoples*, was established, thereby implicitly legitimising the dominant position of the Han. The dual interpretation of *minzu* by the Chinese leadership allowed for an exclusive role of the Han majority in the fixed hierarchy of national relations within Chinese society. The new socialist nation was established on the ruins of the unfulfilled national aspirations of China's multiple ethnic groups, and like its predecessor viewed itself as a transterritorial racial formation. While the socialist government aimed to build an egalitarian classless society, free of divisions and inequalities, the party-state effectively created and institutionalised *minzu* as a new category of domination and exploitation.

'Domestic cosmopolitanism' in socialist nation-building

The communist interpretation of the Chinese nation was different from the one suggested by the reformers and republicans of the Late Qing and Republican periods. Mao Zedong succinctly summarised the core of New China's nation-building vision: 'First the dying out of classes, then the state, finally the nation – that is true of the whole world' (Mao Zedong quoted in Fei Xiaotong 1981a: 85). According according to this line of thinking, throughout the period of socialist revolution, divisions along national lines would gradually fade away together with class distinctions and would be finally overtaken by a single proletarian culture. This overarching idea of shared proletarian values and culture could only be ingrained into the people's minds through intensive ideological and propaganda work advocating the value of thinking beyond fixed and local categories on the part of the population.

After taking over the country, the next objective for the CCP was 'to strengthen nationalities' unity and dissipate nationalities' alienation' (Moseley 1965: 17). The *General Programme of the PRC for the Implementation of Regional Autonomy for Nationalities*, adopted as an official policy in 1952, stated that 'each national autonomous area is an integral part of the PRC' (General Programme 1962: 181). This interpretation of the national question was repeated in the 1954 constitution (Art. 3 of *General Programme*). By the beginning of the 1950s, when all the minority areas were 'liberated', the communist position on the national issue was fully developed and formulated. The subsequent phase was primarily concerned with socialist nation-building, which in relation to national minorities was manifested in the implementation of the national minority identification project (*minzu shibie*) and the introduction of limited autonomy to recognised minorities. The establishment of autonomous areas was an essential political mechanism for fostering a sense of identification with the regime in Beijing. At the same time it was a way of granting political status to the areas identified by the state as inhabited by minorities. In a sense it constituted a form of citizenship for minorities in the framework of the PRC.

The Chinese leadership imported the Soviet idea of internationalism to guide them in their nationality work (Dreyer 1976: 91). However, it was never implemented in the way it was in the Soviet Union, where the system allowed the existence of communist parties for the republics and the nationality policy was officially coined internationalism. In the PRC, the CCP assumed the role of the leader of all ethnic minorities (Moseley 1966: 7). By distancing its interpretation of the national question from the one by the GMD and showing a certain degree of cultural plurality,[4] the CCP had already secured minorities' loyalty during the years of its power struggle with the nationalists. After the communist ascent to power, China's nationalities work aimed to continue strengthening a sense of patriotism and trust in the communist government. In the context of Chinese socialist nation-building, patriotism was synonymous with love for the Party and the central government. The CCP's policies towards ethnic minorities aimed to evoke support for the all-country idea of the 'peasant revolution', across territorial, cultural, ethnic and gender boundaries. The socialist transformations were directed at lifting the minorities out of their sense of belonging to fixed geographical places at the local level, refuting their allegiances of kinship, and uniting the minorities through the idea of the revolutionary struggle. Through the implementation of land reform, social adjustments and organisation of the collectives, the idea of the unity of the Chinese people in the socialist revolutionary mission was instilled among minority populations.[5] Similarly, the introduction of a regional autonomy system was aimed at instilling a sense of unity of national minorities with the communist regime and its leadership (Moseley 1965: 17). In other words, the idea of socialist revolution was a tool to lift the people from their former attachments and unite them around the mission formulated and proliferated by the CCP. These undertakings were intended to eliminate 'colonial, semi-colonial and semi-feudal' traces of the previous systems, 'liberate' the population, and introduce a qualitatively new social system. These efforts of the PRC to detach minority nationalities from their local loyalties in favour of the centrally imposed revolutionary idea are coined here the promotion of *domestic cosmopolitanism*.

It is often observed in the literature that the ideological work carried out by communist governments considered the concept of cosmopolitanism antithetical

52 *Socialist nation-building*

to communist principles. Cosmopolitanism and patriotism from the perspective of Soviet ideology conflicted with each other. Cosmopolitanism, according to this interpretation, renounced national attachments and fostered nihilism. In the Soviet Union this viewpoint resulted in a severe campaign against 'homeless cosmopolitans'. The campaign identified and persecuted citizens, mainly of Jewish background, who were accused of being disloyal to the regime. Soviet academic tradition designated the exact parameters of cosmopolitanism, primarily for ideological reasons. Unlike in the Soviet Union, in China anti-cosmopolitan campaigns did not occur. Prior to the late 1960s, when a major fracture in the Sino–Soviet relationship emerged, China referred to its role in the world revolution as being one of the players in the socialist front led by the Soviet Union. While the communists saw their mission as radically transforming Chinese society, they did not see it in isolation; rather it was presented as part of the initiatives begun and led by the Soviet revolutionaries. This dedication to the Soviet Union was necessary for regarding China as a true internationalist nation; China was expected to defend the Soviet Union along with its own sovereignty. China's symbolic subordination to the Soviet Union was related to the fact that the Soviet Union proclaimed itself the leader of the world's working people; the leaders of the Soviet revolution, especially Lenin and Stalin, were regarded as the leaders of the Chinese toiling masses as well. Chinese leaders were seen as acting within the framework set out by the Soviet leaders. Along the same lines, the mission of China's ethnic minority leaders was attuned to the Soviet Union's and the CCP's perspectives, and thus they were re-educated to be 'emancipated' in accordance with communist ideology in thought-reform schools. Soon after the PRC's establishment, the Party started training minority officials who would represent minorities' interests at different levels of power. A network of nationality academies with one central minority nationalities' institution of higher learning, the Central Institute of Nationalities in Beijing,[6] was founded, and it started providing training for Party members and cadres from minority areas. The state education system shaped by the ideology of the CCP was introduced to the minority areas following the National Conference on Education among the Nationalities in 1951, which announced as its aim to overcome the distinctions between minority nationalities (Mackerras 1996: 133).

There are several specific ways domestic cosmopolitanism was manifested in China. While in the Western tradition the idea of cosmopolitanism is associated with individual sophistication and a person's imaginings beyond his or her own society, at the domestic level in China it was implemented through promoting the 'solidarities' and 'shared values' formulated by the CCP and the central government. The category of class was an overarching concept and the notion of the people emerged as its 'cosmopolitan denominator'. Chinese domestic cosmopolitanism suggested a form of political, social and cultural solidarity across localities, and called for the erosion of the social inequalities and cultural differences specific to different groups and their places of origin. In other words, the point of reference in the system was not the individual but the amorphous uniform collectivity of the people stripped of social and cultural disparities. In Mao

Zedong's formulation, 'countries (*guojia*) want independence, nations (or nationalities, *minzu*) want liberation, and the people (*renmin*) want revolution – this has become an irresistible historical trend' (in Zhou Enlai 1973). The class-defined concept of the people was represented as a driving force of societal transformations, while nationalities, according to Mao, sought liberation from suppression rather than independent rule.

Another related particularity of the PRC's domestic cosmopolitanism was that it promulgated the value of uniformity rather than diversity. Soon after the establishment of the PRC, nationality work was centralised and institutionalised. A special ministerial organ for supervising minority nationalities policies, the NAC, was established. Its duties included implementing the right of regional autonomy of national minorities, which was formulated in the *Common Programme of the Chinese People's Political Consultative Conference 1949* (Art. 51)[7] and in a guarantee of equality for all nationalities in the PRC (Art. 9) (Common Programme 1962). This institution was also responsible for identifying Chinese minority groups and their different stages of economic development, i.e. primitive, slave, feudal, capitalist and socialist. When this project of ethnic identification was initiated in the mid-1950s, it emphasised the common social basis of the minorities who had been exploited by the previous regimes and who were now 'liberated' and 'emancipated' by the struggle led by the CCP. The identification project aimed to determine the level of development, or rather underdevelopment, of the minorities in order to integrate them more 'efficiently' into the all-country modernisation project led by the Han, who were viewed as the most developed of all the ethnic groups.[8] Throughout the identification project, most ethnic minorities were categorised into fixed ethnic groups with 'special characteristics', such as political and economic backwardness, which would be tackled through the acculturation and civilising project. While such categorisation brought to light the diversity of Chinese society, it stressed the uniformity of interests and the aims of the revolutionary struggle, which denied tangible cultural or social boundaries. The first outcomes of the identification project were incorporated into the 1953 census, which designated ten minority nationalities totalling 35,320,360 people, or 6.06 per cent of the total population (Cressey 1955: 388).

The first decades of communist rule were characterised by relative flexibility in the government's approach towards minority nationalities. Because of the ethnic minorities' special characteristics recognised in the course of the identification project and the common communist belief that national unity and uniformity were inevitable in the course of historical evolution and socialist building, identified minority nationalities were given assistance in the development of their respective cultures in anticipation of their ultimate assimilation into the purportedly most economically and culturally advanced Han nationality. However, while there was a realisation that 'modernisation needs the minorities, the minorities need modernisation' (Fei Xiaotong 1981a: 83), the state's modernisation was significantly prioritised over the interests of the minorities. As soon as communist rule over minority areas was secured militarily, the degree of diversity among minority nationalities was significantly narrowed. Selective economic, health, educational and cultural programmes were undertaken to connect minority areas and their populations to the rest of the country. A programme whereby Han specialists migrated into minority areas was gradually introduced. The development of a common language based on Beijing Mandarin was considered indispensable to the development of China as a unified nation.[9] Mandarin was established as the most developed language in opposition to minority languages, one of the designated criteria for minority nationality identification. In cases where minority nationalities did not have their own written language, Chinese communists invented scripts for them in order to better promote communist ideas. The primary goal of the state initiatives directed at the identification of minority nationalities was to overcome the existing social, cultural and historical differences, not their celebration. The denial of differences among the Chinese languages was thought to be critical to the modernisation of the nation. Nationwide political and ideological indoctrination was implemented hand in hand with minority modernisation projects, and served as a means for achieving the goal of a classless society. Socialist nation-building meant Han communist domination, while minorities were simply participants, often involuntary ones, in the project.

The early period of nationality work culminated in 1953 with the Third Enlarged Conference of the Nationalities Commission, which summarised the first results of the work in the minorities' areas and laid the bases for the constitution of 1954 (Dreyer 1976: 122–24). The results of the campaign paved the way for a new approach to nationalities work. There was general agreement among the leaders of the CCP that the preparatory stage of integration had ended, and that a new phase, presupposing closer adherence to single communist patterns, could begin. The conference laid the groundwork for a more refined class struggle, adoption of the Chinese Communist model of economic and social organisation and other measures embodied in the policies of the Great Leap Forward, which symbolised the end to the relatively favourable policies of domestic cosmopolitanism.

'Ethnic internationalism' in overseas Chinese policies

Rivalry between the GMD and the CCP over attracting the loyalty of overseas Chinese, as a way of securing legitimacy and recognition, characterised the years of their power struggle as well as the first decades of communist rule in China. The CCP's work among overseas Chinese began as soon as the troops of the People's Liberation Army (PLA) overran the home areas of overseas Chinese in 1927 (Lu Yusun 1956). The first formulation of the Party's position on the issue of the overseas Chinese was made in the *Common Programme of the Chinese People's Political Consultative Conference 1949* (Common Programme 1962), Article 58 of which stipulated that 'the central people's Government of the People's Republic of China shall do its utmost to protect the proper rights and interests of Chinese residing abroad' (quoted in Tao-tai Hsia and Haun 1976: 17). Consequently, overseas Chinese were included in the United Front of the revolutionary struggle during the time of the Second United Front between the communists and nationalists. At the same time, a special organ within the Bureau of

United Front Work – the Overseas Chinese Affairs Department – was established with the intention to carry out propaganda and organisational work among the Chinese communities abroad (Lu Yusun 1956). Increasingly, in the course of the civil war between the nationalists and communists, the overseas Chinese grew disenchanted with the corruption of the Chiang Kaishek regime and expressed their enthusiasm for a communist victory on the mainland. Such sentiments showed in the armies of young people returning to the mainland to participate in revolutionary construction; their numbers reached about 45,000 in the first five years of the PRC's existence (Elegant 1959: 33).

What is striking about the early Chinese communists' approach to the issue of overseas Chinese, especially in contrast to their policies towards ethnic minorities, is that they never developed their own perspective on overseas Chinese affairs. Chinese communists valued overseas Chinese entrepreneurial success and their awareness of their roots in China and hoped to capitalise on these attributes. Overseas Chinese were regarded by communists as potential builders of socialism in China, who could financially contribute to this construction. The PRC's overseas Chinese policies were thus organised in line with the nationalist model, occasionally seasoned with communist slogans. Although the communists emphasised the overseas Chinese's exceptional role in socialist state-building, they faced serious problems in reaching out to them and incorporating them in the implementation of the socialist projects. First, the majority of the overseas Chinese were subjects of other sovereign states and thus China's involvement with them could compromise the international status of China's young communist government; second, many overseas Chinese did not fall within the definition of revolutionary classes, but rather were actively involved in what communists called 'bourgeois-capitalist' activities. The identification of the overseas Chinese as China's nationals was based on the *jus sanguinis* principle which went against the grain of the communist revolutionary approach organised around class struggle. Application of this originally nationalist principle assumed an unbreakable common bond between all Chinese in China and those abroad, which contradicted the communists' ideological convictions. The census of 1953 listed some 11.7 million overseas Chinese as part of the Chinese population (Cressey 1955: 388). Most of them were emigrants from China's coastal provinces of Fujian and Guandong and differed significantly in terms of their activities.[10]

Like nationalists, Chinese communists widely used the term *huaqiao* to refer to overseas Chinese. The only criterion which was supposed to make this group homogenously united was patriotism towards the motherland, that is, the new government in Beijing. According to the Chinese leaders, 'all patriots belong to one big family' and 'are gradually coming to an awakening and embarking on the road of supporting the socialist motherland' (Zhou Enlai quoted in Lien Kuan 1978: 15). A slogan which stated the principal role of the overseas Chinese in China concluded 'overseas Chinese should join together in great patriotic unity around China' (Fitzgerald 1972: 84). The term 'patriotic unity' implied that overseas Chinese, whichever class they belonged to, were expected to unite with the revolutionary 'masses' within the country into a single front of opposition to the

GMD and to contribute to socialist development in the PRC by investing foreign currency.

The overseas Chinese were first of all viewed by the PRC's leadership as a force which, through its remittances, investments, donations for the 'patriotic movement' and human capital (returned students), would contribute to domestic nation-building rather than to the spread of world revolution. To meet this aim, a range of strategies and special policies were introduced. Since the early 1950s a special system of Overseas Chinese Investment Corporations (*huaqiao touzi zonggongsi*) was operating in locations with a large population of overseas Chinese and their relatives; it aimed to regularise overseas Chinese's 'voluntary investment'. By 1957 eleven provinces had such corporations (T an Tianxing 1994: 31). The great majority of investments in the form of remittances was coming from relatives of the overseas Chinese (*qiaojuan*). There were also widespread instances of forced extortions of funds from the overseas Chinese or their relatives in China. One source indicates that, in 1951, 90 per cent of overseas Chinese living in Chinatown in New York were victims of extortion (Reuter quoted in Lu Yusun 1956: 69). Voluntary and forced contributions in the form of annual remittances and investments by overseas Chinese amounted, according to the official estimates, to around 60 million dollars in foreign currency (Elegant 1959: 29).

The PRC's overseas Chinese policies had to find a compromise between encouraging overseas Chinese to contribute to China's socialist construction and granting them special treatment upon their return to the homeland and displaying commitment to respect and abide by the principles of sovereignty and territoriality in China's relationships with other states in the region. In its aspiration to gain recognised status among Southeast Asian states amid its awareness of its growing clash with the Soviet Union, China formulated a list of principles of peaceful coexistence and downplayed claims to overseas Chinese allegiances. The PRC's international reputation and foreign recognition of the legitimacy of communist rule were more crucial than strengthening its relationship with overseas Chinese communities. These involvements with overseas Chinese can be characterised as China's practice of *ethnic internationalism*. Overseas Chinese remained desired participants in the new socialist China on the basis of their ethnic affinities and roots in China. But when the PRC's overseas Chinese policies started conflicting with the CCP's ambitions to be the internationally accepted government of China, China's leaders had to slow their attempts to incorporate overseas Chinese into their socialist nation-building.

China's development of its strategy towards the overseas Chinese in the first decade of communist rule was devised in light of the objectives of the newly-established government to win diplomatic recognition from the neighbouring states and to consolidate its political and economic authority both domestically and internationally. The Overseas Chinese Affairs Commission, a ministerial organ that dealt with overseas Chinese affairs, was established in 1949 and served the purpose of fulfilling those objectives. Two more special organs for dealing with overseas Chinese matters soon followed: the Commission for Overseas Work of the Chinese Communist Central Committee, which was responsible for communist propaganda work among overseas Chinese; and the Third Office of the UFWD of the Chinese Communist Party Central Committee, which was responsible for organising overseas Chinese into a Unified Front movement. The electoral law promulgated in 1953 provided that the overseas Chinese would be represented in the All-China People's Delegates Conference by thirty delegates.[11] However, representation of almost 12 million overseas Chinese by thirty delegates was nothing more than lip service to providing care to 'overseas orphans'. Ironically, some of the overseas Chinese representatives had never been abroad, others were returned overseas Chinese and permanent residents of the PRC, and none of them had been appointed by overseas Chinese to represent their interests.

The PRC's eagerness to establish links with the overseas Chinese and win their loyalty, as well as China's involvement in the Korean war, led the home governments of the overseas Chinese to suspect that the PRC might use them as a 'fifth column' in the subversion and disruption of these colonial regimes, all in the interests of the PRC.[12] It was assumed that the overseas Chinese were in a position to propagate communist ideas and policies in their home countries, which had the potential to strengthen the international communist presence and contribute to the realisation of world socialist revolution. This realisation gradually led to hostility towards the Communist regime, as well as towards the Chinese population in their host countries. It seriously strained China's relations with the governments in Southeast Asia, especially those who had declared their diplomatic preference for the regime in Taiwan, such as Malaysia, the Philippines and Thailand.

One of the ideas expressed by the communists about overseas Chinese was that they should return to China to serve their motherland, rather than staying abroad. This points to China's cautious desire to avoid deteriorating relations with the neighbouring countries whose recognition it urgently needed. However, China avoided resolving overseas Chinese issues on a legal basis. In the mid-1950s the CCP initiated a campaign to persuade young overseas Chinese with special skills to return to China to serve the homeland in socialist construction. In the first four years of communist rule in China, over 9,000 overseas Chinese students returned to mainland China to get a traditional Chinese education (LuYusun 1956: 42). On top of their enthusiasm for being able to contribute to the socialist revolution, returning overseas Chinese were bringing family money and remittances which were spent on socialist development in China.[13] The established patterns of overseas Chinese education by the Chinese government were an effective means of influencing the overseas Chinese communities; through such education and ideological indoctrination, the attachments of the overseas Chinese to their homeland were renewed and reinforced. As Fitzgerald (1972: 126) put it, 'overseas Chinese education{...}[was] a ready-made vehicle for the export of the Chinese revolution'. However, by 1954, the unresolved nationality issue of the overseas Chinese had become a major problem with the states which had diplomatic relations with the PRC, such as India, Indonesia and Burma. At the same time, disillusioned by the deficiencies of the regime, overseas Chinese were going back to China in decreasing numbers.

58 *Socialist nation-building*

China's overseas Chinese policies were contingent on its international position and foreign policy priorities. In the 1950s and 1960s, when domestic instability was accompanied by the international isolation of China due to the United States' support of the GMD government in Taiwan and the PRC's territorial conflicts with India and the Soviet Union, China was seeking to improve its relations with the states in Southeast Asia, where the majority of overseas Chinese lived. Any activities of the overseas Chinese abroad in support of the communist regime in China would endanger relations with the local governments and be disadvantageous to international recognition of the People's Republic. Having failed to attract substantial contributions from the overseas Chinese, and facing the danger of further upsetting relations with the Southeast Asian states, the PRC, which was winning its battle for legitimacy against the nationalists, took the step of renouncing the dual nationality law in 1955. At the 1955 Bandung Conference, the PRC signed an agreement with Indonesia that rejected the earlier *jus sanguinis* principle and the institution of dual nationality, and embraced the principles of territoriality, sovereignty and citizenship. The PRC's delegation took a conciliatory and friendly approach to the Asian states, many of which were hostile to communism. The conference laid the grounds for the establishment of the 'non-aligned' movement of Third World countries. Consequently, the nationality issue was used as a bargaining tool in China's struggle to win diplomatic recognition. At China's request, a clause repudiating dual nationality for overseas Chinese with foreign citizenship was included in the communiqués signed when diplomatic relations with Malaysia, the Philippines and Thailand were established in the mid-1970s. The Party changed its overseas Chinese policy to one of disengagement and detachment from the overseas Chinese. It was implemented in the 'three good policies of nationality, non-interference and resettlement' and was followed by the nominal exclusion of the overseas Chinese from the People's United Front. These developments were part of China's ambition at the time to assume the role of the leader of the Third World, which was implied in the adopted Five Principles of Peaceful Coexistence, the theoretical basis of China's foreign policy.[14] One of the main adopted principles was noninterference in the domestic policies of other states and respect for their sovereignty. This principle introduced legal limitations on China's policies of ethnic internationalism towards overseas Chinese.

Minority nationalities and overseas Chinese in the socialist experiments of the late 1950s to the late 1970s

The periods of the Great Leap Forward (1958–60) and Cultural Revolution (1966–76) were characterised by countrywide economic and cultural experiments aimed at accelerated development of industry and agriculture, along with extreme homogenisation in the ideological and cultural spheres of society. Preoccupied with boosting economic development and strengthening its strategic and military might, and still concerned with winning political recognition internationally, China threw all of its resources into heavy industry and strategic development. Its policies towards minority nationalities and overseas Chinese were strongly affected by these developments. The variety and divergent nature of these groups conflicted with the strictly uniform character of the policies. Moreover, minority areas occupied strategically important areas of borderlands which served as bases for military 'defence' infrastructure developments (Norbu 2001: 98). Meanwhile, the overseas Chinese remained a festering source of tension in the PRC's relations with Southeast Asian states, forcing the communist regime to further withdraw from overseas Chinese affairs as a condition for improving relations.

While the period of the late 1950s was characterised by the continuing introduction of limited autonomy to minority areas and the implementation of the ethnic identification programme, China's policies were aimed at deepening the minority nationalities' sense of identification with the communist government in Beijing and at assimilating their cultures into the dominant Han culture. An extension of the CCP's bureaucratic control under the guise of granting autonomy to minority nationalities was conducive to domination by the majority Han, and led gradually to the political marginalisation of minorities within the autonomous system. For instance, in the Tibet Autonomous Region, no Tibetan was ever appointed to the most powerful post of Party First Secretary after this position was established in 1965. And, so far, only Han cadres have occupied the post of Party First Secretary in the Xinjiang Autonomous Region.

During the years of the Cultural Revolution, national minority policies turned to the annihilation of minority cultures. The slightest cultural difference or deviation from uniformity was interpreted as a 'class contradiction' which had to be eradicated (Moseley 1965: 16). Many special-treatment measures towards minority nationalities were abolished, and their economies were brought into line with the socialist culture and economy. Monks were uprooted and Buddhist monasteries in Tibet were demolished; national intelligentsia and clergymen were persecuted; national organisations in Xinjiang and Inner Mongolia were closed; and new scripts and language reform were introduced in most of the minority areas. The Chinese communists also conducted a forced Han migration into the minority areas. This, along with industrial and agricultural projects, led to the disruption of the environmental balance of the region and to the destruction of the vast grasslands of Xinjiang and Inner Mongolia. The three largest autonomous regions suffered most from the policy of the Han migration. Thus, in the period of the 1950s–80s, about one million Han moved to the Xinjiang Autonomous Region under a number of population migration initiatives, including the rustication (*xia fang*) campaign and the construction corps (*bingtuan*). By 1990 the number of Han in Xinjiang had increased to 5.7 million people out of a total population of 15 million. In comparison, before 1949, the Han population was no more than 5 per cent of Xinjiang (Toops 2004: 245). With the start of the Cultural Revolution, the minority cadres in Xinjiang dropped from 60 per cent to 40 per cent of the total (Grunfeld 1985: 64). Similar trends took place in other minority regions, most notably in Tibet and Inner Mongolia. As the previous research suggests, in spite of the government's attempt to neutralise the minorities' differences, the resettled Han population did not succeed in integrating or assimilating local populations into the uniformity project (Dreyer 1975).

The policies during the period of the Cultural Revolution adversely affected those who did not easily conform to communist dogmas or who stood out as 'non-compliant elements'. The campaigns of the period aimed at 'four cleanups', one of which targeted 'the ox-monsters and snake-demons' who were 'damaging' socialism. At the national level, the policies heralded a period of anti-Westernism, as well as neglect and suppression of the minority cultures. Nominal respect for cosmopolitan values was negated and renounced as bourgeois. The government's attempt to achieve 'the final goal of the communist society of plenty through mass campaigns' resulted in famine, shortage of raw materials for industry and overproduction of poor-quality goods. Cultural experiments were manifested in the deliberate 'melting together of nationalities' and in coercive restrictions and prohibitions on the use of minority languages, scripts, customs and religion. Similarly, academic institutions involved in research into minority cultures or in training minority cadres were closed down.

But the intensification of China's 'socialist construction' exacerbated the differences between nationalities, and the credibility gap between the Han and the national minorities widened rather than narrowed (Moseley 1965: 16; Dreyer 1976: 175; 2000: 288–89). The costs of economic experiments, the termination of the minority research projects, and the pressure on their cultural practices were perceived by the minorities as imposed by outsiders and dishonouring and obliterating of their distinct cultural identities (Liu, A. 1996: 200; Dreyer 2000: 288). As a result of the extreme and discriminatory nature of the policies, there was growing resentment and resistance on the part of national minorities which took the form of violent confrontations. Although these clashes did not undermine the power of communists in the country at large, they demonstrated the high level of national self-awareness of many ethnic minorities, as well as their discontent with discriminative communist practices in the national minority regions. The Muslim Hui in Qinghai and Ningxia were the first ones to rebel against the CCP's discriminative policies as early as 1952–53 (Liu, A. 1996: 201). In 1958 an armed rebellion by the Huis erupted in Gansu and Qinghai, and the PLA had to be dispatched to suppress it. In 1955, more than 100,000 of the Yi and other ethnic groups in forty-three counties along the Yunnan–Sichuan–Tibet border rebelled against land reform and collectivisation. The subsequent official references to these events stated that 'more than 6,000 battles were fought, more than 20,000 rebel elements were shot, more than 20,000 rebel elements were taken prisoner, while more than 40,000 masses were able to return to their homes' (quoted in Schoenhals 1994). Furthermore, a series of uprisings in Tibet led to the flight of the Dalai Lama to India and the persecution of Tibetan lamas, and an armed conflict in Xinjiang resulted in more than 60,000 people moving to Central Asian republics of the Soviet Union (Grunfeld 1985: 64). In 1969, one third of the Inner Mongolian territory was given to the bordering provinces of Gansu and Ninxia. Overt manifestations of resistance to the hard line of the CCP were evident throughout China's frontier regions, which intensified the struggle against local nationalism and instillation of the principle of 'unity through uniformity'. This situation remained until the early 1970s, when the policy was gradually moderated.

Socialist nation-building 61

In contrast to the early years of the PRC, when its overseas Chinese policies were guided by the *jus sanguinis* principle, since the mid-1950s these policies were translated into class terms. Many overseas Chinese abroad were labeled bourgeois, and maintaining connections with such 'reactionary elements' was declared unacceptable for communists whose revolutionary struggle was directed at bringing down the bourgeois, not aligning with them. [15] As a result, Chinese communist commitments towards overseas Chinese in Southeast Asia were minimised. Overseas Chinese were encouraged:

> 'to mind their own business', 'to stick to their own posts', not to criticise the internal affairs of the local governments, 'to obey the local laws and respect the local customs and habits' and 'to carry out all their work publicly and lawfully'.
>
> (Fitzgerald 1972: 105)

The overseas Chinese policies were formulated in accordance with the 'three good policies' of nationality, noninterference and resettlement, which were introduced in 1958 and remained unchanged until the Cultural Revolution, when the foreign aspect of the overseas Chinese policies disappeared from the Party's agenda. One of the most tragic outcomes of the 'three good policies' was the failure of the Chinese government to protect ethnic Chinese in Pol Pot's Cambodia, where more than 200,000 Chinese were killed by the PRC's 'friendly' regime in less than four years (1975–78).

The last report on overseas Chinese policies was delivered at the overseas Chinese Political Work Conference in Beijing in mid-1966. Soon afterward, the OCAC as a policy-making organ dealing with overseas Chinese issues ceased to function. In the period of the Cultural Revolution the previous work of the OCAC was repudiated as anti-revolutionary and revisionist (Fitzgerald 1972: 90). The overseas Chinese policies were limited to policies towards domestic overseas Chinese and their institutions. While overseas Chinese were encouraged to withdraw from any political activities in their countries of residence, their contribution to socialist construction in the PRC was welcomed. Since the early 1960s, returned and repatriated overseas Chinese schools and special associations for 'destroying bourgeois ideology and fostering proletarian ideology' flourished, and any special treatment or privileges for domestic overseas Chinese were opposed (Fitzgerald 1972: 112). The emphasis was on 'equal treatment' and full integration of domestic overseas Chinese into the proletarian socialist realm of the PRC. As a result, all previous special considerations for domestic overseas Chinese were cancelled. The role of domestic overseas Chinese in the Cultural Revolution was seen as either participating in nationwide movements or being subjected to attack for their style of living (Fitzgerald 1972: 119).

Taken together, the years of the Great Leap Forward and Cultural Revolution brought to extremes the policies of socialist nation-building and signified a departure from the earlier policies of relative cultural plurality and openness. The period marked a triumph of experiments in economy and culture which led not only to the extermination of ethnic minorities' cultural diversity, but also to the impoverishment of traditional Chinese culture and to the exhaustion of the Chinese economy by the military-industrial experiments and indiscriminate collectivisation. An attempt to instil a unified consciousness among the nationalities dominated by the Han resulted in resistance and resentment of the minorities. The campaigns of the Great Leap Forward and Cultural Revolution did not achieve the declared primary aim, created deep lines of division within Chinese society , and left the harmful legacy of socio-economic experiments for the next generation of Chinese leadership to deal with.

Conclusion

From the very beginning of the communist struggle for power , ethnic minorities and overseas Chinese were considered part of the United Front of socialist construction. The principles of class and ethnicity co-existed in the CCP' s designation of the basis of the Chinese revolutionary nation. In the first ten years of the accumulation of power and accommodation by the communists, their policies of 'domestic cosmopolitanism' and 'ethnic internationalism' towards ethnic minorities and overseas Chinese were flexible and tolerable. The two groups were seen as critical participants in the socialist modernisation project in China and were incorporated into it through means that reflected their peculiar positions in the United Front. By granting overseas Chinese and ethnic minorities preferential policies and special treatment, the new leadership emphasised their favourable roles in the United Front. As the ethnic minorities were an inalienable part of the territory of the state, the objectives of the policies toward them were to instil a common communist consciousness and to cultivate a sense of loyalty towards the CCP. The overseas Chinese, while seen as potential contributors as well as propagators of the Chinese socialist-building process, were treated cautiously so as not to damage the PRC' s shaky and uncertain international status. The roles prescribed to the groups showed how the communist leadership viewed membership in them. The overseas Chinese were identified according to a vague and ambiguous principle of racially-defined ethnic affiliation. Chinese ethnic minorities, in contrast, were methodically assigned certain fixed characteristics and ascribed cultural and economic labels. Thus, while in relation to ethnic minorities class struggle was explicitly emphasised, in its appeals to the overseas Chinese the CCP ignored differences of class and economic circumstances until the mid-1950s, when it became clear that overseas Chinese mobilisation was problematic and that further attempts to promote it could af fect China's diplomatic status.

There was an obvious convergence of nationalist and communist arguments in the communists' strategy to legitimise their control over the mainland. Class as a unifying national principle seemed to push out ethnicity as a valid denominator of belonging to the Chinese nation. Class dominated the political language of the communist government, but ethnicity as a basis for socialist nation-building was not completely abandoned. With minority nationalities, ethnicity was translated into 'class struggle' and a socio-evolutionary paradigm to be resolved through socialist construction. At the transnational level, China appealed to overseas Chinese on the basis of their ethnic and blood roots in China despite their often nonproletarian backgrounds. Class and ethnicity were intertwined in an unlikely tandem to form the premises of the Chinese nation. The Chinese government's contradictory and often sporadic engagements with the overseas Chinese and minority nationalities during the period of socialist construction show the ambiguous character of the Chinese socialist nation-building project. The statuses of overseas Chinese and ethnic minorities were hotly debated in the PRC, and the premises of the Chinese socialist project were incoherent and contradictory. The government's ambition to simultaneously solve the class and national questions ultimately led to narrowness and rigidity in both policy directions.

3 Post-socialist modernisation and China's national outlook

Since the late nineteenth century when modernisation first became an important issue – as well as a bone of contention – in the political programmes of Chinese regimes facing an aggressive military challenge from the colonial powers, the goals and mechanisms of modernisation have changed significantly. The current course of economic reforms and modernisation was preceded by a century of war and revolution and upheaval associated with profound national and class struggle. Today, China officially adheres to market economy and the communist ideology as its guiding principles for modernisation. Its new developmental agenda has not completely replaced the earlier socialist rhetoric: instead, the two are synthesised and modified using cultural elements. But the rhetoric of economic development driven by market forces dominates the leadership's political programme.

This chapter considers Chinese nation-making through the analysis of the contemporary debates on modernisation in China. It explores how the dominant formulation of the modernisation process affects the contours of the officially-presented Chinese nation, and looks at the kind of nation that is being produced in the mainstream discourse on modernisation. Specifically, the chapter examines how the dominant perspectives on modernisation compare with those of their Western predecessors as well as official policy directions. I argue that the official interpretation of the concept of modernisation affects not only the direction of particular modernisation policies, but ultimately the format of the Chinese national project. Chinese official perspectives on modernisation do not offer an alternative path of development, but a variation on the modernisation theory without recognising inherent problems. China's official modernisation studies are not scientific calculations of the development progress, but ideological perspectives on what the Chinese state aspires to be nationally and internationally and how, on the path of fulfilling its dreams, it deals with difference. As devised and implemented, the modernisation project rests on a set of ideas and practices which classify certain values as auspicious for modernisation and dismiss others as incompatible with the very idea of a modern subject. The forces articulating these aspired values constitute the moral authority of the society and claim the right to formulate its transformations. With some values assumed to be compatible with modernisation and others in conflict with it, the statuses of the groups associated with these values are, of course, affected. Some groups are considered traditional and conservative, others as vanguards of modernisation. But essentially only those who comply with the prescribed mode of modernity are regarded as its promoters and executors, while those who do not are coerced to participate in the modernisation process or are largely alienated by it. The values officially associated with modernisation become benchmarks for designating the levels of inclusion and the roles of social groups in the national modernisation project. The prioritisation of human attributes conducive to modernisation particularly affects the roles of groups that do not fit neatly into the framework of the Chinese nation-state, including overseas Chinese and ethnic minorities.

The first section of this chapter traces the development of modernisation debates in China's official circles since the start of the period of reform and the opening-up of the country. The second section examines the main tenets of the Second Modernisation Theory informing state-sponsored annual *China Modernisation Reports* and compares them to the earlier Western analogues and the official modernisation discourse. The third section discusses how China's geo-body is employed in the Second Modernisation Theory to explain development processes both in China and throughout the world, and the effects of this politics of identity on China's construction as a modernising nation. The fourth section looks at what human values are celebrated as desirable in the process of modernisation, and the implications of this for the formulation of membership in the Chinese nation. The final section describes how China's modernisation goals are projected onto the international realm, and how the contours of the Chinese nation are shaped by the newly-emergent discourse on international modernisation. The analysis in this chapter shows how China's current modernisation debates are rooted and dependent on the modernisation language produced in the West. While a lot of the official discussions emphasise China's allegedly alternative path of development, there is an inescapable dependency on, in many ways outdated, Western mode of thinking about the development path. This production of ostensibly scientific knowledge reveals how China as a nation is produced not only in opposition to the West, but also through the creation of internal dichotomies and oppositions along the dimensions of territory and ethnicity.

Modernisation as the core

An academic debate on the Westernisation of China and its convergence with traditional Chinese culture has been evolving for over one hundred and fifty years. Themes of the past are echoed in present-day Chinese scholarly discussions. The disillusionment of intellectuals with previous communist 'modernising' efforts in China has plunged some into a crisis of confidence about Chinese society; they question its ability to modernise without complete Westernisation.[1] Yet early attempts at Western-type modernisation were not particularly successful, and culminated in a prolonged, humiliating semi-colonial position still much remembered in China. Thus, the first Western-oriented modernisation experiment, the Self-Strengthening movement of 1861–95, is very much associated with the imperialist phase of the history of China in the late nineteenth to early twentieth century. As a result, since the start of a new modernisation initiative in the late 1970s, a debate over the level of Westernisation of the modernisation process and the place of traditional Chinese values in it erupted again. While some have argued that from the moment of initiating the reforms in the late 1970s the PRC has accepted the Western mode of modernity, albeit not Westernisation as such (King 2002), the prevailing opinion in the Chinese academic debate on the concept of 'socialism with Chinese characteristics' is that China has uneasily integrated the Western concept with Chinese particulars (Radtke 1993: 20; Wakeman 2002: 160).

The PRC's central government took the first steps toward nonrevolutionary modernisation as early as 1965, when Zhou Enlai, then the Chinese premier, declared at the Third National People's Congress that the nation's goal was the realisation of the Four Modernisations – in agriculture, industry, national defence, and science and technology – before the end of the twentieth century. These ideas were abandoned during the Cultural Revolution, only to be reaffirmed in 1975, when, at the Fourth National People's Congress, Deng Xiaoping called for four modernisations. Then, at the Fourteenth National Congress of the Communist Party held in October 1992, the official goal of Four Modernisations was replaced by the formulation of a 'socialist, modernised country which is wealthy, powerful, democratic and civilized', or, more generally, 'socialist modernisation with Chinese characteristics' (Jiang Zemin 1992). At the same congress, Deng Xiaoping's development doctrine was officially recognised as the theoretical basis for China's reforms. The two most important concepts in Deng's theory, stressed at the Fourteenth National Congress, were a socialist market economy and Deng's redefinition of socialism (Zhang Weiwei 1996: 213). The latter confirmed Deng's long-held conviction that market forces are value-neutral and can serve the purposes of both socialism and capitalism. Deng's 'three steps development strategy' (*'san bu zou' fazhan zhanlüe*) rested on principles formulated earlier, such as 'seeking truth from facts' and building Chinese-style socialism. The objective of the first step of his strategy was to double the 1980 total output by 1990, the objective of the second step was to redouble the rate, and the objective of the third step was to achieve the status of a medium-developed country by 2050.

Over the course of over thirty years, the Party slogans and five- and ten-year plans revolved around the key goal of ensuring China's economic growth. The 'theories' introduced by the post-Deng generations of leaders – Jiang Zemin's 'Three represents' and Hu Jintao's 'Building a harmonious society' – prioritised different aspects of China's transformation, but essentially centred on economic development.[2] Jiang Zemin welcomed private entrepreneurs into the Party and recognised their contribution to China's economy, while Hu Jintao emphasised sustained and balanced development, stressing the development of the countryside and the Western parts of the country, and introducing a new 'scientific concept of development' and 'harmonious society'.[3] The Chinese leadership have essentially adopted a developmental mentality in their pursuit of modernisation. The measure of the success of China's official modernisation theory is the GDP rate, which is centred on economic growth and the economic component of development. Chinese state media often emphasise, as the *People's Daily* did in March 2004, that 'China's per capita value of gross domestic product has reached 1,000 USD, and it is expected to hit 3,000 by 2020' (2020 being the deadline for building a well-off society).[4] The media also frequently mention that China's priority is to create the material base for spiritual advancement. Most tellingly, the Party-formulated development strategy and the government's position on development were stipulated in the State Council's (SC) 2005 White Paper on China's Peaceful Development Road,[5] which reiterates the primary role of economic growth. In August 2006, the Central Committee's Foreign Affairs Meeting adopted directives stressing that 'economic development should remain the central theme of [China's] foreign policy'.[6]

The major differences between the new history of Chinese modernisation and the past history of revolution, according to the official Party perspective, lie in the purported driving forces behind historical progress. The idea of class struggle as the principal impulse for social change dominated Chinese discourse from the establishment of the PRC until the start of the reform period. This concept, along with the principle of anti-imperialism, constituted the formula for revolutionary struggle in China. Nowadays, much of Chinese official and scholarly thinking still adheres to the principle of historical materialism in interpreting historical change. However, the driving force of progress is now considered to be the development of the forces of production. These forces are seen as the motor propelling social change and economic development. Recently, the new social strata of private entrepreneurs, small-business owners and managerial-level staff in private or foreign-funded enterprises were praised for their contribution to China's economic development.[7] They constitute the biggest segment of China's growing middle class. Proximity to this class has become a normative designation of social citizenship in China, and is often measured by consumer power and urban residence (Anagnost 2008). The stark differences between the socialist revolutionary and market reform agendas for modernisation, however, do not preclude significant continuity between the two.

The role of ideology as a tool for embellishing and communicating the regimes' values and policies to the Chinese people continues unabated. Although a pragmatic approach to the pace of economic reforms was generally adopted by the Chinese ruling elite, the ideological dimension of Marxist teaching has remained. After the tragic events of 1989, Deng Xiaoping strengthened the Party–government link by exercising firmer Party control over the government. Since then, ideological statements have frequently been used by the leadership to justify the reforms as normatively required transformations (Zhang Weiwei 1996: 2). The relentless role of ideology in the Chinese polity becomes apparent when considering the long-lasting principle of the United Front. The United Front has remained an overarching ideological principle of the Party and government in the reform period. In his 1979 address to the CPPCC, Deng Xiaoping emphasised the importance of strengthening the United Front (Deng Xiaoping 1979). He pointed to a new historical period of United Front work, which should be directed at unifying the 'patriotic elements' around the idea of socialist modernisation. Rather than identifying class struggle as a primary focus of the United Front, Deng extended the concept of the working class to include broad masses of Chinese people, including intellectuals and all those who serve the cause of Chinese modernisation. In 2002 Jiang Zemin further extended the scope of the United Front when he emphasised the role of private entrepreneurs in China's modernisation.

In 1985, the CCP Central Committee's United Front Work Department convened the First National Conference on United Front Theoretical Work, which reasserted the tasks of the United Front that Deng Xiaoping outlined.[8] The defining element of the United Front in the reform period was identified as patriotism, which was equated with supporting modernisation and the re-unification of China. The principal forces of the United Front, including overseas Chinese and ethnic minorities, essentially remained in place. Work to include ethnic minorities in the United Front was emphasised as necessary and separate from the issue of social class. In other words, the class problem was resolved by broadening the term 'working class' to include other social segments. The Party dismissed as 'leftist' the view that the nationality question was a class question, and stressed the unity and harmonious cohabitation of different nationalities. The role of the overseas Chinese in the new period of United Front work was not ignored either: they were now seen as 'playing an increasingly important and positive part in the effort to achieve the great goal of reunifying our motherland, in supporting the country's modernisation and in strengthening the international struggle against hegemony' (Deng Xiaoping 1979). The United Front was revised to serve to unite patriotic forces that would help construct socialist modernisation in China, a strategic goal in the new historical period.

The amended Constitution of the CCP adopted at the 16th CCP National Congress in November 2002 reiterates the rhetoric of the 'the broadest possible patriotic united front' (Constitution of the Communist Party of China 2002). The Constitution also broadens the scope of the Party by stating that it is now 'the vanguard of the Chinese working class and of the Chinese people and the Chinese nation' (ibid.). The Chinese nation (*zhonghua minzu*) as coined by Chinese Nationalists in the early twentieth century is here referred to in its elusive sense. It simultaneously stresses the claim of the Party to the territories secured by the Qing Dynasty and alludes to the non-territorial cultural and racial foundations of the Chinese nation. The conflation of territorial with cultural and racial bases of the Chinese nation and the Party's United Front is also noticeable in Hu Jintao's speech to the 17th National Congress of the CCP in October 2007, when he called to 'reinforce unity, … conscientiously uphold the solidarity and unity of the whole Party, maintain close ties between the Party and the people, cement the great unity of the people of all ethnic groups, and enhance the great solidarity of all sons and daughters of the Chinese nation at home and overseas … '.[9]

Though still influenced by the Party ideology, today's official academic discourse on Chinese modernisation emerged as a criticism of Western theories of modernisation of the 1960s, such as Rostow's (1960) five stages of economic growth. Rostow argued that traditional societies should adopt the characteristics of modern societies in order to modernise their social, political, cultural and economic institutions. Chinese modernisation theorists generally refute the idea that, in order to achieve capital formation, productivity and consumption comparable to developed countries, it is necessary to duplicate the cultural institutions of those countries. On the contrary, the modernisation discourse of the 1990s to early 2000s proposes a culture-sensitive concept, arguing in favour of modernisation that is acceptable in a given culture (*wenhua chengnuo*) (He Zhonghua 1996). This discourse advocates producing an Asian concept of modernisation for the twenty-first century, one which refutes Westernisation as a model for modern development in non-Western societies (Luo Rongqu 1997: 21). As a result, Chinese works have been sympathetic to a new generation of Western modernisation theories that talk favourably of authoritarian capitalist economies (Pye 1985; Bell 2000; Bell and Hahm 2003) and the production of an alternative to the Western mode of modernity (Huntington 1996; Featherstone and Lash 1995). Distancing themselves from Western theories, Chinese scholars have put forward their own interpretations of modernisation.

It is certainly arguable whether the official Chinese model of modernisation can be really distinct from Western theories. Dirlik (2002: 29) contends that attempting to produce a unique form of modernity based on the assumption of distinctive Chinese cultural conditions is futile. Similarly, Eisenstadt (1999, 2000) suggests that the patterns of modernity, or, to use his term, 'multiple modernities', are shaped by a multitude of factors and cannot be isolated in an increasingly globalised world; moreover, they are increasingly undetermined and fluid. Therefore, according to these authors, it is impossible to divorce the underpinnings of the Chinese modernisation model from the ones developed in the West, and to achieve a single uniform form of modernity through the modernisation project. As I will demonstrate below, the current Chinese modernisation discourse is largely built on the traditional Western delimitations of modernity. In essence, the Chinese model proclaimed by its creators as unique is premised on the same assumptions as the orthodox models developed in the West. It is sustained through marginalisation and suppression of alternative modes of modernity. What is more, its formulation relies on and takes as a reference point Western deliberations on modernisation, making China's modernisation model not an alternative to Western theories, but a self-orientalised version of them.

With the regime's encouragement, Chinese scholars enthusiastically initiated the study of modernisation, and attempted to design a unique Chinese model of it. With the start of reforms, it became prevalent in academic circles and government cabinets to explore how to attain China's comprehensive modernisation. Such investigations became even more prominent in the 1990s, when political and social aspects of the reforms were cut short. Modernisation debates were shaped by the political spirit of the 1990s, which, in turn, was affected by the tragic culmination in 1989 of the relatively liberal atmosphere of the 1980s. The discussions about possible modernisation paths were also influenced by the popularisation of the ideology of development, which by the end of the twentieth century had reached most parts of the world. In this environment, the study of modernisation and especially its economic aspects replaced euphoric discussions of China's political transformations. Besides borrowing from outmoded Western theories, the official scholarly discourse on modernisation also reflects the Party's directives to enhance economic development and increase total economic activity and the output of society. In fact, most of the influential modernisation scholars rely on Deng Xiaoping's theory of modernisation as the departure point for their research. An accelerating modernisation craze triggered the opening of numerous research centres and institutes devoted to investigating the meaning and logic of the modernisation process. In the late 1990s China started to publish yearly reports on modernisation and economic development, producing numerical measures of China's progress towards its goals. One of these reports is the *China Modernisation Report*, which includes a modernisation index, a measure of the level of modernisation not only of all thirty-one provinces and autonomous regions in China but also of most countries in the world.

Much dominant discussion on modernisation in China relies on the Second Modernisation Theory, a theoretical foundation of the *China Modernisation Report*. This theory occupies a specific space in official and intellectual fields in China. It is remarkable that the theory, along with the *China Modernisation Report*, is produced within the walls of the most influential Chinese academic establishment for 'hard science', the Chinese Academy of Science, rather than in its equivalent in the fields of Social Sciences and Humanities, the Chinese Academy of Social Sciences. Notwithstanding the proclaimed official focus of 'scientific development' on the people as the centre of China's development project, development is seen as an object for study by supposedly neutral 'hard science'. Another interesting fact is that the *China Modernisation Report* is published by Beijing University Press rather than the China Statistics Press, the official bureau in charge of practically all statistical yearbooks in China. Rather than relying solely on the statistical data produced at different levels of the Chinese government and on ideological directions formulated by the Communist Party and state leaders, the *China Modernisation Report* is the product of intellectual efforts by a team of scholars. It offers 'scientific' knowledge that adds weight to the officially-formulated state policies. While integrating much of the official line, the reports make use of Western theories and data produced by international organisations. The scope of the report goes beyond China, as the aim of the Second Modernisation Theory is to provide a generalised explanation of the development path of not only China but the rest of the world.

This is not to say that there is no alternative to the dominant discourse on China's modernisation path represented by the Second ModernisationTheory and the *China Modernisation Report*. There is an important body of literature highlighting local knowledge and development practices, which hardly fit the prescribed development model. But most of this literature is produced by researchers whose research agendas and goals go against the line of official thinking. There are also other statistical reports produced in China; for example, the Human

Second Modernisation Theory

Behind the creation of the Second Modernisation Theory stands the figure of essentially one scholar. Professor He Chuanqi is the head of the China Centre for Modernisation Research at the Chinese Academy of Social Sciences and the Centre for Studies of World Modernisation Processes at Beijing University. His concept of the Second Modernisation was first put forward in 1998 in a journal article and later served as the basis for a major study published as a book in 1999. His work is predominately influenced by the studies of knowledge and the information economy conducted by Western scholars in the 1970s to 1990s. He Chuanqi also utilises earlier Western modernisation theories, including postmodernist approaches. But he is critical of them due to their alleged inability to explain the situation in developing counties and their confused concept of time, which is referred to as both modern and post-modern (He Chuanqi 2003: 246–47).[10] According to He, post-modernists managed to reflect the new developments that took place in developed societies in the 1970s, but failed to explain the situation of the 1990s and to account for new global developments such as the knowledge economy, the information economy, the network economy and so on.

The Second Modernisation Theory is presented by He as the contribution of Chinese researchers to general theories of modernisation and human civilisation overall (He Chuanqi 2003: 281). He Chuanqi argues that a contemporary world historical analysis which does not take into account China's experiences 'is not a complete world' (He Chuanqi 1999: 389). To fill this gap he offers an examination of China's development history in the context of world development processes. He maintains that China's experience, although unique, can be instructive for understanding the general development process of other societies in the world. The Second Modernisation Theory is thus both China-specific and general enough to explain development processes outside China. He correlates the processes of human civilisation and development and presents the Second Modernisation Theory as the first attempt to view the development of human civilisation through the modernisation process (He Chuanqi 2003: 248–49). Second Modernisation Theory substantially relies and builds on the theories of modernisation developed by Western scholars from the 1950s to the late 1990s. It is presented as a successor of the earlier Western paradigms on modernisation. Chinese studies of the struggles of the Chinese modernisation process from the Republican and socialist periods are neither reflected nor mentioned in He Chuanqi's theory. It sees Western theories on the development process as the only legitimate body of knowledge on which to base the Chinese theory, even if it is critical of them.

He Chuanqi contends that another important reason for developing the Chinese theory of modernisation is that it serves as an expression of China's growing influence. In other words, the theory shows China's capability to develop its own theoretical paradigms of development and to generate new theories, which, in

He's view, are signs of the nation's 'quality' (He Chuanqi *et al.* 2007: 152). In line with his thought, production of knowledge, including in the fields of humanities and social sciences, is a manifestation of high national quality; a population's ability to learn, innovate and contribute to general knowledge is valued as a national asset.[11] A nation's quality is also stressed as the guarantor of China's successful performance at the international level and a condition for successfully tackling future challenges:

> China has a splendid history, an ancient culture and an ingenious people. There is nothing in the world that can stop the advance of China, restrict the wisdom of the Chinese people, contain the momentum of China's innovation, or limit the space of China's development. Innovation, learning, knowledge and human resources constitute the greatest wealth and also the flying wings of the Chinese nation. Although the challenges ahead are unprecedented, history is made by man. A nation that has created a splendid history can certainly create an entirely new future.
>
> (He Chuanqi *et al.* 2007: 145)

Similar to earlier modernisation theories, He Chuanqi divides the process of human development from 2.5 million years ago to the year 2100 into several stages. These include the tool age, the agricultural age, the industrial age and the information age, each of which is also divided into several phases: the start, development, maturity and transition phases. The first modernisation is the process of transitioning from an agricultural society to an industrial society, an agricultural economy to an industrial economy, an agricultural civilisation to an industrial civilisation, and an agricultural age to an industrial age. The second modernisation is the process of changing from an industrial society to a knowledge society, an industrial economy to a knowledge economy, an industrial civilisation to a knowledge civilisation, and an industrial age to a knowledge age. According to He Chuanqi (1999: 257–58), for advanced societies the second modernisation will take more than 100 years (1971–2100). As for developing societies, they have to face the challenges of both the first and second modernisations simultaneously.

The period of the second modernisation in China, according to He, started with the launch of economic reforms in the late 1970s. One objective of the first stage of the second modernisation was to double the total output value by 1990 and then redouble it by 2000. Since 1997, China has embarked on the development of a knowledge economy and innovation systems. To achieve knowledge modernisation, in He's opinion (1999: 404–5), China should consider the comprehensive promotion of learning, innovation and their applications, which will together form the basis of the new infrastructure of society. In the English-language summary of his theory, *China Modernization Report Outlook 2001–7* (He Chuanqi *et al.* 2007), He Chuanqi projects what modernisation will look like in 2050. According to He, China's modernisation strategy should be revised in view of the desired goals. In other words, the process of modernisation should be guided by the vision of modernisation in the future. The linear development He anticipates promises the era of prosperity at the end of the path. This stress on innovation, progressive development, technological achievement and particular scientific knowledge from the perspective of the desired outcome dismisses as 'anti-scientific' other forms of knowledge and visions of development that are often directed at environmental protection.

He Chuanqi's interpretation of modernisation comes down to treating the economy and technological development as the key driving forces of societal development. This approach puts the forms of economic organisation above the values inherent in the society, and diminishes the role of cultural and similar 'spiritual' values in the process. Modernisation becomes a mechanical tool of 'total output value' production, while other aspects of societal life are secondary and serve the main objective. However, as Radtke (1993: 32) observes, 'culture is not an adjunct to social organisation'. Reforms and an open-market economy do not automatically lead to the development of a modern society. The goal-oriented view of the modernisation process leads to disproportionate implementation of specific economic policies, and unrest among segments of society who, culturally or psychologically, do not keep up with economic growth. Moreover, the meaning of modernisation as promoted by the official rhetoric often differs from how it is interpreted by the wider population. For example, Shih's study (2002) shows that some ethnic minorities in China do not understand the meaning of modernisation suggested by the Han-dominated state. On the contrary, modernisation fuels the concerns of ethnic minorities to preserve their distinctiveness and uniqueness in the process of transformation.

He Chuanqi emphasises the process of human development especially for the period of the Second Modernisation, with development strategies focused on the human being. Nevertheless, modernisation progress, including the advancement of human subjects, according to He, can be measured and expressed in numerical or another verifiable form. The criteria for quantifying modernisation are considered to be universal and applicable not only to different regions within China but to most countries in the world. This way of thinking neglects the diversity within China and disregards the importance of it on a world scale. The theory only allows for one standard of modernisation, which must be reached in a certain period of time, and does not ask what will happen after a country or region achieves the necessary modernisation parameters.

The Second Modernisation theory is presented in the manner of a five-year Party political programme, with clear-cut objectives including pre-determined numerical economic goals. This does not allow for much flexibility and adaptability in the process of market reform. However, in the course of historical development, a set goal tends to change into a new aim. Early modern Chinese reformers such as Zhang Jian, the minister of agriculture and commerce in early Republican China, argued in favour of deep systemic changes but did not specify any concrete goal or transformations; Christiansen characterised it as pragmatic thinking (1993: 55). To stipulate, not to mention numerically define, the goal, as history suggests, is short-sighted. To quote Radtke (1993: 15), we are 'unable to discuss history in teleological terms'. It is difficult to predict whether modernisation will bring a country towards an outlined goal. Radtke (1993: 15) elaborates:

> 'Market economy' may be the great winner of the moment; to anticipate 'market economy' as the goal of teleological historical development would betray a near-total insensibility towards the unpredictability of future historical developments.

So, rather than prescribing a definite path of development, modernisation debates in China show how China as a nation is produced through the formulation and pursuit of a particular kind of development model and how difference within and outside China is accounted for.

Appadurai's writing on the modernity of imagination attacks 'social theories of the ruptures of modernisation' on the grounds that they assume a teleological premise for interpreting modernisation as a universal recipe for 'rationality, democracy, the free market, and a higher gross national product'(Appadurai 1997: 9). He also criticises the dominant theories for their preoccupation with prognoses for and outcomes of projects of 'social engineering' (Appadurai 1997: 9). These deficiencies in early Western interpretations of modernisation seem to have been uncritically imported by their more pronounced recent Chinese version. For example, He Chuanqi's theory uses the Western development index as a measure for growth assessment, which makes it dependent on Western indicators, and uses Western countries as a point of reference for Chinese modernisation. The West is referred to as a uniform amorphous entity of progress and development. This concept of modernisation does not permit multiple modernisations, either in different regions in a country or different states in the world. Modernisation is an abstraction, and one that unduly influences how Chinese national goals are formulated and the idea of the modernised Chinese nation is constructed.

The portrayal of modernisation in predominately economic-numerical form is striking. They are even reflected in a trend observed by some studies on contemporary visual representation and official propaganda. One such study by Landsberger concluded that, in the official discussions of the 1980s and early 1990s, there was an almost complete dominance of Western symbols of progress (Landsberger 1993: 188). In the 1980s to 1990s many writings largely undermined the functional approach in social science and disputed the linear conception of universal historical process. These writings are easily accessed in China and, in fact, have influenced a number of mainland scholars (Wang Hui 2003: 141–87). Nevertheless, the dominant scholarly research continues to see modernisation as an evolutionary process, with economics and technological innovations at its core. The modernisation discourse is formulated around Western theories, while earlier Chinese studies, with their underlying emphasis on the interaction between technology and spirit, are made irrelevant. The transformation of the socio-political and cultural systems, which are more inert than the economy when it comes to radical systemic changes and present one of the greatest challenges to the communist regime, remains largely ignored by the Second Modernisation Theory. The production of

China's official national project is informed by the linear vision of history evolving along the development progress, the simplistic interpretation of culture, and the somewhat passive and uncritical acceptance of the experiences in some Western societies as the only legitimate source of development knowledge. China's official formulations of its development process not only have become rooted in and dependent on the Western orthodoxies, but also have produced a generalised vision of the West that suppresses difference within China.

China as a map of the history of civilisation

The Second Modernisation Theory is presented as a contribution by Chinese scholars to general theories of modernisation, but it is also presented in essentially Chinese national terms. He Chuanqi utilises China's national geo-body to draw an analogy with the global modernisation process. He specifically refers to the Yangtze River that flows from the west to the east, which, he argues, spatially illustrates the temporal progression of civilisation and world modernisation: 'From the upper to the lower reaches, the levels of both development and civilisation rise (despite fluctuations). The process of this change is logical, and is highly similar to the process of world modernisation' (He Chuanqi *et. al* 2007: 106, see Figure 3.1). It is interesting to note that traditionally the Yellow River in the north has been presented as a cradle of Chinese civilisation and the birthplace of the Chinese nation. The Yellow River often serves as a symbol of the Chinese nation in scholarly, literary and popular accounts. But He's reference to the Yangtze River is employed for a different purpose. While it illustrates China's unique development model, according to He, it also invites an analogy with China's progression through the whole history of civilisation known to humanity. In He Chuanqi's words, 'As if human civilization had flowed from the upper reaches, to the middle reaches, to the lower reaches, and to the estuary. We call this phenomenon the Yangtze River Model of the long history of human civilization' (He Chuanqi *et al.* 2007: 102). Thus, China is a home to those societies at the beginning of the development of civilisation as well as to those nearing the height of civilisation, as it approaches the post-industrial knowledge society. He Chuanqi employs the following description of the process of civilisation along the Yangtze River Valley:

> In the upper reaches of the Yangtze River, most parts are agricultural regions and some still have the traces and features of a primitive culture. For example, the Mosuo ethnic group, having about 30,000 people and living in the place where Yunnan and Sichuan provinces meet, still preserves the habits and customs of a matrilineal society. Its habits and customs are the basic lifestyle of human society in the late Paleolithic Age about 10,000 years ago. In the Xishuangbanna region in southern Yunnan province, some of the ethnic groups in the mountainous areas still live on slash-and-burn farming. This is the basic mode of production of human society in the Neolithic Age about 6,000 years ago.
>
> (He Chuanqi *et al.* 2007: 101)

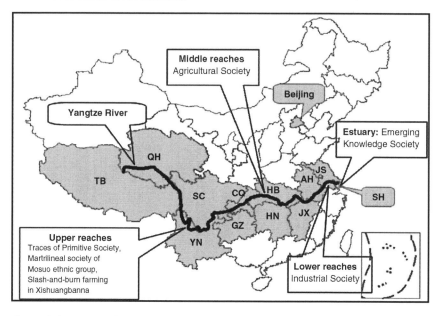

Figure 3.1 Yangtze River model

Source: *China Modernization Report Outlook 2001–2007* (He Chuanqi *et al.* 2007: 101).

The Yangtze River Model is viewed as an 'historical section' for analysis of the modernisation process. Going to the upper reaches of the Yangtze River in Qinghai and Sichuan provinces is, in other words, reminiscent of travelling back in time to the origins of civilisation. The lower reaches and the estuary, with their industrial societies and early traces of knowledge societies, are at the forefront of the modernisation process, but cannot compare to some societies outside China that have higher modernisation indexes. According to the authors of the *China Modernisation Report*, the developments of these societies provide an orientation and trajectory for how Chinese modernisation will evolve.

While the geographical symbols of national territory are usually thought to embody a particular nation and society, He Chuanqi attempts to place the entire historical process known to humanity within the territorial confines of China. China thereby maps out the development process of the whole world, in addition to China's own development. China becomes a reference point for general thinking about development while providing a particular model of development. And through projecting historical time onto China's national space, the Yangtze River Model serves as a 'spatial expression' of the progress of human civilisation. He Chuanqi recognises, however, that this model can only account for the period of human civilisation from the First to the Second Modernisations, as no place in China has completed the process of Second Modernisation yet. The reference point for China's future modernisation is an idealised vision of the modernisation end of other societies, predominately in the West. Not only does He Chuanqi not compare China's experiences to those of developing countries of the global South, the roles of its neighbours, such as Korea, Japan, Russia or India, are not mentioned in the Second Modernisation Theory.

The Yangtze Model, with its fusion of the temporal process with geographical space, deems China's choice of development as the only acceptable one. It thus essentially subscribes to a mode of knowledge that has been produced and already heavily criticised by many in the West. John Agnew (1998) asserts that 'turning time into space' has dominated much of contemporary thinking about 'national development', not only in the spaces subjected to colonialism but also in the parts of the world that were outside of direct colonial rule. Despite his apparently strong commitment to produce a distinctive Chinese theory of modernisation, He Chuanqi submits to the colonised mentality dictated by a particular interpretation of the development experience in the West. Through projecting the entire process of civilisation onto the national map of China, his theory labels certain localities within China as developed and others as backward. And, unavoidably, the theory oversimplifies local experiences and practices through categorising them as 'advanced' or 'primitive'.

While the Yangtze River Model recognises China's cultural diversity and acknowledges that 35 out of China's 56 ethnic groups live in the 12 regions of the Yangtze River Valley, the linear progression of civilisation that it posits leads to a particular mode of thinking about how the development of diverse populations within China should evolve. Each stage of the development of civilisation, neatly categorised into primitive, agricultural, industrial and knowledge societies, is applied to the regions along the Yangtze River, starting from the border between Tibet and Qinghai and finishing in Shanghai. The authors of the *China Modernisation Report* state that the model demonstrates 'the top-down unevenness and orderliness' of the development process:

> From the upper reaches to the lower reaches, social productivity (per capita GDP and the per capita GDP at PPP) rises, the proportion of agriculture declines, and both the proportion of industry and the proportion of the labour force in the service industry rise. The level of economic development in the lower reaches is visibly higher than in the middle and upper reaches.
>
> (He Chuanqi *et al.* 2007: 102)

A similar analysis is applied to social indicators (He Chuanqi *et al.* 2007: 104). This analysis classifies China's regions and groups associated with them according to their particular stages of socio-economic development, an approach that has been identified as one of the tools for 'naturalising' how the development process works (Doty 1996: 10).

The Yangtze River Model of the *China Modernisation Report* displays the politics of representation and identity. On the one hand, it utilises the language of development to present China as a developing country which aspires to follow the development path paved by other, more modern, Western societies. It relies on the dominant language and knowledge system of the West, which results in the marginalisation of other modes of knowledge and experiences of development (Escobar 1995: 13; Dirlik 2002: 36). Its recognition of China's development stage and future orientation legitimises the dominant thinking about the modernisation process, and it a priori rejects any possible alternatives. On the other hand, the Yangtze River Model groups China's regions and diverse ethnic groups into categories along the modernisation vector, producing hierarchies of levels of development and social groups. In this process, it assigns localities and their populations particular characteristics and makes them general and absolute. Not only are the western, central and eastern regions of China organised into a hierarchical relationship, but a binary opposition between the Han nationality (*Han zu*) and minority nationalities (*shaoshu minzu*) is asserted. When the category of *minzu* was attuned to the Stalinist definition of nationality in the 1950s to 1960s, a nationality's level of socio-economic development was considered crucial to the identification and recognition of its minority status. The *China Modernisation Report* and its theoretical framework similarly do not allow space for diverse types of knowledge and experiences of development within China. The report's preoccupation with the production of a particular vision of development for China extends to the individual values considered conducive to the modernisation process.

Humanistic aspects of modernisation

Since the 1990s, the so-called humanistic (*ren de*) features of modernisation have become prominent in the official debates stressing that modernisation also involves nurturing and realising certain nonmaterial aspects of modernisation. At the most basic level, articulation of the humanistic dimensions of the modernisation project can be attributed to the need to fill the niche previously occupied by the ideology of the socialist project. In recent years, talk of these dimensions has been fuelled by the rush to rediscover and revive China's traditional culture and values. Human-centred perspectives on modernisation have most distinctly manifested themselves in the officially-endorsed discourses on spiritual civilisation (*jingshen wenming*), 'population quality' (*renkou suzhi*) and, most recently, 'harmonious society' (*hexie shehui*).

The development of a spiritual civilisation was identified by Chinese leadership as essential for the realisation of the modernisation project in the early days of the reforms and the opening up of China. Material civilisation was considered to provide a crucial foundation for achieving a socialist spiritual civilisation. And the spiritual civilisation defined the orientation of material civilisation (Chang Ching-li 1983: 27). Back in 1981, the central government published a document entitled 'Suggestions Concerning the Promotion of Decorum and Courtesy and the Efforts to Build Socialist Spiritual Civilisation', which delineated 'five stresses and four beauties'[12] aimed at providing general guidance for the daily life of the Chinese people. The introduction and proliferation of spiritual civilisation was an attempt to re-establish the discredited moral authority of the communist regime. It was formulated to fill the post Cultural Revolution moral vacuum, to eliminate ideological confusion, and to secure popular support for the CCP (Chang Ching-li 1983: 40). According to the official explanation, spiritual civilisation was comprised of two aspects: cultural (education, science, art, literature and so on) and ideological (Marxist theory). Spiritual civilisation was 'manifested in a higher educational, scientific and cultural level and in higher ideological, political and moral standards' (Hu Yaobang quoted in Chang Ching-li 1983: 26). In 1982, patriotism encompassing 'three loves' (love for the motherland, socialism and the party) was identified as one of the crucial factors promoting spiritual civilisation and added to the other two aspects of spiritual civilisation (ibid.).

Related to the discourse on spiritual civilisation was the popularisation of the notion of 'population quality' (*renkou suzhi*), which was first used in party documents in the early 1980s. While *suzhi* lacks a uniform definition, it vaguely refers to the physiology, morality, scientific and cultural consciousness, and psychology of a person. It has been employed in Chinese official and popular discourses to refer to what Chinese society lacks. It calls attention to China's 'internalised sense of the lack of development', as Anagnost (1997) characterised it. Low population quality (*renkou suzhi di*) was recognised as one of the main impediments to China's modernisation drive. But the official idea that one can understand China's hampered development by the lack of *suzhi*, as Yan Hairong observes (2003: 496), is essentially tautological, because the lack of development lies at the heart of the *suzhi* notion, and the promotion of development is seen as the only solution. The official formulation of the *suzhi* problem and the advocacy of a developmentalist agenda as a way of overcoming it cover up a multitude of factors that have contributed to the disparities in Chinese society. As an idealised and absolute notion, s*uzhi* designates an attribute of a modern subject, and those with more of it are considered 'more deserving of the rights of citizenship' (Anagnost 2004: 194).

The debate that has recently emerged on humanistic modernisation (*ren de xiandaihua*) builds on and reflects the earlier discussions on spiritual civilisation and population quality. Humanistic modernisation has been presented as the key to the national modernisation quest, and the main engine and guarantor of the modernisation process (Zhang Zhongliang 2003: 359). One of the scholars of the Chinese concept of modernisation, Zheng Yongting (2005: 4), argues that population quality and people's consciousness constitute the two main elements of humanistic modernisation. He stresses that the process of transformation from a traditional to a modern society is aimed at training and advancing people's modern consciousness, ability and mentality (*yishi, nengli, xinli*). These attributes are constituent of the human quality and are seen as an underlying condition necessary for a successful modernisation process (Zheng Yongting 2005: 6–7). Another scholar of modernisation, Zhang Zhongliang, somewhat similarly states that central to humanistic modernisation is the modernisation of physical and spiritual human qualities: physiology (*shengli suzhi*), mentality (*xinli suzhi*) and ability (*neng li*) (Zhang Zhongliang 2003: 345). These qualities are advocated from the perspective of China's broader modernisation goals and framed by a perception of the desired future. While it is understood that human values will change under the external pressures brought about by the modernisation process, it is emphasised that every human being should make an effort to change their values and beliefs in order to achieve the modernisation aims (Zheng Yongting 2005: 5).

Chinese modernisation scholars contend that the successful pursuit of humanistic modernisation is premised on the advancement of a knowledge economy and society, which they see as the ultimate goal of China's current development. Zheng Yongting states: 'The difference between traditional and modern people is that modern subjects can adapt to the demands and development changes quickly and use knowledge and creativity to change the world' (Zheng Yongting 2005: 233). The reorientation of societal values towards the values compatible with the realisation of modernisation goals also constitutes an important aspect of He Chuanqi's Second Modernisation Theory. He asserts (1999: 409) that the construction of a 'knowledge society' (*zhishi shehui*) and a 'knowledge civilisation' (*zhishi wenming*) – the goals of the Second Modernisation – involves a particular way of thinking (*sixiang guannian*), a particular work attitude (*gongzuo taidu*), a particular lifestyle (*shenghuo fangshi*), particular societal relations (*shehui guangxi*) and so forth. He stipulates that the attitude and consciousness of an individual, rather than the actions of the government, are central to this transformation. Knowledge production forces and labour are key to He Chuanqi's formulation of the advancement of a knowledge society (He Chuanqi 1999: 408). A knowledge society constitutes the highest level of human civilisation development and possesses the highest level of human quality.

In these discursive deliberations on the desired advancement of human qualities in the process of modernisation, several dichotomies are produced. There is a general recognition that the origins of modernisation are found in the West, but it is emphasised that the long history of Chinese civilisation and traditions cannot be neglected in the process of modernisation. The pursuit of humanistic modernisation and civilisation is premised on a belief in the glorious Chinese past and an aspired future. Chinese culture, where Confucianism is regarded as the centrepiece of the tradition (with Buddhism and Daoism being supplementary, and Islam and other religions in China considered irrelevant), faces the double challenge of meeting the demands of modernisation and managing well relations with the West. A range of asserted differences between Chinese and Western cultures – in people's mentalities, ways of thinking, characters and lifestyles – is presented as a cultural disparity, and Chinese people are called on 'to adapt to the modern way of thinking' (*shiying xiandai shehui de xitong siwei*) (Zheng Yongting 2005: 219). Although the roots of the problems related to China's development are deemed endogenous to China and not solely attributable to Western imperialism, the generalised West is presented as the benchmark against which China measures its advancement and progress.

The dominant discussions of China's humanistic modernisation stipulate that the whole of China's population needs to raise its qualities and level of civilisation compared to the West. But these discussions also extensively employ oppositional binaries found within China, such as 'China's East in comparison to the West' as Zheng Yongting writes. Zheng also argues that, 'compared to China's interior, the coastal region develops quicker in economic and social terms'(Zheng Yongting 2005: 228). These domestic disparities are presented as the main issues to be resolved to attain humanistic modernisation. The discourse on humanistic modernisation portrays a particular picture of the modern Chinese, and creates a series of hierarchical relationships between diverse groups. Those who have more access to knowledge production (especially scientific and technological knowledge production) and greater ability to contribute to the modernisation process are positioned on a higher step of modernisation hierarchy. These producers of knowledge, who are not located within a particular social group, are favoured as desirable for modernising China. Those who contribute less to knowledge production are lined up behind them in accordance with their contributions to reaching the modernisation goals. Those at the very end of this chain are often blamed for slowing down the pace of modernisation.

In the dominant discourse on modernisation, China's minority populations are referred to as hindrances to modernisation. A deputy head of the Nationalities Commission of Gansu province said that 'minorities' low level of development is often linked to their low level of "civilisation", i.e. to their allegedly backward culture, education, science/technology and human resources' (cited in Zhang Chonggen et al. 1996: 260–63). Chinese scholars have concluded that population quality, however defined, 'is for the most part higher in Han areas than in minority areas' (Li quoted in Yan Hairong 2003: 496). The minority label a priori precludes the possibility that its bearer can take on the role of a generator of knowledge valuable for Chinese modernisation. Hegemonic thinking about modernisation simply does not allow ethnic minorities to be identified with modernity and high population quality. It privileges the Han majority and its dominant views on the modernisation path.

While the image of the overseas Chinese is rarely mentioned in scholarly discussions on Chinese modernisation, their proximity to the West could suggest that they are endowed with higher qualities and have more potential to contribute to Chinese modernisation. They have the highest chances of obtaining useful knowledge and translating it into practices beneficial to China's modernisation. They are the invisible actors in the official modernisation discourse. Their valuable roles are implied through the declared humanistic values of modernisation. They also can be seen as important contributors to China's modernisation at the international level, a new focus of modernisation discourse.

Discourse on international modernisation

Since Deng Xiaoping's inauguration on the reform agenda in 1978 until the mid-2000s, China's modernisation had been largely presented as domestically oriented. Foreign capital and investments had been welcomed in China for the purpose of stimulating economic growth. But the mid-2000s witnessed a shift in China's modernisation orientation, with the leadership emphasising combining modernisation with China's greater engagement with the rest of the world. This shift found its official formulation in Hu Jingtao's call for building a 'harmonious world', which is the foreign policy equivalent of his concept 'harmonious society'.[13] Reflecting this development in the official thinking, *China Modernisation Report 2008* focuses on the favourable international environment for China's economic growth and development.[14]

The report opens by contending that international modernisation is an important ingredient of China's development path, which is restricted by two types of environment. This argument is based on an analogy with genetics, which considers the genotype of an individual who exists within the living environment. Correspondingly, China's national modernisation takes place within the international environment (*China Modernisation Report* 2008: i). The report asserts that, while China has so far concentrated on the national aspect of modernisation, it has recently started looking more closely at the interaction between the international environment and national modernisation, with a view to influencing the international climate in favour of China's modernisation. The authors of the report stress that 'national modernisation is the final destination, while international modernisation is just a measure. International modernisation is a path to enhancing national level, but not the objective' (*China Modernisation Report* 2008: iii).

By the term 'international modernisation', the authors of the report refer to the international interactions in the course of modernisation, and the correlations between national modernisation and the international environment. They argue that international modernisation involves international interactions in the fields of politics, economy, society, culture, international systems, geopolitics and 'national quality' (*China Modernisation Report* 2008: v). A high national quality, echoing the notion of population quality projected onto the whole state, is seen as the key to the pursuit of modernisation; GDP per capita, figures of economic growth, and education (especially in the fields of science and technology) are particularly stressed (2008: v). Importantly, and this is similar to the emphasis on knowledge production as a marker of a modern subject in the discussions on humanistic modernisation, this new turn to incorporate international dimensions of the modernisation process stresses 'strategic profit ... including concepts and knowledge' (2008: iii-iv). The existence of the Second Modernisation Theory itself, as already noted, has been presented by He Chuanqi as testimony of China's growing national quality. The analysis used to outline the particulars of international modernisation is identical to the theoretical line of the Second Modernisation Theory, which informs and structures the *China Modernisation Report*. The analysis in the Second Modernisation Theory at the level of human beings and societies is extrapolated to the level of the international space in analyses of international modernisation. The attributes of modern subjects valuable for China's modernisation are the same: national quality is defined in terms of successful adaptation to the modern currents of life, and measured by economic indicators, the ability to contribute new knowledge, and the production of novel concepts and innovative ideas.

The report presents international modernisation theory as China's alternative interpretation of modernisation and related to dependency theory, world system theory, international relations theory and globalisation theory (*China Modernisation Report* 2008: v). But it is not only an interpretative theory, as its central objective is to make suggestions for developments at the international level to benefit China's modernisation process, including by enhancing China's position internationally (2008: vii). One of the report's central contentions is that success in modernisation is a combination of international and domestic factors. At the international level, the report emphasises taking advantage of opportunities for development and cooperation with developed countries; domestic factors determine the national quality of the country (2008: iii). The report fuses theories of international relations and the Chinese conception of modernisation to produce China's strategy for becoming an important international power.

The report assesses China's international position through measuring its status and performance along a number of dimensions. It concludes that China occupies the rank of a preliminarily developed country according to its modernisation and human development levels and the rank of a world-class power according to its 'objective national power and influence'; its economic power gives it the rank of a medium power; and its per-capita competitive power places it among underdeveloped countries (2008: ix–x). The report also implies that China should strive to become an information civilisation because 'an agricultural civilisation is unable to compete with industrial civilisation, while the latter is unable to compete with information civilisation' (2008: iv). A significant part of the report looks specifically at how to enhance China's international modernisation and puts forward a strategic proposal for this modernisation for the twenty-first century. The twenty-first century is viewed as the period of China's development and revival, in contrast to the twentieth century, which is characterised by China's struggle for national survival.

The report advances a Peace Dove Strategy for China's international modernisation in the twenty-first century, which the authors suggest will improve China's international modernisation prospects (see Figure 3.2). The report reaffirms the key role of the United Nations in leading and guaranteeing the world's peace and development, but proposes to significantly strengthen the role of the Asian region. To this end, it proposes that a new regional oganisation, Asia Association, be set up with its headquarters on the Chinese island of Hainan. Within the framework of this organisation, the report advocates, China should deepen its cooperation with the West and East through APEC and the Asia–Europe Economic Cooperation, which the report proposes to upgrade to the Asia–Europe Meeting. China's next priorities in international relationships are with the countries of the global South, particularly the regions of Africa, Oceania and South America. More specifically, the report suggests that China strategically improve its international relations with 'innovative countries, the resource-abounding countries, the large-population countries, the cultural countries, the friendly countries, and the surrounding countries' (*China Modernisation Report* 2008: xiii).

The report develops the officially-pronounced Chinese foreign policy agenda and presents it in a scientific and theoretical framework as an essential aspect of

84 *Post-socialist modernisation*

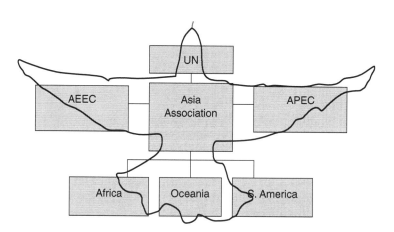

Figure 3.2 Peace Dove strategy of China's international modernisation
Source: *China Modernisation Report* (2008).

China's national modernisation project. The report is a product of the collective efforts of one of China's leading academic institutions, which bolsters the authority of the official policy. The scientific language of the modernisation theory relies on time-series and cross-sectional analysis. The report's research team thus not only generates particular knowledge of the modernisation process, but employs it to present China's official policies in a scientific framework and to represent China's stance in international relations in allegedly scientifically-verifiable terms. Here the power of the apparently neutral modern language of science employed for the production of a particular vision of progress and modernisation is crucial in concealing the workings of power in the words of declared truth. Scientific language serves as a complicit element in the production of the power of China's state.[15] It is palpable in the Modernisation Report's employment of particular 'scientifically reliable' quantitative methodologies to produce 'The Objective Power Index' and to evaluate China's position in the international arena (*China Modernisation Report* 2008: xiv–xv).

The model of global and regional governance suggested by the report is explicitly China-centric, with the final goal to raise China's profile in Asia and the world. It bears repeating that behind this seeming drive to engage more intimately with the region and the world is the pursuit of China's domestic goal of modernisation. A favourable international environment, in other words, would serve China's race to increase its national quality. The final objective of China's advancement of its relations with other countries in Asia and the world is to enhance its material foundation and national quality. But there is an interesting correlation asserted between a favourable international environment for China's modernisation and world peace. By fostering such a favourable international environment through the promotion of new institutions and ideas, the report suggests China can also bring peace to the world (*China Modernisation Report* 2008: xiii). International modernisation theory, with its prioritisation of science, technology and capital as the main components of the development process, strikingly echoes Harry Truman's notion of a 'fair deal' which, at the end of the Second World War, was proposed as an American solution to the world's problems of poverty and underdevelopment (Escobar 1995: 3–4). At least at the rhetorical level, this ambitious programme was presented as being concerned with the problem of poverty around the globe. *China Modernisation Report's* is an equally ambitious attempt to raise the profile of China around the world for the purpose of China's domestic modernisation.

It is remarkable that African and Latin American countries are included in the tail of the White Dove model led by Asia with China in the centre. This view places China in the middle of the global development shift where developing countries are not part of the driving force of transformations, but follow the directions of development set by China. Chinese leaders and scholars not only have adopted the idea of China-led globalisation, but put forward theoretical interpretations of China-led international modernisation. While some Western scholars identify socio-economic and political dangers and opportunities for the world associated with China's rise (Henderson 2008), official discourse in China articulates a new 'Yellow Man's Burden', a mission to develop the countries in the Global South, which China has shouldered on its way to become a great power (Nyíri 2006). This self-professed global role reverberates with the party-state's domestic missionary approach towards its ethnic minorities is discussed further in Chapter 4.

In accordance with the Second Modernisation Theory and preceding *China Modernisation Reports*, the 2008 edition confirms China's status as a developing country yet to catch up with the advanced economies of the West. But the report emphasises China's role as an influential and growing power, whose influence in the world could be asserted through the generation of new ideas and norms as well as the promotion of new international institutions. More assertive engagement at the regional and international levels as well as promotion of its perspective on international processes could compensate for deficiencies in China's development. The authors of the *China Modernisation Report* reiterate the prevalent conceptions and theories developed, popularised, and in some instances treated as the norm in the West, although those ideas have been increasingly challenged. The authors do not question the hegemonic thinking on development, but heavily rely on it in their representations and normative prescriptions of China's modernisation path. And in doing so, they fail to liberate their thinking from the Western mentality about the ways of living in other societies. Indeed, they largely adopt this mentality as the only possible way to conceive issues of progress and development. Rather than developing an alternative model to Western modernisation, Chinese official perspective further perpetuates the hierarchies inherent to it.

Conclusion

The above analysis of how the Chinese nation is constructed and represented in the official way of thinking about modernisation processes emphasises the performative and constitutive role of ideas. The pursuit of modernisation is presented by the official discourse as an omnipresent and inescapable goal, influencing modes of thinking, acting and living at both personal and state levels. The dominance of the modernisation agenda in official and scholarly analyses demonstrates how China's domestic and international realities are conceptualised through the prism of modernisation. China's modernisation discourse, much of which advocates all-around development, is concerned with the politics of representation and identity and the reproduction of the nation. Its vision of the future informs the articulation of the development agenda for Chinese society. The future, and especially its numerical expression, becomes the vantage point for viewing the national condition.

Although the present Chinese scholarly-driven discourse on modernisation is rooted in debates that have taken place since the late 1800s, the political and economic climate of the reform period played the key role in shaping how modernisation is conceptualised. This chapter demonstrated a connection between the elite-formulated programmes of modernisation and the scholarly debates on it. Chinese mainstream modernisation thinking produced within the walls of China's key think tank has become a form of 'religious prophecy' for the Chinese elite, one built upon the orthodox understanding of modernisation developed in the West. Chinese scholarly and official circles in many ways use Western orthodox approaches to modernisation as yardsticks for producing a Chinese version of it, even if they are critical of them.

The narrow understanding of modernisation as a means of production of numerical indicators and a mode of following a certain developmental model inhibits embracing cultural diversity and considering people's well-being and satisfaction. Also, such restricted theorising excludes pursuing multiple types of modernisation or incorporating the voices of different social groups. The Second Modernisation Theory, for example, treats modernisation as a defining feature of China's national character and basically neglects China's peculiar diversity. It subordinates or ignores alternative paths to modernity. A uniform modernisation project is based on the identification of a certain code of values and ideals as showing the only true path to development; it dismisses difference as conservative or backward. Certain sectors of the population are unavoidably labelled the antitheses of modernisation and therefore risk being excluded from the project.

China's official perspective on modernisation not only reiterates China's inferior status in relation to Western societies, who are ahead of China in their development processes, but presents a particular picture of China's domestic situation. It relies on and reproduces a series of hierarchical relationships within and outside China in its articulation of the modernisation process. Despite China's status as a developing nation, modernisation scholars recognise China's growing influence in the international arena, and emphasise the value of knowledge production in the contemporary world, which China, in their opinion, should accelerate. China's growing power in the world could be asserted, in their view, through the generation of new ideas, norms and international institutions. The objective, however, appears to be not the improvement of the well-being of the world, but of China's modernisation.

The modernisation project rests on a certain set of values rather than the nation-state's attributes, such as territoriality and state sovereignty (though these attributes are by no means dismissed). China's official discourse on modernisation defines the 'true' patterns of modernisation and thus predetermines the parameters of change in the nation-state. This process has a nation-shaping effect, as modernisation is based on values greater than those encompassed by the politico-territorial understanding of a nation-state, and yet it aims at their implementation in a territorially-restricted but essentially diverse environment. As norms and ideals, compatible with the modernisation goals are desired as the absolute truth, the carriers of other ideals are excluded from the modernisation project. Ethnic minorities, as will be further demonstrated, are often perceived as a collective embodiment of values inconsistent with the officially-promoted modernisation mode. At the same time, the bearers of an identical cluster of values outside the nominal boundaries of the Chinese nation-state could be brought into the modernisation project within the symbolic and territorial confines of the nation-state. In this sense, the discourse on modernisation reshapes the symbolic and territorial contours of the Chinese nation-state.

4 Ethnic minorities and overseas Chinese in the post-socialist modernisation discourse

This chapter examines the discursive representations of overseas Chinese and ethnic minorities in the dominant modernisation rhetoric in China. Through analysing Chinese scholarly publications and official statements, it traces manifestations of the hegemonic modernisation discourse on the roles of these two groups in the Chinese nation. I seek to identify how particular ways of thinking about the development of the Chinese nation designate these roles in China's national modernisation project.

Modernisation and economic development are certainly not the only themes in the official discourse on the Chinese nation. Equally important and prominent topics are state unity and reunification, sovereignty, stability, security, 'peaceful rise', as well as Confucian-informed ideals such as 'harmonious society'. However, modernisation and economic development have been the most long-standing concerns of the Chinese leadership and central themes in official and public discourse on how China's national project should evolve.

I examine Chinese scholarly articles linking modernisation debates with the roles of overseas Chinese and ethnic minorities, as well as relevant official statements of the state's leaders. In my research, I did not analyse specific academic outlets, but instead used the China Academic Journal database to search for the keywords 'modernisation', 'overseas Chinese', and 'ethnic minorities'. Most of the articles I examined were published between the early 1990s and the early 2000s in the leading national and provincial academic journals.

There are certainly limitations to my analysis as far as how I selected, grouped and analysed my sources. However, my objective here is not to reveal the 'true' representations of ethnic minorities and overseas Chinese in the official discourse, but rather to show the role of these representations in the construction of a seemingly-coherent picture of the Chinese nation. These representations shift and perhaps can be seen as 'partial fixations', in Doty's terms, which produce certain truths and legitimate certain meanings and practices of development (Doty 1996: 167).

This chapter consists of two parts: the first is on the dominant perceptions of the roles of ethnic minorities in academic and official debates on modernisation, the second is on the dominant perceptions of the roles of overseas Chinese. Each part presents a discursive image of the relation of ethnic minorities and overseas

Chinese to the modernisation project across a range of academic writings and official statements. The parallels drawn between the two discourses show a close relationship between the official Party line and mainstream scholarly positioning on modernisation. In both the scholarly and official narratives, the ethnic minorities and overseas Chinese are represented as extreme participant groups, which are situated diametrically opposite to each other. The dominant discourse both fixes their images and reduces their roles to a simple oppositional dichotomy. Ethnic minorities are presented as being at the beginning of the modernisation process, while overseas Chinese are seen as representing the way modernisation should and will evolve. This understanding of modernisation and the roles of these two groups in it is often reflected in the language structures used in the sources I analysed. Across the body of scholarly perspectives, ethnic minorities are referred to as the objects of modernisation projects, while overseas Chinese are constructed as their active subjects and in some cases even as protagonists.

I first turn to discuss four dominant themes in the Chinese official scholarly discussions on ethnic minorities and modernisation: modernisation as an opportunity for unity and development; modernisation as a mission; selective cultural celebration; and de-politicisation of ethnic minorities. I then briefly consider non-official scholarly and popular discussions on ethnic minorities.

Ethnic minorities in the modernisation discourse

Modernisation as an opportunity for unity and development

Chinese ethnic minorities are most frequently included in the official modernisation discourse in the context of unity (*tuanjie*) and development (*fazhan*), which originally constituted the core of Deng Xiaoping's national theory of modernisation. Scholars frequently refer to a quote of Deng Xiaoping's successor, Jiang Zemin, to illuminate the importance of these issues for China's national project: 'If there is no well-off society in minority areas, there is no well-off society nation-wide; there is no nation-wide modernisation until minority regions are modernised' (Yuan Jingxia 2002: 22; Li Qiuxiang 2002: 108; Han Ziliang 2007a: 75). Chinese scholars often emphasise that the imbalance in regional development between the eastern 'Han' region of China and western 'minority' areas is an 'obstruction' (*fangai*) and a 'restriction' (*zhiyue*) to the process of Chinese modernisation (Yang Jingchu 1989:18). The goal of the national modernisation project, according to this viewpoint, can be achieved only when all parts of the country are modernised (Han Ziliang 2007a: 75). In other words, China's ethnic minority regions are held responsible for the success of the national modernisation project as a whole.

China's western region associated with ethnic minorities is renowned for its richness in natural resources, which are in great demand in China's east. But while ethnic minorities' areas are thus commonly depicted as rich in natural resources and land, economically and culturally the people there are characterised as 'tremendously backward' (*daduo shifen luohou*) or 'traditional, few, remote, and poor' (*lao, shao, bian, qun*) (Yuan Jingxia 2002: 22). One of the commonly-suggested opportunities for a more vigorous modernisation drive by ethnic minorities is to engage them in the greater opening of the region's natural resources (Zeng Yuming 1993: 51). In this light, the period of reforms, especially the 1999 central government's WDP, is presented as providing more opportunities for ethnic minorities' regions to develop (*fazhan jiyu*). The WDP is depicted as a chance for supposedly poor minorities to eradicate poverty and achieve common prosperity (*fanrong*) (Yuan Jingxia 2002: 22). In this context, China's national modernisation project is viewed as a two-level process of opening up: on the one hand, it refers to the opening up of China to the world; on the other hand, it refers to an opening up of the western regions of China for exploration, business, and tourism by the people from the eastern parts of China and foreigners. As one author contends: 'The density of population in Han regions is very high, exploration and use of the natural resources started very early, the supply has significantly dropped, therefore, with the further progress in development, China is relying upon the natural resources in the Western part of the country' (Aireken Aihemaiti 1999a: 27).

The WDP is perceived by many Chinese scholars as a minority development project and an opportunity to resolve a long-standing national question, thereby guaranteeing the success of modernisation (Zhang Zhizuo 2003; Yuan Jingxia 2002; Long Yi 2003). From their point of view, this national question is how to guarantee the stability and preserve the unity of the country. Development of the minority areas is presented in an economic light as much as a political and strategic one (Yuan Jingxia 2002: 22). The modernisation initiatives in China's western region, such as the Three Gorges Dam or the Tibetan-Qinghai railway, are depicted as fostering the economic and social development of the region (Zeng Yuming 1993: 48). Many Chinese scholars assert that these modernisation initiatives provide an opportunity for ethnic minorities to engage more fully in modernisation and contribute to the overall modernisation of the country. Moreover, closer exchange and cooperation with the supposedly more developed eastern regions of China is deemed to 'strengthen national consciousness' among the minorities (*zengjia guojia yishi*) (He Xingliang 1996: 77). In the opinion of some Chinese scholars, the reform period introduced more chances for China's ethnic minorities to interact on cultural and economic bases with the Han majority, gave them more opportunities for cultural exchange, and promoted better mutual understanding and influences. As one scholar observes, 'a more advanced culture can impact backward cultures' and 'form new cultural models which are compatible with the ideals of economic modernisation, among which there are new values for minorities, such as competitiveness and profit-making' (He Xingliang 1996: 72, 77).

Taken together, the opening up and development of the market economy are seen as potentially facilitating a dialogue between minority nationalities and the Han majority, pushing them closer together. In the course of this process, so some Chinese scholars believe, ethnic minorities will change their attitudes towards modern ways of thinking and behaving. As one scholar writes: 'Differences are also disappearing. At present, no matter interior or coast line area, or minority border areas, the differences in youth culture, clothing, the concept of beauty, and so forth are becoming less and less significant' (He Xingliang 1996: 77).

Overwhelmingly, modernisation is presented in Chinese scholarly publications as a solution to China's ethnic problems, an all-encompassing answer to the problems of regional and social inequality, ethnic cohesion, cultural development and potential ethnic strife. Modernisation is seen as a unifying force in China's vast and diverse geo-social space, one driving the development of China's ethnic minorities forward. The capacity of ethnic minorities to formulate and come to grips with the challenges which modernisation poses is neglected in the majority of these studies. The emphasis is placed on the positive and progressive nature of the state-formulated projects. The minorities are presented as groups in need of development programmes. This rhetoric unavoidably confines ethnic minorities' development choices to the ones formulated by the state.

Modernisation as a mission

The rhetoric of including ethnic minorities in the modernisation drive often has a missionary tone. The mission to develop or civilise ethnic minorities has deep roots in Chinese imperial and modern history, and has been informed by a mix of Western social evolutionary theories, Confucian thought and the ideology of Marxism (Harrell 1995b). One of the most illustrative examples of the missionary rhetoric is different variations of the following statement: 'The party and the government attach a great importance and are concerned about the economic development and people's livelihood in the minority areas' (Han Ziliang 2007b). The notion of the salvation of ethnic minorities is a continuation of a theme dominant since the establishment of the PRC, and even earlier since the Long March of the PLA across central and western parts of China. It is generally accepted among Chinese scholars that since the 'liberation' of the country, ethnic minorities, with the help (*bangzhu*) and support (*zhiyuan*) of the party and the government, have achieved equality and economic, political and cultural development. The process of reform and the opening up of the country and western regions is viewed as both a revolutionary strategy and a continuation of the earlier policies to guarantee the development and unity of all nationalities. The missionary understanding of ethnic minorities is even manifest in legal documents. For example, the 1982 Constitution of the PRC states that 'the state *helps* the areas inhabited by minority nationalities speed up their economic and cultural development in accordance with the peculiarities and needs of the different minority nationalities' (Par. 1, Art. 4, my emphasis). The WDP is similarly interpreted as an opportunity for development *granted* by the central government (Zhang Haiyang 2001: 253).

Not only the authorities, but also the Han majority – often presented as an elder brother of other nationalities – is seen as a source of support and inspiration for minorities. With the diminished power of the central authority, the saviour 'mission' moved to the provincial governments, predominantly in the east, which are interested in the vast resources of the west. The modernisation initiatives in the west are depicted as guidelines or directives given by the fast-developing provinces in the east to the lagging western regions, so that the western regions can catch up with the eastern coastal areas. Eastern provinces are often referred to as conductive forces (*chuandao xing*) transmitting the state's will to achieve an even modernisation. When in 1993 the Ministry of Agriculture launched a project of east-west cooperation by building enterprise establishments in the west, it was underlined that the initiative had received the full support and promotion of famous entrepreneurs from the east (He Xingliang 1996:74). The following is emblematic of the missionary view of modernisation: 'With the *help* of the state, *support* of the Eastern provinces, and ethnic minority regions ef forts, we will definitely achieve the objective of prosperity among all nationalities' (Yuan Jingxia 2002: 21).

Within the dominant discourse, the local minority elite stands out as a link connecting the centre and the provinces, the eastern region and the western region, and the Han majority and the ethnic minorities.[1] Chinese official documents and academic literature portray minority cadres as a unique type of leadership familiar with the situation in the minority regions, who understand local customs, culture and traditions. When their unique knowledge of local situations is coupled with special training in line with the Party and its spirit of modernisation, these leaders constitute an irreplaceable force supportive of the Party and government ideas of modernisation, opening up, reform, and the transfer of science and technology to the minority localities (Ma Shipin 1996: 3). These leaders are seen as having the potential to energise a minority cultural spirit of modernisation.

The passive role of ethnic minorities as the recipients of the development policies formulated by the Party and the state, and already practiced by the Han majority, precludes seeing the minorities as playing active roles in the state-led project. Such portrayals of ethnic minorities in dependent roles does not allow for the possibility of them engaging critically with or opposing the modernisation project. They are not recognised as being capable of actively interpreting and advancing their own modernisation practices. Such representation does not attempt to reflect the reality on the ground and, of course, conveys a negative view of China's ethnic minorities. There is strong evidence of rich entrepreneurial skills and innovations among many ethnic minorities, whose relationship with the market systems differs from that of the majority group (Heberer 2007). Ethnic minorities' active engagement with development practices often leads to a strengthening of their ethnic consciousness and local attachments (Gladney 1995, 2004; Shih 2007). The dominant representations by Chinese scholars do not recognise the legitimacy of already-existing alternative forms of knowledge about development paths. The prevalent discourse fails to appreciate the irreducible diversity of development experiences, and prefers to refer to ethnic minorities as a whole. This way of thinking justifies and legitimises the state-initiated development programmes, which are presented as benefiting ethnic minorities and having been designed with ethnic minorities in mind. It also reproduces and normalises a particular perspective on the Chinese nation, which is presented as composed of the modernisation-oriented Han majority and passive ethnic minorities who have to be led and guided to achieve better living standards. This mode of thinking and the politics of representation associated with it lock ethnic minorities into unequal and hierarchical relationships. They produce ethnic minorities as objects of the modernisation project, inhibiting the possibility of developing a perspective of equality and appreciating diversity as a constituent quality of the Chinese national project. These representational practices make possible the politics of domination and submission.

Selective cultural celebration

The modernisation project of the period of reforms and opening up has been accompanied by a 'cultural fever ' (*wenhua re*) for ethnic minorities' cultures, which suddenly flourished after the years of suppression during the Cultural Revolution. Minority cultures were now supported, codified, promoted, popularised, commodified and utilised by the state. They became a symbol of an open, multicultural and plural Chinese society, which is the image that China's leadership wants to project to the outside world. Ethnic minorities became symbols of China's embrace of multiculturalism and plural values, often associated in the Chinese scholarship with the societies of the West, and of the ideals of a modern society (Aierken Aihemaiti 1999b: 3). Indeed, diversity and multiculturalism have been viewed as aspects of China's modernising process, because the 'multicultural society is prone to a quicker opening up, democratisation, and prosperity' (Aierken Aihemaiti 1999a: 28). Another scholar views marketisation of minority cultures as part of the transformation from 'traditional to modern society' (Yang Qingyu 2004: 21).

Although the multicultural character of the Chinese nation has become more widely celebrated, the role of the Han majority group is still often stressed as the most important in setting the pace of China's development. The roles of ethnic minorities are restricted to marking China's cultural diversity, not its development advancements, as they are not recognised as being capable of sufficiently contributing to the latter. Some authors do acknowledge, however, that while the Han occupy an 'exceptional' place in Chinese culture, they 'cannot negate or substitute [for] traditional cultures of minorities' (Yang Jingchu 1989: 18). With the start of the reform period, there was a realisation that exotic, distant, unfamiliar minority cultures could provide modernisation investment opportunities. People suddenly discovered that all fifty-five ethnic minorities were 'talented in singing and dancing' (*neng ge shan wu*) and had their own particular clothing, cuisine, architecture, festivals, customs, and written and spoken languages (Aierken Aihemaiti 1999b: 3). This awareness resulted in the publication of numerous minority photo albums, or ganisation of minority sports competitions, minority beauty contests, tourist tours of minority areas, and the construction of minority parks in Beijing, Shenzhen and other parts of China. Ethnic minorities have become an imperative feature of the national holiday celebrations, such as the annual spring festival TV gala, and other nationally important events, such as the opening ceremony of the Beijing Olympics (Gladney 2004; Leibold 2008). While ethnic minorities have always featured in the PRC's national celebrations, in the post-Mao era their participation does not symbolise the ethnic unity in the face of common class struggle, but multicultural diversity which, in the eyes of China's leaders, is an inalienable feature of a modern society. However, the ways ethnic minorities feature in such state-sponsored representations show the crystallisation of a particular image of ethnic minorities in the Chinese national imagery. It is telling that the children who were dressed in minority costumes in the 2008 Beijing Olympics opening ceremony were all representatives of the Han nationality. The authorities dismissed any attempts to criticise such bogus celebrations of minority cultures by calling them 'normal' practice in the Chinese tradition (Leibold 2008).

Despite general acknowledgement of the importance of the rich and diverse traditional cultures of ethnic minorities for China's national project, a significant number of Chinese scholars assert that the culture of ethnic minorities can either advance or hinder their development and the country's development (Yang Jingchu 1989: 19; Ma Shipin 1996; Li Qiuxiang 2002: 109; Han Ziliang 2007a). Therefore, these authors see a necessity for minorities to overcome 'cultural obstacles' and a 'conservative minority mentality', and to develop positive aspects of their cultures, while eliminating those which are difficult to accommodate to the modernisation process (Yang Jingchu 1989: 19; Li Qiuxiang 2002: 109). They call upon ethnic minorities 'to open up their minds' to overcome prejudices and old traditions, and to embrace new values compatible with China's reform and opening up (Li Qiuxiang 2002: 110; Han Ziliang 2007a: 77). Ma Shipin, for example, believes that certain aspects of minority cultures are backward and go against the very grain of the modernisation project (Ma Shipin 1996:1). These elements of their cultures, particularly slash-and-burn agriculture (*daogeng huozhong*), in Ma's terms, are anti-scientific (*weibei kexue*) and primitive (*daogeng huozhong*). One of the often-cited examples of backwardness among ethnic minorities is their supposedly conservative attitude towards profit making and competition (*bu hui jingshang, bu yuan yu ren jingzheng*) (He Xingliang 1996: 77). Chinese authors often posit the need to further develop ethnic minorities' modernisation practices so that they are in line with the state's overall formulation of the modernisation project. These authors often contend that such selective approbation of the traditional cultures together with technological advancements of modernisation can advance the modernisation process in the minority regions. Ma Shipin (1996), for example, believes that there is a conditional relationship between modernisation and traditional minority cultures, and that the latter should accommodate to the demands of the former. He argues that only by adapting their cultures to the nature of the state modernisation project can ethnic minorities develop 'pride, eliminate backward elements, and promote their development'. In other words, minorities should review their cultures and traditions in light of China's modernisation goals. Ethnic minorities are called upon to develop a new 'political culture' synonymous with such principles as 'secularism' (*shisu xing*), 'independence' (*zizhu*), 'openness' (*kaifang*), and 'progress' (*jinqu*) (Ding Zhigang and Han Zuozhen 2003: 123–24).

Such analyses subject minority cultural practices to the developmental logic of the state's modernisation paradigm. Cultural practices are only recognised as legitimate if they reinforce the rationale of the modernisation project and serve its implementation. Culture becomes the predicate of economic development, and is interpreted within its framework. Minorities' cultures are also subjected to the power of the Party, as only their sanctioned aspects can be displayed and practiced. The unwanted aspects should be silenced and, more radically, confined to the past.

De-politicisation of ethnic minorities

In the late 1990s a new trend in Chinese scholarly writings and official publications on ethnic minorities emerged. A number of scholars pointed to the importance of reviewing the status of ethnic minorities within the Chinese state (Zhou Chuanbin 2004; Ma Rong 2007; Ruan Xihu 2008). They proposed treating ethnic minorities as cultural groups participating in the larger socio-political project of China, rather than as nationalities according to Stalin's criteria. Since the late 1990s there have been at least three nationwide conferences specifically examining the nature of the terms *minzu* and *zuqun* (ethnic group) (Zhou Chuanbin 2004). While the use of *zuqun* to refer to China's ethnic minorities is still a hotly disputed issue within Chinese academic circles, the majority of scholars point to the similarities between the Chinese term *minzu* and the English term 'ethnicity' or 'ethnic group', rather than to the similarities with the previously-used Soviet notion of nationality (see, for example, Ruan Xihu 2008). This new trend in how China's ethnic relations are viewed was especially apparent in the translation of the Chinese term *shaoshu minzu* into English, which now became 'ethnic minorities' rather than 'minority nationalities'. This shift in the use of the term of course evokes new connotations. The preferred English translation used by the Chinese authorities indicates a new direction in the official discourse and policies underlying it. The fact that the language of the foreign variant of the Chinese term has changed indicates a shift in the utilisation and application of the Chinese concept rather than simply being an end in itself (Barabantseva 2008).

This language shift is invoked by Chinese scholars to downplay the political status and rights of ethnic minorities and to stress instead their cultural origins in China. This new wave of scholarly writings could be partly attributed to the collapse of the Soviet Union and Yugoslavia and the explosion of ethnic wars in many former socialist states, which Chinese scholars often interpret as the result of the defective ethnic policies. The emphasis on the cultural rather than the political status of ethnic minorities has been regarded by some authors as a possible preventive measure against a feared disintegration of China. Ma Rong, the key promoter of the idea of the 'de-politicisation' of ethnic minorities, was one of the first to suggest that the ambiguity of the term *minzu* in Chinese could affect ethnic relations and the unity of China.[2] He suggests avoiding possible problems by revising the use of *minzu* and presenting it in cultural rather than political terms (Ma Rong 2007: 202). As Ma states, 'by emphasizing the cultural characteristics of ethnic groups, their political interests are diluted' (2007: 202). Such 'de-politicisation' of ethnic minorities, in his view, would help stabilise the Chinese state and make it more cohesive. It would also, he argues, minimise the chances that ethnic minorities will seek greater autonomy and independence from China.

Ma suggests that imperial China's approaches to dealing with cultural differences were a more natural, correct and historically proven way of managing ethnic relations in China. He sees the introduction of the Soviet-type national model in China as politically and historically problematic. Instead, he proposes viewing the Han majority and ethnic minorities as constituting one Chinese civilisation. He argues that the 'barbarian-civilised' distinction between ethnic minorities and the Han majority referred to differences between their stages of development rather than to cultural differences (Ma Rong 2006: 203). In suggesting a rethinking of the model of managing ethnic relations by turning to the Chinese imperial past, Ma curiously fuses Confucian cultural arguments with the Morganian socio-economic evolutionary thesis. He reduces differences between ethnic groups in China to 'the distinction between highly developed and less developed civilizations with similar roots but at different stages of advancement' (Ma Rong 2007: 203). In other words, he narrows the understanding of ethnicity to the crude opposition between the 'more civilised' and 'less civilised' groups. Ethnic differences for Ma are attributed to different levels of socio-economic development. In his analysis, ethnic minorities' subordinated relationship to the Han is presented as a historical fact.

Ma's writings have recently become very important in China and have gained recognition outside China as well, with his articles appearing frequently in English-language academic journals (Ma Rong 2006, 2007) and cited by scholars in the West (Leibold 2008; Callahan 2009; Sautman 2009). He is often quoted as the leading scholar of ethnic relations by Chinese colleagues, who subconsciously sanction his voice as representative of Chinese scholarship on ethnic relations. Ma's solution to China's ethnic issues lies in rethinking ethnic relations in cultural-developmental terms, whereby development measures play the determinant role in designating a group's place within the Chinese nation. Ma's influential proposition to view China's ethnic composition in terms of cultural rather than political values emphasises developmental distinctions between different ethnic groups. According to Ma, 'cultural achievement' becomes a measure of conformity to the development standards set by the assumed Confucian core or the dominant Han culture. Ethnic minorities become denigrated as apolitical social groups lacking 'proper' culture and development.

Non-official discourses on ethnic minorities

Critical views on China's engagement with its ethnic minorities find marginal but important expression in academic and popular circles in China. It is interesting to examine the terms and framework within which such critiques of China's policies towards ethnic minorities are based.

Critical Chinese scholarship on China's minority policies demonstrates that the modernisation model suggested by the centre and the modernisation projects undertaken not only threaten traditional cultures, historical heritages and the environment, but are often unwanted, misunderstood and misinterpreted by the local people (Zhang Haiyang 2001; Xiong Jingmin 2002). This scholarship challenges the consumerist model of growth and development presented by the government as the only valid path to modernity . In fact, this critical scholarship regards the 'development' imposed on minorities as a new form of the penetration of the dominant culture into the western region, one which violates the indivisibility of people and their cultures, and endangers the wholeness of distinctive otherness.

Zhang Haiyang (2001: 258) and Xiong Jingmin (2002: 130), for example, ague that the western provinces of China have a unique and fragile environment which is not suitable for either extensive farming or large-scale settlements or industries. They both assert that it is no accident that the region occupies over 54 per cent of the total territory of China, but that only 23 per cent of the Chinese population inhabit the area. Nevertheless, the authors lament, the region is already overdeveloped, overpopulated and significantly damaged. The soil of the region is becoming less fertile. Local people live according to the natural rules of the region, adapting to the severe conditions of powerful rivers and mountains, preserving and protecting forests and grasslands (Zhang Haiyang 2001: 258). Zhang stresses that any changes to the ecosystem may cause major ecological upheavals, which in the end could lead to the stagnation of the modernisation process.

Rather than looking at ethnic minorities as poverty-stricken and backward, these critical studies emphasise their role in modernisation, seeing the minorities as providers of the continuity of traditional culture and even as motors of advancement (Zhang Haiyang 2001: 264; Xiong Jingmin 2002: 130). Zhang also points out that instead of pursuing a selective approach to the culture of minorities in the region, and seeing a division between its backward and advanced features, we should understand it as a complex system, as its diversity and complexity reflect nothing less than the richness of civilisation (2001: 259). He asserts that pursuing modernisation should be restricted to means rather than ends in the process of building a better, dignified life for ethnic minorities.

This critique of the of ficial interpretation of the role of ethnic minorities in China's national project is nevertheless located within the state-formulated framework of modernisation. It reasserts the power of the dominant discursive practices to set the legitimate grounds on which the critical analysis is carried out. The hegemonic discourse of modernisation determines the conditions on which its critique is formulated and advanced. And so, while the critical accounts dispute how ethnic minorities should be included in the state-imposed modernisation framework, they contribute to and reproduce the dominant vision of modernisation (and its twin term, development) shaping the Chinese national project. The critical accounts treat the state-imposed framework as foundational and normal.

Popular sentiments on ethnic relations in China also reflect the power of the official national discourse. To illustrate this, I will briefly turn to Internet-based discussion of ethnic relations in China. In September 2006, Li Dezhu, the head of the Ethnic Affairs Commission, made a speech in which he contended that the

Chinese government respects ethnic minority cultures and traditions, but cannot provide their absolute protection (*baohu jueduihua*) in the midst of globalisation. Globalisation, Li argued, was an overarching issue affecting everybody, and China's ethnic minority groups would naturally encounter and engage with the manifestations of such global processes. Following Li's speech, the Chinese section of the BBC invited the Internet community to comment and reflect on these commentaries made by this top Chinese official. The forum attracted more than fifty responses, predominately from overseas Chinese netizens.[3]

The main strands of the official discourse were reproduced in these online discussions on ethnic minorities. A number of responses commented favourably on China's minority policies, characterising them as 'successful overall' and somewhat more generous than those in other countries in the world. Others were rather sceptical about even discussing the issue of ethnicity in China. For example, one respondent pointed out that the Han nationality was the only major group in China and that the discourse on ethnic minorities was 'parasitic'. The same respondent noted that switching ethnic affiliation is a matter of rational choice and opportunism, and that people in China register as ethnic minorities to qualify for preferential treatment. Another respondent claimed that the topic of the Chinese BBC discussion forum was 'political' and suggested that it might provoke certain ethnic minorities to call for China's disintegration. This sentiment was echoed by yet another netizen who called for the assimilation of ethnic minorities, as the government's beneficial treatment of ethnic minorities was allegedly conducive to strengthening minorities' identities. These lines of arguments mirror and reiterate at the popular level the recent trend of Chinese academic works to downplay the 'political' component of ethnic groups and view them in cultural terms.

Notably, several respondents questioned the relevance of the discussion forum because they felt, in tune with Li Dezhu's comments, that all Chinese, whatever their ethnic affiliations, were experiencing Westernisation, and that therefore all Chinese, including ethnic minorities, were becoming 'assimilated' by the West and its culture. A more urgent concern, according to these netizens, was to study how the West influences China with all its ethnic groups. In other words, these netizens sought to re-direct the topic of the discussion forum to the West and its cultural influences as a common 'threat' to the 'vulnerable' Chinese culture. They saw successful adaptation to the conditions of globalisation as a task for all Chinese people. Preserving the lifestyles of ethnic minorities is, in the opinion of these netizens, a 'violation of human rights', as it would mean denying these ethnic minorities the benefits of modern life. This reasoning resonates with the missionary perspective of the official discourse that criticises ethnic minorities for being ungrateful of the new lifestyle which 'we' (Han Chinese) introduced to the ethnic minorities, who are now unthankfully accusing 'us' of assimilating them. Ethnic minorities, one netizen argues, are not 'living fossils' or 'specimens' and would like to pursue a modern life (*xiandaihua de shenguo*). The respondent called for the ethnic minorities to 'use modern concepts and styles to attain a new level of development'. This person did not see any possibility for ethnic minorities to 'understand the contemporary world' and enjoy the fruits of modernisation advancements unless they are expressed through particular forms and practices and in standardised Chinese, the official language of the Chinese state.

Such discussions of the roles of ethnic minorities in China's modernisation project rarely draw distinctions between the conditions and traditions of China's fifty-five ethnic minority groups. Most sources employ the concept 'ethnic minorities' to refer to all ethnic groups that are different from those officially regarded as the Han (Han Ziliang 2007a). This has ideological implications. It endows the problematic Han majority with the values of an advanced, developed community with the 'right' modes of development and a moderate level of development. Hart (1985: 37–39) contends that, while the terms 'modern', 'developed' and 'advanced' are similar concepts, 'developed' and 'advanced' have hidden ideological connotations. By and large, minorities are those who are falsely associated with stagnation and who in some way complicate China's national modernisation project.

The use of the term 'ethnic minorities' in the context of modernisation strikingly resembles the dominant discussions of modernisation in China discussed in Chapter 3. Such use relies on the production of several dichotomies: the predominately Han eastern part of the country is set against the minority west; the Han are generally considered to have reached a moderately modernised stage, while ethnic minorities are predominately referred to as backward; and those who are referred to as the Han in the national context of China are seen as providers of modern values, while ethnic minorities are viewed as deeply traditional. Culture is regarded as an inferior, secondary value relative to modernisation, and one that to a certain extent should even be suppressed to meet the needs of modernisation. Therefore there is not much room for articulating the differences between the minority cultures in the dominant picture of the position of minorities in modernisation. There is also not much room for seeing potential sources of development within the minorities themselves. Therefore, they should seek inspiration for development in the successful experiences of the eastern provinces, and dutifully follow the directives of the centre.

The above discursive portrayals of ethnic minorities and their roles in the modernisation project show the minorities' largely marginal and derogated status in the project, and the failure of the official debates on modernisation to reflect and appreciate the cultural and ethnic diversity of the Chinese nation-state. The representation of ethnic minorities in the dominant modernisation discourse illustrates the domination of a particular national identity insensitive of difference, and based on silencing and suppressing it. Cultural and ethnic diversity is denigrated and subordinated to the all-encompassing language of modernisation and economic development.

Representations of overseas Chinese in the modernisation discourse

Since the early modern period in China, overseas Chinese have been seen as a source of motivation, support, knowledge and new ideas for the realisation of

China's modernisation efforts. As discussed in Chapter 1, the GMD and the early CCP heavily relied on Chinese diasporic populations in the formulation of their revolutionary programmes for China. Later, during the heyday of the People's Republic and its grand experiments, overseas Chinese were excluded from the government's agenda and deemed 'class enemies'. However, with the start of the reforms and the process of opening up, overseas Chinese have been included again in the official discourse as one of the immediate forces in Chinese modernisation. From the beginning of the reform period, Deng Xiaoping and subsequent Chinese leaders attached great importance to the role of overseas Chinese in China's development. This is reflected in the abundance of related scholarly publications in China. Several themes stand out in the academic and official characterisations of the roles of overseas Chinese in China's national modernisation project: overseas Chinese as the drivers of Chinese modernisation; overseas Chinese as patriots; the 'Chinese heart' of the overseas Chinese; and overseas Chinese as a political force.

Overseas Chinese as the drivers of Chinese modernisation

Across the spectrum of official publications, the greatest and foremost contribution of overseas Chinese to contemporary China is seen in the material realm. This contribution was a response to Deng Xiaoping's invitation to overseas Chinese to come back to China and contribute to the national modernisation project. Deng's call was based on the assumption that overseas Chinese understand China and have the right 'business-minded' orientation (in Chen Fei 2002: 45). Deng formulated his policy agenda on the assumption of overseas Chinese support of the Chinese government and its policies, and the strong belief that 'they will enthusiastically support our efforts to build the country' (Deng Xiaoping quoted in Chen Fei 2002: 45). Chinese scholars commended the overseas Chinese for their vigorous response to the government's call and their generous investments.[4] In He Jiasheng's words (1997: 30), 'South-East Asian Overseas Chinese turned Mainland China into an arena for their enthusiastic (*rezhong*) investment'. Another scholar contended that 'overseas Chinese activities in the Mainland China met the need and the spirit of modernisation' (Chen Fei 2002:43).

The overseas Chinese are frequently depicted as a crucial driving force of China's modernisation, and a source of knowledge and investments in China's economy. In the 1990s, overseas Chinese were seen as the main contributors to the actually used foreign direct investment (FDI)[5] in China (Zhu Huiling 1998). Overseas Chinese poured capital into China and opened up China's vast expanses for the international market (*dakai guowai shichang*); helped increase tax revenues; provided employment in China; guaranteed payment for workers; and introduced advanced foreign technological and managerial experiences (Zhao Heman 1994: 8; Chen Zhihong 1997; Wu Qianjin 2000: 27; Chen Yunyun 2009). One author suggests that expectations of overseas Chinese involvement are held not only by the Chinese government but also by ordinary people (*laobaixing*) who expect to receive assistance from overseas Chinese communities (Feng Ertang 1999:158).

Overseas Chinese are portrayed as promoting a deepening of the reforms and giving dynamism to modernisation and urbanisation (Lin Xiaodong 2000: 29–30; Chen Yunyun 2009). Increasingly, overseas Chinese participation is seen as crucial for the development of the central and western regions of China as well as for China's development initiatives abroad. Overseas Chinese are sometimes referred to as the expression of the PRC's 'soft power' (*ruanshi li*) and bearers of Chinese national interests, whose role abroad is becoming more pertinent with the shift from domestic to international aspects of China's modernisation (Zeng Yunhua 2008: 44).

An understated issue in Chinese scholarly writings on overseas Chinese investments in China is the rationale behind the apparently keen involvement of overseas Chinese in economic activities in the mainland. The most common explanation given in these writings is a combination of profit interest and strong attachment to the motherland, with the emphasis on the latter. These scholars stress the spiritual, psychological attachment of overseas Chinese to China, their awareness of their origins, their common ethnicity, and their knowledge of Chinese culture and language (Zhao Heman 1994: 11; Zhu Huiling 1998: 18). Some scholars assert that overseas Chinese activities have been historically driven by a desire to assist China to gain more power and influence in the world arena. Overseas Chinese concern with China's domestic and international success is seen as improving the status of the overseas Chinese in their countries of residence (Chen Fei 2002: 43; Chen Lijuan 2004: 15).[6]

There is overarching agreement among Chinese scholars that overseas Chinese contribute positively to the cause of modernisation. They are seen as enthusiasts of China's modernisation project who contribute investments, innovation and knowledge, and who, through their involvement, reflect the spirit of China's modernisation. The manner in which overseas Chinese engage in the modernisation project mirrors, as Chinese scholars suggest, the government's aspirations of China's modernisation, setting an example for Chinese people in China to emulate. Their involvements are largely presented as an expression of patriotic feelings, another common characteristic ascribed to the overseas Chinese.

Overseas Chinese as patriots

A member of the Standing Committee of the Political Bureau of the CCP's Central Committee and the chairman of the CPPCC mentioned four traditions of overseas Chinese, which made the 'deepest impression' on him. One was the tradition of 'deep affection for the motherland and hometown'.[7] He explained:

> They constantly show concern for the economic, political, and the social development of the motherland, as well as the living conditions of their beloved ones, consider it as an honour to be able to make contributions to their fellow countrymen, and take pride in the magnificent and long-standing history and culture of their nation.[8]

The early post-Mao calls for overseas Chinese to take part in China's modernisation were underpinned by the assumption of overseas Chinese's 'love for country, love for native place' (*ai guo ai xiang*). At the start of the reform era, Deng Xiaoping contended: 'China is unique in comparison to other countries.{...}For instance, we have tens of millions of patriotic Chinese living abroad. They have made a lot of contributions to China' (quoted in Chen Fei 2002: 45). On another occasion, Deng Xiaoping maintained that 'we also have several million compatriots loving their country whilst living abroad. They hope that China will thrive in its development, it is a unique case in the whole world' (quoted in He Jiasheng 1997: 23).

There is a widespread assumption in Chinese writings that all overseas Chinese care about their motherland (*xinxi zuguo*) and strive for a strong country (*panwang guojia fuqiang*), which will be their 'strong back-up'(*jianqiang de houdun*) where they can 'pay back their tributes' and 'help to achieve its aspirations' (*baoxiao zuguo de yuanwang*) (Feng Ertang 1999: 156). Chinese scholars have also frequently argued that in the past overseas Chinese were 'overseas orphans' (*haiwai gu'er*), neglected and abandoned by their motherland as it experienced difficulties. With the opening up and reforms in China, the country has embraced and appraised the potential value of the overseas Chinese for China. Since then overseas Chinese have been seen as 'China's sons' (*zhonghua minzu de zisun*) who 'have always worked hard, sacrificing their lives for the prosperity , unity, and development of their motherland' (Xiang Dayou 1993: 4).

The discursive representations of overseas Chinese closely link their patriotic sentiments with their ethnic identity. The two are often seen as intimately related (*minzu zhihun*; *aiguo zhixin*) and crucial to the Chinese nation (Xiang Dayou 1993: 4–5). At the same time, some scholars assert that in contemporary Chinese history patriotism is synonymous with contributing to socialist modernisation (Xiang Dayuo 1993: 4–5). Modernisation is interpreted as a process of strengthening China's self-respect, self-confidence and national self-consciousness (ibid.: 4–5). Therefore, as verification of their love for and attachment to their native place and country, overseas Chinese are often presented as generous donators of remittances and aid to their places of origin and country .[9] As evidence of their patriotism, overseas Chinese are portrayed as supporting China's symbolic modernisation projects, such as the hosting of the Olympics.

Some scholars, such as Wu Hongqin (1996: 6), offer an interpretation of overseas Chinese involvement in China which could precipitate criticism of China's recruitment of overseas Chinese as spies to serve China's aspirations in the area of science and technology.[10] In February 2008, when Chung Dongfang, a retired US aerospace engineer of Chinese origins, was charged with economic espionage benefiting China, he explained his motivation as wanting to 'contribute to the Motherland'.[11] Wu Hongqing argues that overseas Chinese's patriotism should be distinguished from their loyalty (*xiaozhong*) to their host country . Wu contends that economic, cultural and psychological commonalities between mainland China and overseas Chinese do not necessarily mean that overseas Chinese are loyal to their motherland. Nevertheless, China attempts to employ members of the Chinese diaspora to gather intelligence for Chinese authorities on the basis of their patriotism. A letter from the Chinese authorities to the convicted spy Chung said in part that it was Chung's 'honor and China's fortune' that he was able to realise his wish to serve his country (Lewis 2008). The sensitive and contested issue of overseas Chinese's loyalty to their country of origin rather than to their country of residence historically caused problems in China's bilateral relations with Southeast Asian countries, and is now souring its relations with the United States. For Wu Hongqin, one way out of the deadlock is to draw a clear-cut distinction between sentiments of patriotism and loyalty. He is not explicit about how to differentiate between these sentiments.

Related to patriotism is the assumed Han-Chinese identity of overseas Chinese that links them to mainland China on the basis of their lineage and blood, which we turn to next.

The 'Chinese heart' of the overseas Chinese

Qian Qichen, a member of the Political Bureau of the CPC 15th Central Committee and Vice Premier of SC, pointed out:

> Although the broad masses of our overseas Chinese (*huaqiao*) are residing abroad, their hearts are linked with the motherland. They throw all their energy into opening up, the development of economic and trade cooperation, science and technology, cultural exchanges, the development of foreign relations of their country, and the building of the two civilisations in their cities and towns in China.[12]

In Chinese scholarly circles, the portrayal of the level of Chineseness of overseas Chinese echoes the Party's observations. Xiang Dayou (1993: 2), in his analysis of Western claims about the emergence of overseas Chinese neo-nationalism, argues that the majority of overseas Chinese share a 'common national consciousness and sentiments' (*minzu yishi, minzu gangqing*) rather than nationalistic feelings. Xiang argues that overseas Chinese 'are aware of their belonging to the Chinese nation, and even their self-identity is organised around their national attribute' (Xiang Dayou 1993: 2). He is certain that all overseas Chinese have a very strong attachment (*zhizhao de qinggang*) to Chinese history, character, language, art and traditions (Xiang Dayou 1993: 2). He compares the vitality of the attachment of overseas Chinese to China to the attachments of the 'spring for water and the root for a tree' (Xiang Dayou 1993: 2).

Overseas Chinese are seen by scholars not only as practitioners and consumers of Chinese culture, but also as promoters of Chinese culture, philosophy, ethics, arts, traditions and food to the wider world (*zhonghua wenhua xianshen de zhuanbozhe*) (Xu Zhaoling 1996: 24; Zhou and Long 2002: 46; Chen Lijuan 2004). They are, in other words, bodily representations of Chineseness and physical channels through which Chinese culture finds its multifarious manifestations around the world. Importantly, these expressions are traced back to mainland China as the main source of Chinese culture.

One Chinese scholar goes so far as to claim that 'overseas Chinese' is both a racial and cultural concept (Wu Hongqin 1996: 3). He dismisses 'state' as a suitable definition for the collectivity of the 'Chinese race', and argues that 'nation' more accurately characterises its nature (Wu Hongqin 1996: 3). He also draws a distinction between the Chinese nation (*zhonghua minzu*) restricted by the territorial borders of the Chinese state and the Chinese nation (*huazu*) which is a cultural nation of all ethnic Chinese; the heart of the Chinese nation is situated in China, or more precisely within the Han culture (Wu Hongqin 1996: 5). In his account of the differentiation between the Chinese state and the Chinese nation, Wu expresses the difference between the territorial Chinese nation and the non-territorial Chinese nation by stating 'Malaysian Chinese have both different and common features with the Han'. In other words, Malaysian overseas Chinese are indiscriminately included in the problematic conglomeration of the Han Chinese.

Other authors refer to 'Greater China' rather than to the Chinese nation as an appropriate linguistic expression for overseas Chinese (Feng Ertang 1999: 156; Zhang Weiwei 2005). Nevertheless, the core of this identity formation is emphasised as lying in symbols associated predominately with mainland China and glorified in songs such as 'My Chinese Heart', which appeals to all overseas Chinese.[13] Although some scholars have difficulty accepting the notion of 'Greater China' as a clearly-defined political or economic construction, the majority of scholars, following a seminal article by an American-Chinese scholar Tu Weiming (Tu 1991), agree that culturally 'Greater China' is conceivable (Le Shui 1997: 16; Chen Lijuan 2004; Zhang Weiwei 2005). Culture in this case is conceived in terms of blood relatedness and common lineage. It is imperative among Chinese scholars and official publications to indicate that all overseas Chinese are descendants of the Yellow Emperor.[14] In this respect, the problematic Han culture, traditions and values constitute a bond between overseas Chinese communities and the Chinese state.

Overseas Chinese as a political force

Some Chinese authors portray the role of overseas Chinese as a collective human force (*ji renli ziyuan*) encompassing a political element (Zhang and Jiang 1997: 21). As discussed in Chapter 2, in the Maoist period the overseas Chinese were seen as part of the revolutionary class struggle of the United Front. In the period of reform and opening up, the rhetoric of class struggle has been replaced by the official formulations of the modernisation drive that now constitute the epicentre of the United Front rhetoric. In addition to advancing the PRC economically and technologically, the modernisation agenda includes rejuvenating and reunifying the Chinese nation. To quote the former Vice-Premier Qian Qichen: 'The 21st century is a period for rejuvenating the Chinese nation. ... The role of overseas Chinese will become even more important. ... Overseas Chinese are a force that cannot be neglected in promoting China's peaceful reunification'.[15] Similarly, Wang Zhaoguo, a member of the Political Bureau of the Communist Party's

Central Committee, encouraged 'the overseas Chinese youth to link their personal careers with the country's prospects and make contributions to the great cause of China's rejuvenation'.[16]

This prescribed political role for overseas Chinese was tailored to fulfil other political goals. He Jiasheng (1997: 23) points out that among the sizeable number of overseas Chinese all over the world, there are at least ten thousand highly qualified intellectuals who work in the top North-American universities. He refers to them as 'a precious treasure of the Chinese nation' (*zhonghua minzu de baogui caifu*) and suggests that using this potential human capital effectively can contribute to modernisation and the 'revival of China' (*zhenxing zhonghua*).

Chinese scholars see overseas Chinese as potentially playing an active role in implementing political tasks as part of the agenda of peaceful reunification of the PRC with Taiwan and other campaigns intended to improve China's political image and foster stability in China. In the early 1990s, Deng Xiaoping called on all overseas Chinese and their descendants to strive to 'reunify the motherland' and revitalise the nation (Deng Xiaoping 1990). Chinese scholars stress the potential of mobilising overseas Chinese in support of China on such pertinent issues as Taiwanese and Tibetan independence and the East Turkistan movement, all of which China opposes (Zeng Yunhua 2008: 45). Overseas Chinese are seen as representing China's interests and supporting China's principles outside of its territoriality. Chinese officials and scholars have pointed out that the Taiwan issue can be resolved through more active economic involvement of the overseas Chinese, including through investments by them on both sides of the Taiwan Strait. After the Tibetan riots of April 2008, the overseas Chinese around the world who protested against the 'misrepresentation of Tibetan riots' by the Western media were praised for their 'patriotism and love for the nation' by the Chinese leaders.[17]

As in the case of ethnic minorities, discussions in China about the role of overseas Chinese in the country's modernisation produce a collective portrayal of the overseas Chinese as promoters and model participants in the PRC's national modernisation project, and key players in China's economic development. The Chinese official scholarly accounts rarely draw distinctions between the varieties of overseas Chinese, who include dissidents, assimilated people, cosmopolitan highly-skilled individuals, illegal migrants and Chinese students. Mobile, successful and pragmatic overseas Chinese who are potentially useful for China are predominately referred to by Chinese scholars as motherland-loving The fact that these people might be driven by personal pragmatic motives rather than by their Chinese origins and patriotism is ignored. But when overseas Chinese get involved in China's projects, many respond to the calls of the motherland and represent a source of knowledge of what is modern and how to become modern. They are considered a source of capital, management skills and technological know-how, and a growing political force. Overseas Chinese are viewed as united under the slogan of the 'United Front' of patriotism for their motherland and native place. Their perceived role is also gradually expanding: the most prominent of the overseas Chinese are expected to contribute to the resolution of some crucial political issues, such as the Taiwan question, and to foster the PRC's positive image around the world.

In discursive terms, overseas Chinese are considered an active part of China's modernisation project, and indeed are often referred to as its defining elements. While culturally and ethnically overseas Chinese have always been considered an inalienable part of the Chinese nation, their economic and political links to China have grown substantially and acquired new manifestations since the advent of the PRC's reforms. They are now seen as those who have successfully incorporated the modern practices and values of advanced capitalism and are introducing them to people in China.

Conclusion

Across Chinese scholarly writings, the discursive portraits of overseas Chinese and ethnic minorities in China's national modernisation project reinforce the positions of the two marginal groups in China's modernisation. The scholarly publications treat overseas Chinese as an ethnically conscious group that loves its motherland, and inspires and promotes modernisation in the economic, technological and socio-psychological realms. In contrast, ethnic minorities are portrayed as inhibiting and slowing down China's development, and as having to adapt to the modernisation projects introduced to them. Variations within each of the two groups are neglected.

Although the modernisation discourse prescribes particular identities within the Chinese nation, these identities are not the only possible ones. They might well be either denied, opposed, refused or accepted by those to whom they are directed. However, the negotiation of identities takes place in relation to the dominant representational practices of the Chinese state. In this way, the dominant representations define the production of meaning and identities (Doty 1996: 168).

The seemingly marginal statuses of overseas Chinese and ethnic minorities that link them in China's pursuit of modernisation have both positive and negative qualities. On the one hand, ethnic minorities are a source of hampered development and difference which can pose a threat to social stability, undermine unity and slow the progress of Chinese society. On the other hand, overseas Chinese are celebrated as an ethnic and cultural extension of the territorial Chinese nation-state. They are represented as contributing to the Chinese national project in a positive way through preserving and popularising the very essence of Chineseness, and through introducing practices associated with modernity and advanced capitalism to China. They are presented as a force fuelling China's modernisation.

The ways the identities of the marginal groups are developed in the dominant discourse reflect how the Chinese nation is reproduced. These identities shape the contours of the nation not only in relation to the modernisation goals, but also in terms of ethnicity and territoriality. Ethnicity and territoriality have always been inalienable pillars of China's national project, but their political interpretations have varied over time. The discursive analysis of the roles of the overseas Chinese and ethnic minorities in Chinese scholarly discussions reveals the indeterminate nature of the territorial and ethnic boundaries of the Chinese national project.

The structure of the representational discourse of ethnic minorities and overseas Chinese resembles how the West represents the Third World. There is a certain oppositional dichotomy built into both discursive practices. They implicitly and explicitly draw upon a series of hierarchical relationships defined in terms of 'what and who is in, and what and who is in but not quite' (Doty 1996). The superior qualities of the overseas Chinese are juxtaposed to the lack of these qualities in ethnic minorities. Overseas Chinese are called upon to be more patriotic and politically active through their opposition to the pro-Tibet movement, support of the resolution of the Taiwan issue, and projection of a positive image of China abroad. The solution to the ethnic minority issue is presented in missionary terms and is seen to lie in the process of 'de-politicisation' which reduces ethnic minorities to the status of 'sub-cultures' within the Chinese nation-state, and in the implementation of a series of modernisation projects in minority areas. The Chinese national project is constituted across almost symmetrical oppositions between self and other. The overseas Chinese are more like us, and modern, and therefore constitute part of the Chinese nation. Ethnic minorities, on the other hand, should strive to be more like us and to adopt our modern ways, and then they will be worthy of inclusion in the Chinese nation.

5 Transnationalising Chineseness
'Overseas Chinese work' in the reform period

Globalisation is commonly associated with processes that complicate both our understanding of national and ethnic affiliations and our theorisation about such established concepts as nation and nation-state. Indeed, in the age of widespread human mobility and information fluidity, the meanings of place, space, community and nation are unstable and contestable. This is especially pertinent when one considers the fates of those who, by free will or force, seek to live outside the place they would normally call 'home'. One phenomenon of buoyant global capitalism is how, for the people of the diaspora, transnational identity seems 'empty' or lost in the time and space between themselves, their homeland, and their place of residence (Vertovec and Cohen 1999: xiii).

In this chapter I examine how the Chinese state works to fill in this space in the minds of its former subjects and to incorporate them into its projects oriented towards all-around modernisation. Of course, the migrants themselves conjure up images of their departed homes and reproduce histories of them. In fact, it has been suggested that the act of displacement or exile itself can generate 'powerful attachments to ideas of homeland that seem more deeply territorial than ever'(Appadurai 1997: 177). But these imaginings are conditioned by tangled processes in which states are active players. And not only can a state influence the minds of its former citizens, who are now accustomed to global opportunities, but it can reach out in new ways to them. In doing so, it also initiates new forms of citizenship and negotiates how a nation-state is constituted, operates, and consequently is imagined.

In particular, this chapter discusses how the Chinese state exercises its policies toward overseas Chinese in the context of the PRC's modernisation and broader globalisation. It looks at the mechanisms of incorporating the overseas Chinese into China's modernisation strategy, which fall under the so-called 'overseas Chinese work' (*qiaowu gongzuo*) and the practices of the relevant government institutions. In addition, the chapter considers how the Chinese leadership utilises the global regimes of migration, transnationalism, mass media and, in certain cases, multiculturalism to affirm the CCP's political legitimacy, increase China's political standing, assert Chinese culture, and enhance China's economic performance. The chapter shows how the Chinese state travels outside its national space using contemporary global processes to preserve its power over the identity of Chinese transnationals, and to legitimise and reinforce itself outside its territory.

The Chinese state appeals to ethnicity and cultural sentiments as potential community building-blocks across borders, but with the goal of integrating the PRC into the global economy under the leadership of the CCP. I argue that the Chinese leadership's adaptability to the changing global economic system represents a departure from its position as a single, territorially-restricted unit. It employs the ideology of ethnic nationalism and allows flexible forms of citizenship for its audiences abroad, as it engages in a uniform but territorially-dispersed project resulting in the transnationalisation of the Chinese nation-state.

This chapter builds upon the themes elaborated in earlier chapters about Chinese modernisation discourse and the place of the overseas Chinese in the vision of modernity put forward by the central government. The policies and tactics of the Chinese government towards the overseas Chinese can shape the subjective identity of Chinese transnationals. But how successful these policies and tactics are in attaining their goals is beyond the scope of this study. Instead, I seek to demonstrate that the strategies of Chinese authorities are directed at nourishing and maintaining a particular kind of Chinese identity auspicious for the PRC's economic, political and social transformations. I consider dominant discourses and policies as mutually reinforcing and constitutive in producing a particular kind of the Chinese nation.

The Chinese state resorts to multidimensional, flexible and nonterritorial practices to assert its position in the globalising world. However, this does not mean that territory is no longer relevant. On the contrary, the state's assertion of its position through flexible means is accompanied by the pursuit of uniform modernisation strategies towards ethnic minorities to foster national cohesiveness. As will be shown in Chapter 6, the Chinese nation-state frames itself within its geographical boundaries through 'localisation' of the ethnic minorities. The outcome of these intermingled practices of localisation and transnationalisation exercised under the guise of modernisation is the propagation of a specific kind of Chinese identity by the Chinese authorities. By doing so, the authorities prompt the reshuffling of identities and attempt to manipulate those identities, redraw boundaries of belonging, and shift the modes of inclusion and exclusion.

The first two sections of this chapter look at the organisation and content of overseas Chinese work after the start of the reforms. I argue that the re-establishment of extensive overseas Chinese affairs policies were part of China's efforts to deal with economic and political issues that arose after China opened up to the outside world. The third section examines how China re-appropriates the identity of newly-departed Chinese students and the so-called 'new migrants' to legitimise and reinforce their attachment to the motherland as they are adapting to their host society. I argue that China accommodates new, flexible forms of participation in China's modernisation by the overseas Chinese, ones that to a certain extent circumvent limitations on noncitizen membership in the nation-state. The fourth section explores other channels that China uses to export its symbolic or actual presence overseas. The section shows that China both accommodates the identity of the transnationals to its vision of Chineseness and exports the unifying model of the Chinese nation, as formulated by the central government, to the overseas Chinese communities. The fifth section describes how China's economic and business connections with the overseas Chinese are translated into political leverage to address some of the political concerns in China's modernisation agenda. The last section expounds the centrality of ethnicity in China's overseas Chinese policies. My discussion of Chinese ethnic minorities overseas (*shaoshu minzu huaqiao huaren*) and growing official discourse around their issues reiterates that the PRC's overseas Chinese policies are predominantly governed by ethnic considerations catering to the Han Chinese.

The re-establishment of the 'overseas Chinese work' policy mechanism

With the age of reform and the opening up of the country, China's overseas Chinese policies were revised. In December 1977, the CCP held a nationwide overseas Chinese conference in Beijing for the purpose of reviewing overseas Chinese policy in light of criticism of the activities of the 'Gang of Four'. The conference called for the revival and reinforcement of overseas Chinese affairs. Different aspects of China's policy on the overseas Chinese were brought together under the slogan 'all patriots are one family', indicating the government's intention to persuade the overseas Chinese to serve their motherland (Wang Chun 1980:16–18).[1] In these early years after the reforms were launched, the patriotism of the overseas Chinese was still understood in terms of 'class struggle':

> Since the people in the old China could hardly earn a living, some of them were compelled to ... cross the seas and work as coolies abroad ...The vast majority ... are still labouring people ... They are also oppressed and pushed around by imperialists, colonialists and monopoly capitalists.
> (*Peking Review* 3, 1978: 14–16)

The first conference was followed by two more nationwide conferences held by the CCP in 1978: the All Overseas Chinese Affairs Conference and the Second Nationwide Conference of Returnee Delegates. Li Xiannian, the representative of the CCP Central Committee, stressed the importance and urgency of implementing the overseas Chinese policies at different levels of government. At the same time, he called on the overseas Chinese, their families living on the mainland, and the returned overseas Chinese 'to jointly strive for achieving the socialist modernisation of their motherland' (Wang Chun 1980:19). Liao Cheng Chih delivered a report entitled 'Seriously implement the policy of overseas Chinese affairs and strive for building a modernised socialist fatherland'. Among other points, he declared:

> As of 1979, the focus of party work will be shifted to the modernisation of socialist construction. So will the battlefront of overseas Chinese affairs, whose attention will be focused on the vigorous grasping of modernised socialist construction. The paramount task is to wholeheartedly carry out

the party policy on overseas Chinese affairs, to actively elicit and raise the socialist aggressiveness of overseas Chinese returnees and their families. Plunge into serious studies to elevate the standard of politics and ideology as well as that of science and culture. Liberalise the thinking mind and go all out to run well overseas Chinese enterprises. With open arms we welcome the overseas Chinese support for socialist construction. Keep the party in close association with overseas Chinese returnees. Expand the activities of the federation of overseas Chinese. Strengthen party leadership and overseas Chinese affairs to insure a sound structure.

(Liao Cheng Chih quoted in Wang Chun 1980: 20)

These conferences marked a significant shift in overseas Chinese policy, which after years of stalemate and ignorance of overseas Chinese affairs turned to one of liaising with the overseas Chinese for the purpose of economic construction. While the calls for the overseas Chinese to come back to China or to make a contribution to socialist modernisation in China were largely embellished with the revolutionary lexicon of the old days, the message peeping out of the stream of class-struggle slogans was different. It was a message of uniting Chinese people for the cause of socialist modernisation in China and of giving up the principle of class struggle that had served to designate the confines of belonging to the Chinese nation during the revolutionary years. In the new context of the reforms, the United Front of revolutionary and class struggle was giving way to the United Front of modernisation. But the contours and agenda of the Front were yet to be specified.

The early work of re-engagement with the overseas Chinese involved rehabilitating the status of the overseas Chinese's relatives. They were given special treatment and their rights were protected in the 1982 Constitution[2] and the special protection laws of 1990 and 2000 (see Table 5.1). To revive the links between overseas Chinese relatives and returnees with the overseas Chinese communities, a number of governmental and nongovernmental administrative organs were re-established that were responsible for protecting the rights and interests of the returned overseas Chinese and their relatives. In 1978, a nationwide overseas Chinese managing mechanism was set up under the SC: The Overseas Chinese Affairs Office (OCAO) (*qiaoban*).[3] The ex-director of the OCAO characterised the purpose of the office simply: 'The OCAO has been set up for the sake of overseas Chinese'.[4] Overseas Chinese affairs had come to be regarded as a matter of Chinese national interest. In most official statements and publications on the overseas Chinese, it is no accident that the phrasing emphasises that China has a claim on the identity of the overseas Chinese. For example: 'China has got 30 million overseas Chinese worldwide' (*zhongguo zai shijie ge di you sanqianwan huaqiao huaren*) (Zhao Heman 1994: 8). In other words, there is an assumption that the overseas Chinese belong to China. The overseas Chinese are referred to as an aspect of China's 'unique national condition' that puts China in a superior position in comparison to other countries, and grants China legitimacy to incorporate the overseas Chinese into its modernisation project and other national endeavours.[5] It also legitimises the work aimed at enhancing the symbolic

112 *Transnationalising Chineseness*

Table 5.1 Overseas Chinese law and documents

Laws and regulations	Date of promulgation	Date took effect
Decree of the SC on Implementing the Policy of Protecting Remittances by Overseas Chinese	23 February 1955	23 February 1955
Circular on Beneficial Treatments in Housing for Returned Overseas Chinese and Relatives of Overseas Chinese and in Education and Employment for Their Children	20 March 1983	20 March 1983
Rules of the SC on the Encouragement of Investments by Overseas Chinese and Compatriots from Hong Kong and Macau	19 August 1990	19 August 1991
Law of the People's Republic of China on the Protection of the Rights and Interests of Returned Overseas Chinese and the Family Members of Overseas Chinese	7 September 1990	1 January 1991
Circular by OCAO of the SC, Ministry of Personnel, Ministry of Labour, Ministry of Finance, Ministry of Public Security on Treatments to Returned Overseas Chinese Exiting China to Visit Families	9 April 1992	9 April 1992
Implementing Measures of the Law of the People's Republic of China on the Protection of the Rights and Interests of Returned Overseas Chinese and Family Members of Overseas Chinese	19 July 1993	19 July 1993
Law of the People's Republic of China on Protection of the Rights and Interests of Returned Overseas Chinese and the Family Members of Overseas Chinese	31 October 2000	31 October 2000
Implementing Measures of the Law of the People's Republic of China on the Protection of the Rights and Interests of Returned Overseas Chinese and Family Members of Overseas Chinese	4 June 2004	1 July 2004

Sources: Xiang Biao (2003: 43); OCAO website, www.gqb.gov.cn/node2/node3/node5/node9/userobject7ai1271.html.

affiliation and material contributions of the overseas Chinese to their homeland. This work is central to the activities of the overseas Chinese bodies and is exercised at all levels of Chinese government. Since 1978 every province, autonomous region and municipality (except Tibet) established their own OCAOs.

The OCAO's work is complemented by the activities of a mass or ganisation that acts in parallel to the of ficial or gans of the central authorities. All-China's

Federation of Returned Overseas Chinese (ACFROC) (*qiaolian*) was set up in 1956, but during the years of the Cultural Revolution it suspended its work. In 1978 ACFROC was back in place, serving under the slogan '*yi qiao da qiao*', which literally means building a bridge out of overseas Chinese connections. In other words, ACFROC's objective is to use returned overseas Chinese, their family members and overseas Chinese as a channel for gaining manpower, intellectual, financial and other resources from abroad for socialist modernisation. By 2009 more than 15,000 organs of the ACFROC were established at different government levels of the state.[6] Since 1984 the National Congress of Returned Overseas Chinese and Their Relatives has taken place every five years, with the one held in Beijing in July 2009 attracting over 1,100 delegates.[7]

In 1983 the PRC's representative organ, the National People's Congress (NPC) established a special Overseas Chinese Commission (*huaqiao weiyuanhui*, or *renda de qiaowei*) (NPCOCC) of 14 members responsible for research, recommendations and observations on government policies towards the relatives of overseas Chinese, returnees, and the overseas Chinese. There is also a party, Zhigongdang (*zhigongdang*),[8] which unites those Chinese subjects who have an overseas Chinese link, primarily returned overseas Chinese and overseas Chinese's relatives (*guiqiao qiaojuan*). It has intimate relationships with the CCP and ostensibly serves the interests and rights of overseas Chinese, as well as training the overseas Chinese affairs personnel.[9] In 1979 at its 7th congress, one of the Zhigongdang leaders delivered a report called 'Common Heart, Common Mind: To Strengthen the Contribution Forces for the Promotion of the Transformation of State-Building into Socialist Modernisation of Our Country'. The report outlined new agendas and objectives of work, with an emphasis on the need to serve socialist modernisation in China. Chinese People's Political Consultative Conference (CPPCC) set up its own Taiwan, Hong Kong, Macao and Overseas Chinese Affairs Commission (*zhengxie tai gang qiaowei*) (OCAC) to provide research, surveys and consultations on the formulation of overseas Chinese policy.

The establishment of the administrative organs on overseas Chinese affairs represents an attempt by the government to institutionalise different areas of overseas Chinese work in China and abroad: from the party responsible for the development and promulgation of the general scope of the work, to the level of mass nongovernmental organisations with instructions to implement the work on the ground. Such an extensive bureaucratisation of the apparatuses of overseas Chinese affairs shows the urgency and importance of the overseas Chinese element in China's formulation of policies conducive to modernisation.

The government's move to institutionalise overseas Chinese work also suggests that behind the aspirations for immediate economic benefits is a broader political agenda. The five bodies responsible for overseas Chinese affairs – OCAO, ACFROC, Zhigongdang, NPCOCC, OCAC – are often referred to as the 'five bridges' of the central government. They all pursue the objective of incorporating the overseas Chinese into the process of modernising China. The PRC's invitation to the overseas Chinese to take part in socialist modernisation presumes that they are part of China's family, and that China's interests are also their interests. This family is grouped around the Party and its communist government in Beijing. To serve 'common heart, common mind' and to work for the sake of the Chinese family, supposedly with common interests and desires for prosperity and unity, became paramount in the work of governmental and nongovernmental institutions. The objectives of serving the interests and needs of the overseas Chinese and implicitly coaxing their contributions to the modernisation project in China have remained fundamental throughout the reform period. The methods and scope of this work, however, have changed significantly. As the next two sections reveal, the Chinese nation-state's handling of overseas Chinese policies reflects the adaptation of strategies to the global developments of accelerated communication, mobility and technological innovation. These developments go against the grain of earlier arguments that migration constitutes a challenge rather than an advantage for a nation-state, and that a nation-state's natural condition is characterised by 'sedentariness, not mobility' (Joppke 1998: 6). The Chinese case shows that the state-led national project can be produced through the combination of mobile and sedentary practices which serve as mechanisms of adapting to the challenges of the time, as the state asserts its power at national and transnational levels. The participation of immigrant workers challenges the traditional view of the regime of citizenship in host societies, which presupposes 'a specific set of rights and duties' shared by the members of the political community (Soysal 1994: 2). Here, of course, the focus is on a receiving rather than a sending state. However, while human mobility could disrupt the foundations of a receiving nation-state, the ensuing discussion demonstrates that it could also advance the position of the state exporter of migration.

The content of the 'overseas Chinese work'

In the early reform years, overseas Chinese policies primarily targeted returned overseas Chinese and the relatives of the overseas Chinese who were seen as an important channel of their remittances and donations. In the period from 1978 to 1990, the central government passed more than fifty laws and regulations, all of which reflected a sixteen-point directive to pursue overseas Chinese affairs. This directive stipulated 'equal treatment without discrimination, considerations according to the particularities' (*yi shi tong ren, bu de qishi, genju tedian, shidang zhaogu*) (Wang Gongan 1999: 289). The early reform of overseas Chinese law established a special position for returned overseas Chinese and overseas Chinese's relatives, and outlined certain privileges, such as university quotas. It was complemented by the construction of overseas Chinese native places, or *qiaoxiang*, defined by the ratio of residing dependents and returnees. They were an instrument to nurture the emotional attachment of the overseas Chinese to China, as well as a destination for overseas Chinese remittances and investments (Thunø 2001: 918).[10] It is estimated that from 1979 to 1995 the overall value of the overseas Chinese remittances surpassed 15 billion *yuan* (Chen Fei 2002: 45). According to Chinese official sources, about US$11 billion of remittances in workers' payments and compensation of employees[11] was received from 1982 to 1999 (see Table 5.2).

Table 5.2 Overseas Chinese remittances to the PRC, 1982–99 (US$m.)

Year	Workers' remittances	Compensation of employees	Total remittances
1982	541	75	616
1983	446	96	542
1984	317	86	403
1985	180	91	271
1986	208	199	407
1987	166	51	217
1988	0	35	35
1989	0	53	53
1990	124	0	124
1991	207	0	207
1992	228	0	228
1993	108	0	108
1994	395	0	395
1995	350	0	350
1996	1,672	0	1,672
1997	4,423	166	4,589
1998	247	97	344
1999	384	146	530
			11,091

Source: Qiu Liben (2004: 16). Qiu's table is based on the data accumulated from IMF's *Balance of Payments Statistics Yearbook*.

By the mid-1980s, remittances and donations ceased to be adequate sources of foreign currency to China, due to their insignificant rate. Although the amount of remittances increased significantly in the mid-1990s, on a global scale the contributions of overseas Chinese to the PRC are generally less impressive than the remittances of less populous migrant communities, such as Mexicans, Indians or Filipinos (Qiu Liben 2004: 17). For example, in 2000 alone, Indians worldwide contributed more than US$1 1.5 billion in remittances to the Indian economy (ibid.: 9).

In the 1980s to early 1990s, the Chinese authorities turned to the development of new strategies to attract investments from overseas Chinese communities. The establishment of Special Economic Zones and open cities in the eastern coastal area of China, characterised by the high concentration of *qiaoxiang*, served this purpose. This economic arrangement was supplemented by 1983 legislation and 1985 SC provisions that granted special privileges to overseas Chinese citizens (including those in Hong Kong and Taiwan) and ethnic Chinese who wanted to invest in China. Appealing to the profit-oriented nature of the overseas Chinese, these initiatives were called 'call back' policy, and were formulated to advance the economic development of China (Sie Hok Tzwan 1997).[12] Jing Shuping, the

116 *Transnationalising Chineseness*

Table 5.3 Overseas Chinese foreign direct investments in China, 1979–2000 (US$m.)

Period	Total FDI	Overseas Chinese FDI	Proportion of overseas Chinese FDI
1979–1991	26.885	17.932	66%
1992–1997	196.810	127.600	65%
1998–2000	126.633	82.200	65%

Source: Zhuang Guotu (2001: 380).

chairman of the All-China Federation of Commerce and Industry, called upon Chinese entrepreneurs overseas 'to take advantage of their common roots by seizing the vast opportunities available in China' (quoted in Liu Hong 1998: 595). These early calls to contribute to economic construction in China primarily targeted overseas Chinese concentrated in Southeast Asia due to their acclaimed economic prominence. In the 1990s it was estimated that the private wealth of Southeast Asia's 20 million ethnic Chinese exceeded US$200 billion. Of 1,000 leading companies listed in the region, about 517 were owned by ethnic Chinese. Ethnic Chinese owned nearly 80 per cent of Indonesia's private wealth and 40–50 per cent of Malaysia's corporate assets (Liu Hong 1998: 594). In the period 1993–96, Chinese government institutions dealing with overseas Chinese work received 1.5 million people of Chinese origins who came to China for business matters (Zhuang Guotu 2000: 9). The outcome of the call back policy was the predominant position of overseas Chinese capital in China's market throughout the whole period of 1979 to 2000 (see Table 5.3).

In the early 1990s, a major break from the initial strategy of relying on overseas Chinese nationals, returnees and their dependents took place, showing a flexible and de-territorial interpretation of citizenship by the PRC. In 1989 at the Nationwide Overseas Chinese Conference, the delegates underlined that:

> ... the cooperation between OCAOs and overseas Chinese of foreign nationality has been continuously expanding. Overseas Chinese and overseas Chinese of foreign nationality have differences and commonalities. To continue successful overseas Chinese policies, our work should also pay considerable attention to the overseas Chinese of foreign nationality.
> (*Summary of the State Council's Overseas Chinese Work* 9 May 1989, quoted in Zhuang Guotu 2000: 6)

Subsequently, the SC issued a number of internal documents that broadened the agenda of overseas Chinese work to include all ethnic Chinese living abroad (Thunø 2001: 921). The ambiguity of the official language does not clearly indicate whether these calls were directed at both Han and non-Han overseas Chinese. While in the past the statuses of overseas Chinese citizens and overseas Chinese of foreign nationality were treated differently than when the nationality law of

1980 prohibited dual citizenship, in the 1990s there was a resur gence of calls appealing to overseas Chinese's supposed common descent, blood and culture. This move was prompted by the fact that 90 per cent of the overseas Chinese were of foreign nationality. In this respect, overseas Chinese citizens (*huaqiao*) and ethnic Chinese abroad (*huaren*) have received the same consideration in the PRC's overseas Chinese policy (Zhuang Guotu 2000: 6; interview with an oficial from the OCAO, July 2003). For example, a regulation 'About Strengthening of the Work towards Overseas Chinese and Foreigners of Chinese Descent' stipulated two aspects of the work: the need to take into account dif ferences in the nationality status of the overseas Chinese and ethnic Chinese, and to not treat ethnic Chinese and 'common foreigners'(*yiban waiguoren*) similarly. The second aspect involved cherishing the national feelings of the overseas Chinese and ethnic Chinese, and protecting their interests and close relations with China (Zhuang Guotu 2000: 7).

The amorphous definition of the overseas Chinese subsequently dovetailed with the strategies of re-appropriating the identities of the new migrants and Chinese students studying abroad. In the course of the migration of PRC citizens to Western societies after the start of the reforms and the end of the Cold War, the departed nationals especially attracted the attention of the relevant bodies. In 1996 the SC circulated directives to emphasise the new migrants' work (Thunø 2001: 922). While making a report at the national conference on overseas Chinese affairs in January 1999, Jiang Zemin pointed out that:

> ... of the large number of students studying abroad over the past 20 years, some have acquired either the rights of residence in the countries where they are staying or the citizenship of these countries after completing their studies. In cooperation with relevant departments, departments of overseas Chinese affairs should strengthen contacts with them and guide them to devote themselves to the construction of the motherland in various forms.[13]

All organs in the system of overseas Chinese work have gradually switched to establishing and strengthening links with new Chinese migrants. As one official from ACFROC pointed out: 'In recent years *Qiaolian's* (i.e. ACFROC's) work tends to be broadened. A great deal of *Qiaolian's* work targets overseas Chinese, no matter whether or not they come to China, and even Chinese students studying abroad'.[14] The official also indicated that there are no legal provisions for applying similar policies to different types of overseas Chinese. However, it is evident that a green light for such policies was given from above. Qian Qichen, the vice premier of the SC, stated:

> Federations of returned overseas Chinese at all levels should carry out activities in light of their own characteristics, make full use of their own assets and resources, and mobilize the initiative of overseas Chinese, people of Chinese origin, returned overseas Chinese, and families of

overseas Chinese, in order to make greater contributions to comprehensively building a well-of f society and to the great rejuvenation of the Chinese nation.[15]

In other words, during the years of reform and the opening up of China, the work of the Chinese government to integrate overseas Chinese into the PRC's national modernisation project changed significantly . The tar gets of overseas Chinese work and the scale and scope of the work all changed. This shift in overseas Chinese policies, from rehabilitating the status of overseas Chinese returnees and their relatives and providing extra rights and privileges to overseas Chinese citizens abroad to formulating a broad strategy to unite and serve the needs of all overseas Chinese on the grounds of their ethnic origins, represented a partial return to the pre-1957 policy of treating all overseas Chinese as Chinese nationals. While renouncing the binding treaty of Bandung (1955) would threaten bilateral relations with Southeast Asian states, acting within the existing international regime and allowing certain flexibilities in the interests of regional economies served as a favourable framework for the application of what Duara has called 'de-territorialised ideology of nationalism' (Duara 2003: 14). This mode of ideology departs from the territorially-restricted model and involves a fuzzily applied form of cultural-ethnic conver gence attuned to 'the intensified quest for global competitiveness' (Duara 2003: 14). By way of illustration, the next section looks at the Chinese state' s policy toward new Chinese migrants who leave the country.

Claiming the transnationals: new Chinese migrants and Chinese students abroad in the 'overseas Chinese work'

The so-called 'new Chinese migrants' (*xin yimin*) have been playing an important role in shaping the overseas Chinese policies of the Chinese government. Their pivotal role is underscored by one of the leading mainland scholars on overseas Chinese issues, Zhuang Guotu, who designates them 'the elite of the Chinese nation' (*zhongguo minzu de jingying*) (Zhuang Guotu 1997: 5). The potential human and economic capital concentrated outside China has led the government to welcome and assist future migrants.

The term 'new migrants' refers to Chinese immigrants from China, as well as from Hong Kong, who left their places of residence for foreign destinations after the start of the reforms in the 1970s (Zhuang Guotu 1997; Chong Erkang 1999; Zhao Hongying 2000). New migrants constituted 60–80 per cent of the overseas Chinese population in developed countries in the early 2000s (Zhuang Guotu 2001: 361).[16] Chinese scholars estimated that there were about 5 million new Chinese migrants in 2008.[17] This group is far from homogeneous. The motives of the new migrants for leaving their countries and their procedures for doing so are diverse. However, Zhuang Guotu echoes other Chinese authors when he states that 'from the racial and cultural points of view , new Chinese migrants are a similar group' (*cong zhongzu, wenhua yiyi shang jiang xin yimin shiwei tonglei qunti*) (Zhuang

Guotu 1997: 6). Their ethnic identity is 'stable and strong' (*chijiu, qianglie*), and believed to constitute the basis of their attachment to their homeland (ibid.).

Going abroad was facilitated by the relaxed policies on leaving and entering the country set forth in the PRC's law on the Administration of the Exit and Entry of Citizens adopted in 1985.[18] It is estimated that from the late 1970s to the late 1990s, about 4 million Chinese people left mainland China, Taiwan and Hong Kong for other countries. Between 2.5 and 3 million of them went to developed countries (Zhuang Guotu 2001: 352–253). There is disagreement over the exact number who legally left mainland China for the West. Chinese estimates vary from 600,000 to one million (Zhuang Guotu 2001: 356–257). According to the official sources, since the start of reforms more than 30 years ago, over 1.36 million Chinese students have studied abroad.[19]

In the 1980s, when the first groups of highly skilled professionals and Chinese students went abroad to pursue further studies and then settled down in their host countries, a lot of mainland scholars dubbed the trend a 'brain drain' (*zhili liushi*) and were sceptical about the relaxed policies on going abroad (Zhuang Guotu 2000: 10). But over the next ten years, many of these scholars came to promote overseas study programmes and advocated strengthening the links between those who stayed abroad and mainland China.

In this respect, the experience of Taiwan was illustrative of China's own. In the period from the 1960s through the 1980s, hundreds of thousands of Taiwanese students ended up in the United States after going there for a research degree. Following this trend, the Taiwanese government developed a comprehensive system of policies and regulations to get Taiwanese students abroad to contribute to Taiwan's economy in a variety of ways (Liu Quan and Dong Yinghua 2003: 17–19). As a result, Taiwanese students became a significant force in Taiwan's technological boom in the 1970s to the 1990s. Upon looking at the Taiwanese experience, the PRC's leaders started emphasising the importance for China's future of an overseas education for Chinese students in the early 1990s. In the offices of government officials and academics, a belief that students could contribute to their homeland from overseas, by cooperating with mainland research institutes, making research visits to China and or ganising joint conferences, became common (Zhuang Guotu 2000: 10). As a result, instead of just encouraging students to come back to China, the Chinese government started promoting and strengthening close relationships between the students and the government. In the summer of 1993, it adopted a twelve-point policy towards Chinese students studying abroad, which included 'support study overseas, promote return home, [uphold] freedom of movement' (*zhichi liuxue, guli huiguo, laiqu ziyou*) was adopted (Cheng Xi 1999: 43). Yet sending Chinese abroad for primary and secondary study is not approved by the state, on the grounds of avoiding premature exposure to Western culture (Sun Wanning 2002: 3). In other words, the government is in favour of sending only mature and nationally aware citizens abroad for study.

The Chinese government also encourages Chinese migrants with professional or business ties in both China and overseas to regularly travel back and forth

(Xiang Biao 2003: 31). Xiang Biao documents a series of government provisions and programmes aimed at promoting short visits or exchanges by Chinese migrants. For example, in 1997 the National Education Committee launched the 'Spring Light Plan' (*chunhui jihua*) to encourage scholars to return to China for short academic visits. The 'Changjiang Plan' funds one-year residences in strategic centres in China for leading Chinese scholars living overseas. In 2000 a new programme was introduced to bring overseas Chinese to China during summer vacations with the payments of five times their salaries (Zweig 2006: 197).At the end of 2000 the Ministry of Foreign Affairs distributed the 'Circular on Issuing Long-term Multiple Entry Visas to Overseas Chinese Students and Professionals' to assist the returnees' re-entries. In 2001, the Bureau of Public Security in Shanghai began to issue multi-entry visas valid from three to five years to enable overseas Chinese professors with foreign passports to enter China any time. Similar policies are practiced in Beijing, where the city authorities issue Chinese professionals of foreign nationality or residency the so-called Beijing 'green card' (*lü ka*), or 'host card' (*jizhu zheng*), which grants its holder a two-year multi-entry visit in Beijing accompanied by a series of favourable treatments equivalent to those accorded Beijing residents (Liu Quan and DongYinghua 2003: 16). In 2000 the Ministry of ForeignAffairs published a survey according to which only 44 per cent of 551 returned overseas Chinese who set up enterprises in 13 industrial parks reside in China permanently (Xiang Biao 2003: 31). [20]

In other words, the government's policies increasingly encourage flexibility toward overseas Chinese serving the cause of the PRC's modernisation, without necessarily adjusting national law. In December 2003, theAssociation for Science and Technology held a 'Forum on Putting Overseas Chinese Wisdom and Might into the Service of the Nation' with representatives of overseas Chinese scientists.[21] The forum discussed an 'Action Plan for Putting Overseas Chinese Wisdom and Might into the Service of the Nation' that would promote certain forms of overseas Chinese involvement in the PRC's modernisation. It considered flexible forms of involvement for overseas Chinese, such as special discussion groups, short-term part-time jobs, exchanges, consultation and so forth. The main idea behind these undertakings was to provide ways for overseas Chinese scientists 'to serve the country'. Also, to facilitate the participation of overseas Chinese in the PRC's modernisation drive, Overseas Chinese Chambers of Commerce were established in half of China's administrative regions.[22] These initiatives were part of the broader government policy integral to its modernisation goals 'to strengthen the country through human talent' (*rencai qiang guo*).

The adoption of these regulations and policies signifies several developments in the PRC's dealings with the overseas Chinese. First, it seems that the PRC exercises a flexible form of citizenship for overseas Chinese to establish favourable conditions for the participation of the overseas Chinese in the PRC's modernisation project and to foster an emotional sense of belonging to the PRC. Second, the accelerated geographical mobility that results from technological advancements in transportation and the relaxed policies on leaving and entering the country also contributes to strong attachments to the homeland due to the possibility of frequent visits and active involvement in matters in the PRC. On the move between their homeland and other parts of the world, Chinese communities with the Chinese government's support 'do not feel that they have stopped being part of China' (Nyíri 1999b: 67). 'Closeness' to home, or the PRC's poignant presence among the Chinese migrants abroad, is possible through the advances of the modern age, with its inexhaustible cyber terrain and improved conditions for human mobility. These are favourable conditions for the Chinese state to make itself felt in its communities abroad. A Chinese scholar living in Australia remarked that '"leaving" may never be complete, just as "return" may never be total' (Sun Wanning 2002: 214). These processes are conducive to retaining the concept of a sovereign state and national history prominently in imaginations of place and belonging (ibid.: 215). The imaginations of belonging of Chinese transnationals are reproduced and sustained through the production and consumption of national products of the PRC as well as by communication with compatriots; occasional 'othering' of non-Chinese people in their country of residence occurs when the transnationals refer to them as *lao wai*, or foreigners. As discussed below, the establishment and activities of overseas Chinese organisations also contribute to crafting a particular type of overseas Chinese identity.

The Chinese government has certain expectations of its overseas vanguards, such as to 'come back to visit the country often and tell overseas Chinese, students, and their American friends about China's progress and achievements and relevant policies in a comprehensive and objective manner '.[23] Chinese scholars echo the government by identifying a number of ways that new migrants can be beneficial to their motherland. In 1998, during a seminar on Chinese reform and the role of Chinese students abroad at the University of Maryland, a number of Chinese scholars expressed the opinion that the role of the new immigrants – students who have become young professionals – had changed from 'to return to serve the country' to 'serving the nation' (*huiguo fuwu, weihua fuwu*). That is, they were now to serve the cause of the Chinese nation from abroad (Chong Erkang 1999: 158). Chong Erkang (ibid.) contends that a new trend in overseas Chinese affairs is that the government expects that the overseas Chinese will contribute to 'the cultural expansion of the Chinese nation' (*zai wenhua shang guangda zhonghua*). In 1999, Vice-Premier Li Lanqing stated at a meeting with visiting overseas Chinese students that China expects those who stay abroad to contribute to China's modernisation. 'Those [Chinese people] who remain overseas will also be encouraged to serve the country in various ways', he said. [24]

In his recommendations for government policies towards new migrants, Zhuang Guotu stresses the importance of government support for legal immigrants and governmental assistance for the establishment of relevant organisations for the overseas Chinese in their countries of residence. These organisations would establish contacts with the existing overseas Chinese associations and become the central force in the Chinese community (Zhuang Guotu 1997: 6). Chong Erkang (1999: 159) also suggests that the Chinese government should play a central role in unifying new overseas Chinese communities. Zhuang and Chong both recommend to the government that the new Chinese migrants should become the focus of the work of the overseas Chinese departments. Zhuang advises that investment in new Chinese migrants' education, promotion of their culture, and development of the cultural and national consciousness of the second generation of migrants should be the most important aspects of overseas Chinese work (Zhuang Guotu 1997: 6). He urges the establishment of links between the new migrants and the existing overseas Chinese organisations, among new migrants, and between new migrants and their homeland, by helping establish the overseas Chinese associations, unions, and cultural and educational organisations. In Zhuang Guotu's (1997: 6) words, 'every new migrant should become a member of one of the Chinese organisations'. Chong sees the role of the government as an intermediate one between promoting overseas Chinese integration into their local communities and accelerating the spread of Chinese culture and traditions there (Chong Erkang 1999: 160). On the recommendations of academics, the OCAO in 2002 initiated a three-year plan called 'Developing Motherland and Benefiting-Assisting Overseas Chinese' (Xiang Biao 2003: 28). This plan is twofold. First, it seeks to promote interaction between old overseas Chinese communities and new Chinese migrants. Second, it aims to enhance connections between overseas Chinese communities and China. This plan is one example of a series of strategies employed by the Chinese nation-state to attach the overseas Chinese to China's national modernisation project. Another part of these strategies is to export the PRC's ideological presence to the Chinese communities abroad, which I will consider in the next section.

Other potential contributions by the new Chinese migrants are more pragmatic. Seeking to 'invigorate China through science and education' (*ke jiao xing guo*), China turned to the overseas Chinese. The Chinese leadership is aware that, while in the 1980s the majority of the Chinese studying for IT degrees in the United States were from Taiwan, now more and more are from mainland China, whose students are taking over from the Taiwanese in the IT professions in the States. Thanks to these incoming students from mainland China, the overseas Chinese presence in high-tech industries in North America will significantly increase (Zhuang Guotu 1997: 4). According to Chinese official statistics, at the beginning of this century there were 600,000 scientific and technical experts of Chinese descent around the world; they were distributed mainly in developed countries. About 450,000 of them lived in the United States. Further, about 20 to 30 per cent of the top-ranking American professors in the sciences and technology were of Chinese origins (Zhuang Guotu 2000: 2). They have been identified as role models (*bangyang*) for newly departing hordes of Chinese students. The high-tech specialists from mainland China, plus about 20–30 per cent of the new immigrants from Taiwan and Hong Kong, are potential 'investment immigrants'. Their potential economic benefit to China is highly valued by Chinese leaders (Zhuang Guotu 2000: 3).

There are special government-backed arrangements to help Chinese professionals become involved in China. The Chinese Personnel Minister Zhang Xuezhong stated that overseas Chinese professionals have been 'a priority for the Chinese central and regional governments for more than a decade' and that 'it is the best time now for overseas Chinese trained professionals who live abroad to come back to China to start up businesses or take up an academic career '.[25] The Overseas Chinese Worldwide Forum sponsored by the Chinese government was held in Qingdao in 2000 with the theme 'Prospects for the Economy and Science in China'. It brought together public figures, businessmen, economists and scientists of Chinese origin from over 20 countries and regions. The 'go outside' (*zou chu qu*) strategy ardently pursued by the Chinese government since China's accession to the WTO makes provisions for a special role for the overseas Chinese in helping China promote its goods on the world market (Zhejiang Province Overseas Chinese Office 2002). Since 1998 the Convention of Overseas Chinese Scholars in Science and Technology has been held annually in Guangzhou. Vice-Mayor of Guangzhou Lin Yuanhe characterises the event as 'a major channel for exchange and cooperation between overseas Chinese intellectuals and domestic universities, research institutions and enterprises'.[26] In 2002 over 2,000 overseas Chinese scholars registered for the event. They offered more than 1,300 programmes primarily in the fields of information technology, biotechnology, new materials, new energy and environmental protection. In 2002 a new high-tech development zone for enterprises was built in Shenzhen using the funds of overseas Chinese. The director of the Shenzhen OCAO, Zhang Xingxuan, said this move was 'to accommodate the upsurge of investment by overseas Chinese living abroad'.[27] It is estimated that, with the help of the government, the overseas Chinese have established over 3,000 enterprises in various economic development zones in China since the mid-1990s.[28]

The regime of citizenship is traditionally based on discrimination between the members and nonmembers of a political community, which is tied to the principle of the sovereignty of a nation-state. In this legal sense of citizenship, members of the political community are assigned a specific set of rights and duties denied to nonmembers (Soysal 1994: 2). Furthermore, citizenship is a 'nation-related component' of a nation-state (Joppke 1998: 9) that provides members of the political community with a collective identity. However, in social and cultural senses, in contrast to the legal sense, citizenship does not always correspond with legal and political citizenship. Citizenship here is understood as a set of practices which impart meaning and a sense of being socially and culturally included in a country of residence (Marshall 1992: 25; Ong 1996: 738). In this broader meaning, citizenship could be either restricted to the territorial boundaries of a nation-state or go beyond them (Siu Lok 2001). Siu Lok (2001), for example, illustrates how the Taiwan-oriented Chinese diaspora in Panama exercises cultural citizenship transcending the territorial and legal confines of their state of residence. In the case of the new Chinese migrants, however, the Chinese state rather than a diasporic population produces a situation where citizenship as a type of collective identity is divorced from the territorial limits of the nation-state. Flexible participation in the cause of China's reforms by the assumed nonterritorial members of the Chinese nation is given priority over their physical presence in the territory of the sovereignty. Given the dislocated position of the Chinese migrants, the PRC pursues flexible policies encouraging de-territorialised participation in the modernisation project. It claims the allegiances of the Chinese transnationals through their extra-territorial links, and thereby extends the regime of citizenship and its national project beyond its politico-territorial boundaries.

The channels of the PRC's exported presence

Douw (2000: 6) suggests that any government that engages with its diasporas can significantly influence how these overseas communities are organised. Before the 1970s, the overseas Chinese had been increasingly assimilated into local society. Chinese scholars call this phenomenon 'from Chinese nationals to Overseas Chinese to assimilated society' (Zhuang Guotu 1997: 5). However, the majority of the new wave of migrants from the PRC after 1979 were in their 20s or 30s, and because of their skills and age they adapted more easily to their host societies. Because most of them grew up and spent their youth at universities in China and maintained strong family links in China, their attachments to their homeland, including its traditions and culture, are believed to be quite strong. Zhuang Guotu argues that the new Chinese migrants 'have strong identification with China and hope that China will become stronger and influential on the world arena'(Zhuang Guotu 1997: 5). These new Chinese immigrants, Zhao Hongying points out, 'were born in New China, and grew up under the red flag' (*sheng zai xin zhongguo, zhang zai hongqi xia*) (Zhao Hongying 2000: 12). With the new wave of overseas Chinese, not only has the overall number of overseas Chinese increased, but the overall sense of Chineseness, in the form promoted by the regime in Beijing, has become stronger among the old Chinese diaspora (Zhou Lüe 2002: 345). The new Chinese migrants 'continuously pour fresh blood into the overseas Chinese communities', as Zhao Hongying notes (Zhao Hongying 2000: 13). At the opening of the OCAO's National Directors' Meeting, Qian Qichen asserted: 'We must make an effort to increase our work with overseas Chinese, especially those living abroad, in order to raise the enthusiasm of more than 30 million overseas Chinese and to fully develop their advantages'. [29] Others also advocate increasing enthusiasm and fully developing the advantages of overseas Chinese in order to increase their attachment to China. The Chinese government recognises that migration helps revive Chinese consciousness in the Chinese communities abroad, and helps change people's perceptions from being simply overseas Chinese (*huaren*) to being part of the Chinese nation (*huazu*) (Zhuang Guotu 1997: 5).

While economic conditions and a high standard of living in their new societies are among the most crucial factors appealing to the new Chinese migrants, multiculturalism is advantageous to preserving Chinese culture and traditions, and lays favourable foundations for conjuring national images. Multiculturalism as practiced in some Western countries inhibits assimilation into the culture of the host society and permits preservation of the cultural differences of immigrant groups. Soysal (1994: 3) argues that immigrants' membership in a host community does not necessitate participation in the national collectivity of the host society. While some see multiculturalism contributing to the erosion of a coherent identity of a nation-state, challenging the citizenship regime of a receiving state, and upseting the correspondence between political and cultural boundaries (Joppke 1998: 31), it may well be conducive to preserving links to the departed land. By claiming that the new migrants belong to China, the PRC's leadership creates a rationale to export its own image of a unifying force for the Chinese nation. The new migrants also became executors of the PRC's overseas strategies through the activities of the newly-established Chinese associations in their countries. The PRC adapts to global processes of migration, transnationalism, and multiculturalism to address the issues of overseas Chinese identity and the involvement of the overseas Chinese in the modernisation project in China.

The particulars and the results of this work are readily apparent when we consider the transformation of the so-called 'three pillars' of the overseas Chinese communities – overseas Chinese organisations, schools, and periodicals (Liu Hong 1998: 582). These institutes and symbols of the collective identity of the overseas Chinese communities have undergone significant alterations in their structures and orientations, which can also be credited in part to the PRC's policy shift towards them.

Apart from the growing frequency and size of the meetings of overseas Chinese organisations and the increased intensity of their activities, there have been more pertinent changes in the nature of these organisations. These changes have resulted not only from global technological developments but from the repositioned role of the PRC towards overseas Chinese and ethnic Chinese communities. One recent trend is growing approval and support for overseas Chinese organisations and their activities by the Chinese government, which prompted a general re-orientation of the overseas Chinese communities towards the PRC. The newly-emerged Chinese overseas organisations, as well as their activities, have been increasingly oriented towards the PRC (Nyíri 1999a, 1999b), or even been set up with the PRC's direct involvement and endorsement (Nyíri 1999b: 110). Over 2,000 overseas Chinese students' associations and more than 300 professional associations for overseas Chinese scholars were established with the help and direct involvement of Chinese authorities (Zweig 2006: 195). When the European Association of Chinese Organisations was established in 1992 out of the desire of 21 Chinese associations from ten European countries, the formation of this group received high praise from the government. It applauded the association's organisers for 'uniting the overseas Chinese organisations, protecting the rights and interests of the overseas Chinese, facilitating and strengthening the dialogue with European states, and assisting newcomers to integrate into local society' (Zhao Hongying 2000: 13). The PRC's involvement in setting up the association was critical for keeping it together (Christiansen 2003: 125). In Australia, the most influential organisation of the new Chinese migrants, the Australian Chinese People's Consortium, was set up in 1992 to unify the Chinese community in Australia. Over 90 per cent of the consortium's members come from mainland China. The participation of governmental representatives from the mainland in the gatherings of overseas Chinese of all levels has facilitated success in their business-oriented activities. In a similar vein, meetings with local

Chinese communities are usually part of the schedules of China's leaders during foreign visits. The PRC gives impetus to the globalisation and intensification of Chinese networks and associations, which often choose China as the site of their regular meetings. The pro-Beijing organisations attempt to shift the orientations of other overseas Chinese associations from their host countries to the PRC (Nyíri 1999b: 58).

The overseas Chinese associations have also become increasingly institutionalised (Liu Hong 1998: 590; Siu Lok 2001) and centralised (Nyíri 1999a, 1999b; Siu Lok 2001). In the past, overseas Chinese organisations were characterised by their strong kinship and local orientations, which were used to expand business networks. In the reform period, there was close interaction between the overseas Chinese associations and their *qiaoxiang.* The purposes and characters of the organisations varied. There were native places associations, family name associations, and organisations of a professional or religious nature. Since the 1990s there has been a tendency to bring the regional organisations together under one unifying body, and to systematise and coordinate their activities through the organisation of regional gatherings. In August 1997, the European meeting of the Chinese media bodies attracted 35 organisations from 12 European states; since then it has held meetings annually. In 1995 the American Association of Chinese Schools was established. It brought together 150 schools with more than 40,000 students and teachers from 33 states. In May 1991, 280 Chinese associations attended a Chinese congress in Canada. Five hundred attended a congress in Mauritius one year later (Fang Xiongpu 1997: 1 1). In 2003, the OCAO and the Chinese Association for Overseas Exchanges sponsored the '2003 Get-Together of Organisations of Overseas Chinese and Foreign Citizens of Chinese Origin All Over the World', which brought together representatives of overseas Chinese organisations from 100 countries and regions. [30] These developments were products of favourable policies at the supranational level that facilitated the establishment of Chinese organisations across national borders, with the European Union being the most illustrative example (Christiansen 2003: 5). The PRC's policies help build common foundations based on allegedly shared culture, history and traditions, and nurture symbolic association with the government in Beijing and its modernisation goals.

The leaders of the new overseas Chinese associations differ significantly from the old generation of leaders, who earned their recognition in the community through economic success (Liu Hong 1998: 591). Today's overseas Chinese leaders have compensated for their lesser economic prominence by their connections with the PRC's authorities in their countries (Nyíri 1999a: 255). At the same time, the PRC reaches out to the overseas Chinese communities through the leaders of the overseas Chinese organisations who are incorporated into the political institutions in the mainland, and influences the ways their identities are shaped (Christiansen 2003: 12). The image created by the Party of the new Chinese migrants' leaders underscores their assumed political loyalty to their countries of residence along with their cultural identification – their 'devotion and care'(*re'ai*; *guanxin*), as the Party puts it – towards China and its traditions (Zhou Lüe 2002:

343). For example, Cao Yanling, a Danish Chinese and the first female president of the 10th European Association of the Chinese Organisations, was named a 'heroine' and included in the list of the officials of the All-China's Women's Federation, the Party-led mass organisation for women in China.[31] The Chinese party-state makes an effort to instill commitment to the PRC and its policies of modernisation on the part of the overseas Chinese. The party-state shapes the cultural side of their identity and breeds emotional attachment to the PRC.

The intensification of the economic activities of the overseas Chinese and the spread of their pro-Beijing associations was accompanied by an upsurge in the overseas Chinese media. The multicultural nature of Australian society has been especially favourable for the growth of Chinese media. New Chinese migrants there started 43 Chinese periodicals, a 24-hour Chinese business radio station and a TV channel (Zhao Hongying 2000:14). In Europe in the early 2000s there were more than 30 Chinese newspapers published; to name just a few: *European Times* (*Ouzhou shibao*) (France), *Europe Daily* (*Ouzhou ribao*) (France), *Worldwide Chinese* (*Tianxia Huaren*) (United Kingdom), *Chinese Communicator* (*huaqiao tongxun*) (the Netherlands), *United Business Paper* (*lianhe shangbao*) (Hungary), *Romanian Chinese* (*lüluo huaren*) (Romania), *Chinese New Paper* (*hua xin bao*) (Spain) and *Austrian Chinese* (*Ao hua*) (Austria). In Japan there are more than 40 different Chinese media bodies. In 1999, when a new newspaper of the new migrants, *Japanese New Chinese Paper* (*Riben xin huaqiao bao*), was initiated, its aims were outlined as follows: 'to serve as a bridge between new and old Chinese communities, to serve as a bridge between China and new migrants, between Japan and new Chinese migrants, as a bridge between China and the world' (Zhao Hongying 2000: 14). In 2003, Liu Yunshan, the head of the Central Propaganda Department, addressed the Annual Convention of the World Chinese Language Press Institute and expressed his hope for exchange and cooperation with overseas Chinese language newspapers.[32] The official rationale for the Press Institute's cooperation with the overseas Chinese publications was to promote the development of Chinese language newspapers and make them more influential in the world. However, a more important reason seems to be to 'help the world understand China better' – that is, to communicate an officially-approved interpretation of developments in China.

The PRC also appeals to the Chinese communities by the means of modern technology. On 7 January 1997, Rupert Murdoch's Phoenix Chinese-Language Satellite Television Station based in Hong Kong started broadcasting a 12-part full-length television series, 'Deng Xiaoping', to the Asia-Pacific region.[33] It was estimated that 150 million viewers were able to watch it. Most importantly, the 'Deng' documentary could be watched in Taiwan, unlike other mainland television programmes. The documentary presented detailed information on the life of Deng Xiaoping, China's programme of reforms and the opening up of the country.[34] Other PRC-based media projects, such as coverage of Beijing's successful bidding for the 2008 Olympics, as well as Star TV's broadcasts of Chinese programmes worldwide and China Central Television (CCTV) drama series, are produced with both PRC and 'absent' audiences in mind. In her study of how the

Chinese media shape the identity of the new Chinese migrants, Sun Wanning (2002: 9) does not draw a dividing line between 'China' and its 'diaspora'; instead, she argues that the global age has witnessed the emergence of one 'mediatised' Chinese community. She stresses that this is the result of the power of the PRC as well as the prevalence of the Chinese collective memory. She also argues that while the movement of the new Chinese migrants takes place in accordance with global patterns of flexibility, mobility and de-territorialisation, the symbolic attachment of the immigrants to the PRC is possible because of the PRC (Sun Wanning 2002: 11).

In 2009 the work on improving the PRC's image abroad through the overseas Chinese communities and Chinese presence in electronic media intensified. In the wake of the 60th Anniversary of the PRC, a forum entitled 'Nation, Image, Media' was held at Beijing University. At this forum, Fang Li, the founder of *Asian Week* and the *Independent News*, offered her views on the role of overseas Chinese in shaping China's image abroad. Every overseas Chinese, according to Fang Li, serves as 'a representative of China abroad and their behaviours and performance form the image of China'. At the same forum the director of the 7th department of the National Information Office announced that the mission of Chinese media should be to use the 'opportunities created by the financial crisis' in advancing China's media presence abroad. [35] As if pre-empting this official's view, in July 2009 Chinese entrepreneurs purchased two overseas TV stations – one in Los Angeles, one in Great Britain – with the aim 'to broadcast Chinese language programmes promoting Chinese culture in the US and Europe'. [36] In other words, overseas Chinese have become incorporated, and play an important role in the ambition of official Beijing to project a more favourable image of the PRC abroad. This ambition is most pronounced in the Chinese government's plans to set up a Chinese international TV channel to complement the coverage of the world news by British and American forerunners such as BBC and CNN (Ford 2009).

Close ties between the overseas Chinese and the PRC are often emphasised through the official coverage of the overseas Chinese' celebrations of Chinese memorial days and holidays. Annually, overseas Chinese worldwide celebrate the PRC's national day (Zhao Hongying 2000: 12). In addition, there is the traditional October 1st grand reception for overseas Chinese in the Great Hall of the People in Beijing organised by the OCAC. The importance of the event is marked by the presence of the PRC's leading figures. Similarly, Chinese embassies worldwide regularly take part in the events organised by the local Chinese communities. At one such reception in conjunction with the 60th Anniversary of the PRC in London, a representative of the British Chinese highly commended on China's development success such as Beijing Olympics and launching of the Shenzhou VII manned spaceship and said that these achievements are a 'source of pride for Overseas Chinese community'. [37] Through celebrations of memorial days and holidays for overseas Chinese, the PRC makes tangible the sense of community established with the overseas Chinese communities. At the same time, the Chinese nation-state reiterates the importance of the PRC-bound sense of identity among these communities. This identity must be maintained and reproduced through exercising the collective memory in celebration of events that are significant for all members of the Chinese nation.

In addition to promoting overseas Chinese organisations that are sympathetic and loyal to the government in Beijing, the authorities make a considerable effort to revive and preserve the sense of Chineseness among young people of Chinese descent abroad. In the 1990s the OCAO initiated the organisation of annual 'Summer Camps for Foreign Youths of Chinese Origin on a Root-Seeking Trip to China', which aimed to 'disseminate Chinese culture'. In 2001 the camp attracted about 3,000 people.[38] In 2000 the OCAO organised the 'Solidarity of Overseas Chinese and Foreign Nationals of Chinese Origin in the New Century'. As evaluated by official Chinese sources, the event, which gathered more than 220 organisations of overseas Chinese and foreign nationals of Chinese origin from 60 countries and regions, was 'another successful attempt on the part of the OCAO to forge closer ties with overseas Chinese and foreign nationals of Chinese origin'.[39]

Sport is another means that China uses to establish unity with the Chinese overseas. China's authorities have often emphasised that the overseas Chinese are expected to proliferate and promote China's sport-related endeavours. For example, at a meeting with overseas Chinese in 2002, Beijing's mayor at the time, Liu Qi, expressed his hope to 'see more overseas Chinese working with the Beijing Municipal Government for the first Summer Olympic Games in the nation'.[40] Earlier, overseas Chinese had demonstrated their unconditional support for China's efforts to become a respected sporting nation. In 1991 hundreds of thousands of Chinese in more than 50 countries supported Beijing's application to host the Olympics in 2000. In 2000, during the Olympics in Australia, about 4,000 Chinese supported China's team, whose athletes were guaranteed free transportation and free food in the local Chinese restaurants (Wang Gongan 1999: 306). In the course of Beijing's preparations for the Olympics in 2008, the local government started accepting donations from overseas Chinese communities. In 2003 the Beijing Municipal Government received notice of intended donations totalling RMB320 million. The director of the Beijing Overseas Chinese Office characterised the donations as an embodiment of the 'spirit of solidarity among Chinese all over the world' (*Beijing Today*, 18 July 2003). In 2006 the Beijing government reported that the donations from overseas Chinese from 57 countries and regions around the world exceeded RMB500 million, and that the total estimated donations of overseas Chinese towards the Beijing Olympics had risen to RMB900 million.[41] After the Olympics it was officially announced that overseas Chinese donated around RMB1.08 billion for the cause of the Beijing Olympics.[42]

All these developments suggest that the Chinese government has been successful at bringing together Chinese of all walks of life and origins under the banner of patriotism toward the motherland and the unity of all Chinese. The government's success has been facilitated by the fact that in the majority of the developed countries, the regime of multiculturalism provides favourable conditions for maintaining the original ethnic identity of the immigrants.[43] One Chinese scholar argued that the 'international character of Chinese Associations became an example of a cultural sap for a group identity' (Zhou Lüe 2002: 343). Indeed, it seems that an intensification of global mobility, trade, communication, technological advancements and other aspects of globalisation benefit the modernising agenda of the Chinese nation-state. The authorities in Beijing have been successful at seizing onto global trends to serve their cause. The national idea propagated by the Chinese state remains strongly in place, and its form has become increasingly transnational as the state has adapted to the new realities of a global age. Nyíri (1999a: 255) illustrates the diversity of Chinese people who have recently become supportive of the mainland government. For example, the first association with an ambition to represent the interests of all Chinese in Hungary was chaired by a Hong Kong businessman from England, who after one year of his presidency was replaced by a Qingtianese from the Philippines. And the leading Chinese association in Belgium, The Friends' Society, brought together Chinese people from Hong Kong, Taiwan and Belgium.

By satisfying the demands of the overseas Chinese all over the world, and those demands are largely centred on economic profits, the PRC has been successful in extending its presence abroad and culturally uniting the overseas Chinese with the regime in Beijing. In the perception of the Chinese leaders, 'Trade contacts are cultural contacts',[44] and they can work in both directions – to extend trade interdependence and to disseminate and elevate ethno-cultural ties.

Political dimensions of the 'overseas Chinese work'

The PRC's economic interests prevail in its organisation and implementation of its overseas Chinese work. However, the Chinese have long adhered to the formula of promoting 'politics through business, to influence government through people' (Liu Hong 1998: 596). Thus, while overseas Chinese work serves the primarily economic cause of modernisation, it also embraces the political realm. During the 1980s, Tong Djoe, an Indonesian-Chinese tycoon living in Singapore with substantial investments in South China, played a significant role in the re-establishment of diplomatic relations between China and Indonesia (Liu Hong 1998: 591). American ethnic Chinese made a considerable effort to influence the US government to grant China the status of most favoured nation. There is a record of 250,000 cases of relevant actions by 28 Chinese associations to influence the decisions of the American president and Congress (Wang Gongan 1999: 305). The authorities in Beijing quickly realised the potential political assets concentrated outside China's sovereignty and worked hard to win the overseas Chinese's loyalty.

Although the potential political contributions of the overseas Chinese to the PRC are not overtly discussed in Chinese official publications, work to involve the overseas Chinese in political consulting and lobbying is well under way. Some leading organisations, including governmental organs, employ overseas Chinese as consultants.[45] In December 2000, a special consultation group consisting of 30 Chinese experts and entrepreneurs staying abroad was set up to offer consultation and suggestions to Beijing's city authorities on issues related to its economic and social development.[46]

Intrinsic to China's modernisation project is a quest for reunification and rejuvenation of the Chinese nation. Reunification and rejuvenation were identified by the Chinese government as China's key political objectives in the twenty-first century, and the overseas Chinese were targeted to play an active role in accomplishing these goals. The former Vice-Premier of SC Qian Qichen stated on one occasion in 2001:

> Officials doing overseas Chinese affairs will shoulder an arduous mission as to how to organise overseas Chinese in order that they play a bigger role in rejuvenating the Chinese nation and promoting the reunification of the motherland in the new century.[47]

Overseas Chinese are seen as essential to the reunification process. At one meeting of overseas Chinese organisations in 2001, it was pointed out that 'historical experience has shown that the rise and regeneration of the Chinese nation cannot do without the participation and support of overseas Chinese and foreign nationals of Chinese origin'.[48] In an interview for Beijing News Centre, a director of the OCAC of the SC, Chen Yujie, outlined four aspects of her office's work. She emphasised the importance of 'inviting overseas Chinese to come to China'; 'going abroad to meet them'; 'uniting the broad masses of overseas Chinese and Chinese residing abroad to promote the great cause of the peaceful reunification of China'; and 'strengthening exchanges with the overseas Chinese and Chinese residing abroad, including pro-Taiwan people'.[49]

Historically, the states on both sides of the Taiwan Strait have competed with each other to unify the overseas Chinese and provide the best model of Chinese modernity. To date this rivalry has not been resolved. Beijing works hard to win the loyalty of the overseas Chinese using the slogan 'Chinese cultural roots are in China not in Taiwan' (Wang Gongan 1999: 281). During her interview with the Beijing News Centre, Chen Yujie stipulated that the work of the overseas Chinese organisations should

> enable them [pro-Taiwan overseas Chinese] to personally experience the rapid development of their motherland (ancestral homes) and hometowns, publicize among them and introduce to them the principles of 'peaceful reunification' and 'one country, two systems,' and expose the words and deeds of the Taiwan authorities, which have ignored overall national interests, created separation, and schemed to seek independence.[50]

One hundred and ten 'China Councils for Promoting Peaceful Reunification', which organise regular conferences to promote 'China's Peaceful Reunification', were established in more than 70 countries around the world.[51] Since the first steps in this direction were taken in the 1990s, there have been significant victories over Taiwan. In May 1996, when a group of senior leaders from San Francisco's

Chinese Association paid a visit to mainland China, this act triggered a negative reaction from Taiwanese authorities and members of the Chinese community who were leaning towards Taiwan. However, after a report of the delegation was published outlining the results of the visit, the achievements of Chinese reforms, and the advantages of these developments for San Francisco's Chinese community, attitudes towards the government in Beijing turned positive. In 1995 the Fujian-American Association and the United Chinese Association of New York, after a struggle with the Taiwan-oriented United Chinese Charities, won the right to sponsor a parade on the PRC's national holiday (Nyíri 1999b: 111). This celebration of the 46th anniversary of the PRC was also marked by the first-ever hoisting of the Chinese flag in front of the building of New York City authorities (Wang Gongan 1999: 305).

Since the Taiwan issue has assumed uppermost importance in China's domestic and foreign concerns, all relevant bodies have been directed to contribute to this work. In May 2000, the ACFROC held a workshop on anti-Taiwan independence promoting the reunification of China. The chairman of the ACFROC at the time proposed that his organisation play a role in promoting cross-straits economic and cultural exchanges.[52] A conference held in Moscow in September 2003 adopted the 'Moscow Declaration', which called upon 'overseas Chinese to play a role of a bridge in maintaining and developing ties across the Taiwan Strait and make new contributions to the peaceful reunification of China' (*China Daily*, 13–14 September 2003). In August 2002, the leaders of overseas Chinese organisations united in a series of events condemning the motions of Taiwan's president, Chen Shui-bian, to organise a referendum on Taiwan's independence. Overseas Chinese organisations in the United States, the UK, Germany, Spain, Panama, Canada and Thailand organised rallies and issued declarations condemning the separatist attempts of Chen Shui-bian.[53] Pro-Beijing overseas Chinese in Central and South America organised a conference to promote China's peaceful reunification in March 2003 that culminated in the establishment of the Association of Central and South American Overseas Chinese and Chinese Community for Promoting China's Peaceful Reunification.[54]

Mainland China also pays considerable attention to spreading propaganda with the help of the overseas Chinese communities. The central authorities give instructions to the organisations abroad to provide their assistance to the PRC's efforts to promote its positive image around the world. In the late 1990s and early 2000s, many such efforts were made in handling the religious organisation *Falungong*. In October 2001 the World Federation of the Organisation of Overseas Chinese and Foreign Citizens of Chinese Descent was set up in Hong Kong. The federation works to achieve China's complete reunification, promote Chinese culture, and foster the unity of overseas Chinese and foreign citizens of Chinese origin worldwide. The spokesman of the organisation declared that 'exposing and criticizing Falungong by overseas Chinese and foreign citizens of Chinese origin all over the world constitutes the best action for loving the country, native place, and Chinese nation at the moment'.[55] The spokesman pointed out: 'It is necessary to bring into play the advantages of the overseas Chinese circles and the role of overseas compatriots and unite all forces that can be united to expose the sophistries and heresies' of Falungong.[56] These crude examples of state propaganda remind the overseas Chinese communities of the real and virtual omnipresence of the Chinese nation-state. In 2001, 38 overseas Chinese organisations replied to the call of the Chinese government to denounce Falungong by issuing a letter which pointed out:

> The Chinese Government represents the maximum interests of all Chinese people (including Chinese living in overseas areas), and it serves the 1.2 billion people in China and 40 million Chinese living in overseas areas. It is totally necessary and absolutely correct for the Chinese Government to, upon the strong request of the Chinese people, denounce the 'Falungong' as a religious cult ... We would like to show our resolute support and total approval for what has been done in this respect. We, the vast numbers of Chinese living in overseas areas, strongly demand that based on China's relevant laws as well as the international consensus of fighting against religious cults, and for the sake of the fundamental interests of the greatest majority the Chinese people and Chinese living in overseas areas, the Chinese Government should crack down harder on the handful of 'Falungong' members in all seriousness.

While it is doubtful that this message really originated overseas, China's attempts to create a friendly front of pro-Beijing sympathisers among the overseas Chinese reflect China's desire to obtain political and ideological legitimacy in the eyes of certain circles abroad, and to demonstrate to the domestic public the scale of support for the regime in Beijing. Such territorially-dispersed propagandistic activities of the Chinese nation-state have become a manifestation of what Billig (1995) terms 'banal nationalism', which is directed to the recurrent reification and reproduction of the party-state-driven nation. The importance of moral support by the overseas Chinese can be credited to their unique position in between time and space, and being Chinese and non-Chinese at the same time. Securing the sympathy of the Chinese transnationals can pay off for the Chinese nation-state in the form of a more favourable image of the PRC's economic and political programmes.

Chinese ethnic minorities overseas

The PRC's transnational quest for mobilising Chineseness is tailored essentially for the Han overseas Chinese. While, at the domestic level, the PRC promotes itself as a multicultural entity encompassing diverse cultures, faiths and traditions, its transnational attempts to solidify a common Chinese identity rely on predominately Han audiences. Chinese scholars have recently focused on the Chinese ethnic minorities overseas (Xiang Dayou 1993; Li Anshan 2002; Zhao Heman 2004). This topic also became one of the research priorities of the Research Centre for Overseas Chinese (*haiwai huaren yanjiu zhongxin*), which was established in 2002 at the Institute of Ethnology of the Chinese Academy of Social Sciences.[57] The rationale for researching this issue was scholars' dissatisfaction with the exclusive focus of overseas Chinese studies in the PRC on the Han-Chinese communities abroad. They argue that China is not a Han-Chinese country and that it hosts fifty-five other ethnic groups that historically moved across the borders and deserve the attention of Chinese scholarship as manifestations of China's plural nature. Mainland scholars estimate that there are anywhere from 3 million Chinese ethnic minorities overseas (Xiang Dayou 1993) to 5.7 million (Li Anshan 2002: 93). Li Anshan proposes to use the name of a particular ethnic group and to attach *huaqiao huaren* (overseas Chinese) to it to refer to the communities of the overseas Chinese ethnic minorities (see Li Anshan 2002:91). For example, *zangzu huaren* and *huizu huaren* would translate into English as Tibetan overseas Chinese and Hui overseas Chinese, respectively.

However, it seems that there are some inherent problems in claiming that the multimillion ethnic groups are all Chinese, despite the fact that we assume that China, or z *honghua*, designates a multiethnic society. Firstly, such astonishing numbers of ethnic Chinese minorities overseas count even those groups which left China in the distant Middle Ages (Li Anshan 2002: Table 1). However, China is a modern construct born out of the political struggle in the nineteenth century, and it had not operated as a politically- and territorially-coherent unit before then. Furthermore, during certain periods in the thirteenth and fourteenth centuries, China was part of a greater political formation known as the Mongolian Empire. Consequently, people who left the empire at that time could not be claimed as Chinese, but rather as subjects of the Mongolian Empire. People who departed China before the twentieth century could hardly be considered bearers of Chinese identity in the way the Chinese nation-state utilises this concept nowadays. It is not feasible to assume that their origins in China would be meaningful to them, as even if they were aware of their origins in the territories which are now encompassed by the PRC, they would refer to a particular locality or region that their ancestors came from. Similar reasoning would apply to overseas Han Chinese, as mobilisation of their Han and regional identities (Fujianese, Zhejiangese, Cantonese) preceded appeals to their common Chinese, or *zhonghua*, sentiments.

Another problem with making the case for Chinese origins of the overseas Chinese ethnic minorities is that it clashes with other identities that could be primary for those who left China. For example, it is hard to imagine that Kazakhs who left China in the 1950s could be receptive to the discourse that emphasises their links to China while there is another political entity, namely Kazakhstan, which could be considered their historical home. It is also difficult to imagine how groups like Tibetans or Uyghurs, who fled Chinese persecution and discrimination, could be incorporated into the rhetoric on the Chinese ethnic minorities overseas. Arguably, an act of exile for them is not only a physical departure from the territorially-demarcated PRC, but also an act of disassociation and refusal to be emotionally linked to it. As soon as they leave the politico-territorial limits of China, they are on their way to becoming part of another national collectivity of their own choice. Tibetan group identity is also transnational, as it revolves around the figure of the Dalai Lama, and is sustained and reinforced by the group's resistance to China's occupation of Tibet (Houston and Wright 2003). Similarly, the overseas Uyghur communities are united by their opposition to the PRC's regime and its policies, their work for the independence of 'Eastern Turkistan' and their assertion of Islamic identity (Gladney 2004: 238–57). [58] An attribute of *hua* derivative from *zhonghua*, could hardly be used to refer to Hmong communities or Miao overseas Chinese, who number , according to Chinese scholars, 1.2 million, with their roots in present-day China. As Louisa Schein observed in the preface to her volume on the Miao in China, outside the territory of the PRC, Hmong are united in their 'dispersal' around the world: in Laos, Vietnam, Thailand, Myanmar, France and the United States (Schein 2000: xii). Nicholas Tapp (2003) emphases the sense of nostalgia for their lost home, i.e. an Hmong kingdom, which unites transnational Hmong communities.Though these and other transnational ethnic minority communities practice their identities both because and in spite of the Chinese nation-state, even at a rhetorical level it is inconceivable to find premises on which China could attempt to win the loyalty of these groups.

Despite research seeking historical links between China and Chinese ethnic minorities overseas, in practical terms it is seemingly taboo for the Chinese government to claim the identity of these groups. While researchers estimate that the number of some ethnic Chinese minorities overseas exceeds one million people, China silently acknowledges that it does not have enough legitimacy to seek the loyalty of these groups. The government might also realise the problems outlined above. However, as we have seen, Chinese ethnic minorities overseas are hardly ignored by PRC officials. In the early 2000s, OCAC commissioned an academic study on whether ethnic minorities should be part of overseas Chinese work and fall within the OCAC's scope (Wang Lian, no date). In one of the reports summarising the research findings, the authors emphasise that ethnic minorities overseas work should become an integral part of the WDP and be aimed at helping develop the western part of China. The report also stresses that successful implementation of this work would enhance the stability and security of the border regions. Chinese ethnic minorities overseas and their transnational activities are often criminalised through official reference to them as unpatriotic forces or 'splittists' and instigators of ethnic separatism who seek to undermine the PRC government. Ethnic minorities overseas work, in the opinion of scholars, could prevent disruptive activities by them.

Another kind of official rhetoric stresses the common origins of ethnic minorities in the bordering countries and their importance for local economic development. These calls emphasise the benefits of border trade and cooperation to people on both sides of the territorial dividing lines.They are meant to strengthen the economic ties of Koreans, Mongolians and different Muslim groups in China. However, the outcome of this strategy of ethnic mobilisation for economic development is not always the one expected or desired by the PRC. In the case of Chinese Koreans, it was often difficult for them to establish a partnership or brotherly relationships with South Koreans due to the resemblance of the Chinese

Koreans to North Koreans and the derogatory attitude of South Koreans towards North Koreans (Luova 2006: 53). As revealed by Fogden (2003) and Gladney (2004: 310), economic links that were fostered between Muslim people in China and the outside Islamic world led to the revitalisation and strengthening of the Muslim identity of the Muslim minorities in China. As a result, rather than using their links to benefit the economy of the Chinese nation-state as such, they prefer to use them to strengthen their Islamic religious identity through building mosques and advancing Islamic education.

The Chinese government is not in a favourable position to claim the identities of the overseas Chinese ethnic minorities, as it can upset relations with countries that have ties to these groups and is unlikely to elicit an adequate response from the groups. Moreover, when a common cross-border identity is mobilised for economic benefits, it can potentially lead to the emergence of alternative identities that are not beneficial to the Chinese. Furthermore, these processes might have unexpected or even unwanted outcomes that undermine the state's ability to strengthen the common identity of its peoples. Thus, instead of pursuing potentially counterproductive policies, the Chinese government's ethnic minorities overseas work largely consists of measures to curb potential separatist activities which spill over the Chinese national border, to maintain border security and stability, and to guarantee the smooth running of the WDP.

Conclusion

The Chinese nation-state participates in the global mobility of people, images and ideas to influence the imaginations of Chinese transnationals. The intricate intersection of the party-state nationalism and transnationalism changed the way the Chinese nation-state is imagined. Not all Chinese transnationals have a cosmopolitan nature, but this can be evoked by their subjective affiliations as much as by outside forces, including the state (Sun Wanning 2002: 202). The PRC's authorities make considerable efforts to win the loyalty of the overseas Chinese and to organise them into a strong, ethnically conscious and politically sympathetic pro-Beijing front of Chinese people outside the sovereignty of the PRC. Among the newly-available channels to accomplish these goals, the new Chinese migrants stand out as a coalescing force; through them China pursues its interests and asserts its symbolic and ideological presence abroad. Migration from China is often perceived by the Chinese government as a modern and patriotic gesture in line with the current Chinese modernisation project (Nyíri 2001, 2002).

Expatriating nationals as a way to expand China's presence in the world under the leadership of its central authorities has seemingly become an essential part of China's modernisation project. While this project involves the economic and technological advancements of the PRC, in practical terms it transcends the territorial limits of the state. The present dynamics of migration and the regimes of multiculturalism in developed countries are manipulated by the Chinese government to promote Chinese nationalist ideas supportive of mainland China under the leadership of the CCP. By claiming the Chinese identity of all ethnic Chinese, not only those who originate on the mainland, China seeks to mobilise not-so-cosmopolitan transnationals to serve its own national cause of economic modernisation and its political ambitions.

The PRC's 'de-territorialised nationalism', to use Duara's term (2003), is not at odds with its long-pursued ideology of territorially restricted nationalism, which has been manifested in numerous territorial disputes and in the PRC's desire to reunify with Taiwan. Historically, nationalism and transnationalism were always intertwined in China's modernisation project. The two strategies continue to be combined and have attained new relevance in the age of global transformations. Ideologically, the principles of transnational and territorial nationalism are compatible and mutually reinforcing rather than conflicting, as they are both directed at enhancing the PRC's political and economic power, and boosting the legitimacy of its leadership. Territory as such is not irrelevant to China's pursuit of its modernisation project, and China hardly ignores its significance; it acts in spite of it. The starkest difference between the projects of transnational and territorial nationalism, apart from their geographical dimensions, is how they are positioned in relation to ethnicity. It seems that transnational nationalism rests exclusively on the assumption of common and rather narrowly-defined ethnicity. The territorial-political construct of the Chinese nation-state is purportedly founded on the principle of diversity, but with a rigid view of territoriality. The combination of territory and ethnicity, and their flexible utilisation by the dominant power, forms the basis on which the Chinese national modernisation project is constructed.

6 The politics of localisation
Ethnic minorities in post-socialist modernisation

Since the start of the reforms and the opening up of China, the state has mobilised ethnic minorities as a symbol of China's multiculturalism. Minorities' traditions, festivals, music and food have showcased China's plurality and exoticism.[1] Minority cultural sites have also become centrepieces of much of the PRC's tourism and cultural celebration. While ethnographers and anthropologists have examined these functions of ethnic minorities in the framing of the Chinese nation-state, the state's utilisation of ethnic arguments in China's national modernisation project has not been studied to the same extent.Yet, the modernisation project goes hand in hand with redefinition of China's cultural identities and symbolic boundaries, or, as Ong (1999) put it, with the 'remoralisation' of the nation. The PRC's promotion of itself as a plural multiethnic nation-state in cultural terms shapes its implementation of the national modernisation project, and also affects how participation in the national modernisation project is formulated. [2] Along with the discursive practices discussed in Chapter 4, how the prevailing policies of modernisation account for ethnic minorities reflects the articulation of their participation in the national project. Therefore, this chapter examines the role of China's ethnic minorities in the country's national modernisation project. Specifically, the chapter looks at how the notion of the 'ethnic question' changed since the start of the reforms. It also examines how the central government utilises the concept of ethnicity (*minzu*) in formulating and implementing its modernisation strategies, and the ways through which ethnic minority groups are included in the national modernisation project.

This chapter illustrates that the ethnic question in the PRC's modernisation project is essentially linked to 'development' problems of ethnic minority groups. The ethnic question and its solution are closely related to the issues of poverty reduction, economic development, the promotion of openness and the maintenance of stability. The strategies to overcome the underdevelopment assume a dichotomy between the ethnic minorities and the Han majority, and between the geographical areas associated with them. Diversity in development strategies is seen as a problem, and all minority groups are viewed the same way when it comes to modernisation. The promotion of ethnic diversity has taken a uniform format, neglecting important content and meaning. The state's preferential policies perpetuate the minority status of non-Han ethnic groups, allotting them a limited number of rights, reinforcing their limited position within the geo-social space of modernising China.

I show that the PRC's leadership, through developmental strategies and policies tailored for ethnic minorities, essentially demarcates ethnic minorities as localised elements of the Chinese nation-state. I borrow the term *localisation* from Appadurai (1997), who calls it a 'primary concern' of the nation-state. In Appadurai's interpretation, *localisation* manifests itself in attempts to exert power over subjects and national spaces to legitimise a regime's control and domination. It is commonly produced and maintained by the ruling power through the formulation and interpretation of the particularities of a place, its culture and its social practices. In Appadurai's account, localisation is becoming more problematic due to the changes brought about by globalisation. However, as the ensuing analysis demonstrates, the Chinese leadership relies on and reproduces localisation as an essential and natural ingredient of its modernisation project.

The first section of this chapter examines the ways that the 'ethnic question' has changed since the start of reforms. Specifically, it traces how class interpretations of the 'nationality question' in the official discourse disappeared and were replaced by development explanations, which are now at the centre of ethnic policies. I also show how the term *minzu* in the context of the PRC connotes minorities with derogatory characteristics. The second section looks at the nature, goals and some intermediate effects of the WDP, the central government's initiative to accelerate development of China's western region. The third section examines more closely the link between the WDP and state policies on the 'ethnic question'. The fourth section critically analyses the minority connotations associated with the western region and challenges the 'ethnic' label attached to this part of China in the formulation of the WDP. I show that the implementation of the WDP assumes a binary opposition between the majority Han and ethnic minorities and between the regions with which they are associated.

The 'ethnic question' in the reform period: from class interpretations to developmental explanations

Most Chinese officials and scholars do not refer to the period after 1978 as a new stage in the PRC's policies towards ethnic minorities. On the contrary, they see it as a continuation of the work started after the establishment of the New China in 1949 (Wang Hongman 2000). As Chapter 2 illustrated, ethnic policies, or in the Maoist formulation 'nationality work' (*minzu gongzuo*), have been high on the agenda of the communist leadership ever since the establishment of the CCP in 1921. However, it is widely acknowledged that at some periods in recent Chinese history there were negative trends in minority work due to the activities of the 'counter-revolutionary' Gang of Four during the years of the Cultural Revolution (1966–76). Thus, for the CCP, the reform period per se is not a new epoch in dealing with ethnic issues. [3] Though the aims and objectives of post-1978 minority work are seen as identical to those in the early 1950s, in light of the opening up of China and modernisation, 'nationality work' has undergone ideological and policy readjustments.

Almost immediately after the task of nationality identification had allegedly been accomplished in the late 1970s, the Party and government organs embarked on a new mission.[4] They revised the concepts they had used earlier in adjusting economic policies in the early reform period. One of the notions that underwent significant rethinking since the opening up of China was the 'ethnic question' (*minzu wenti*).[5] Stalin's class interpretation of the ethnic question employed before the start of the reform period did not fit the new modernisation and market economy proposed by the new leadership. Therefore, with the economic system moving from a planned to a market socialist economy, the interpretation and handling of the ethnic question had to be changed. One justification stemmed from ambiguities in Marx's ascription of the peculiarities of the ethnic question to certain stages in social development.

A number of Party-led conferences revised the ethnic question and identified the tasks of ethnic work in the post-socialist era. In May 1979 the NAC held the first of such conferences. Among the tasks identified for the new era of the construction of socialism with Chinese characteristics were: to help ethnic minorities catch up with the economic and cultural development of the Han; to train specialists and cadres among ethnic minorities; and to overcome the problem of inequality (Wang Tiezhi 2001: 4). These tasks were reiterated in the CCP Central Committee's Summary of the Report on Ethnic Work in Yunnan issued in 1981.

At the same time, the earlier class underpinnings of the nationality question were refuted. In June 1979, Deng Xiaoping emphasised that 'in our country each nationality takes the course of democratic and socialist transformation; they adhered early to the path of socialism, built the ethnic relationship of socialist unity, fraternity, mutual help and cooperation' (quoted in Wang Tiezhi 2001: 6). Deng's speech was soon followed by an editorial in the *People's Daily* in July 1979, which declared that, in contrast to the earlier formulations of the ethnic question, it was actually 'a relationship between working people of nationalities'. Soon thereafter the 1980 'Summary of the Discussion Meeting on the Work in Tibet' contended that the assertion that the 'ethnic question is in fact a class question' was wrong (Jin Binghao 1999: 89). Class explanations of ethnic issues were now replaced by interpretations of developmental inequalities.

Documents issued subsequently by the central government reflected the new spirit of ethnic work. For example, in 1987 the CCP's Central Committee and the SC published a 'Report on Several Important Issues of Ethnic Work', which reaffirmed that economic construction should be at the centre of ethnic work (*yi jingji jianshe wei zhongxin*). It also stressed the importance of creating a 'spiritual civilisation' (*jingshen wenming jianshe*) and implementing the Law on Regional and National Autonomy (LRNA). Related to the issue of spiritual civilisation was the 'emancipation of ethnic minorities' minds' through the proliferation of qualities compatible with the principles of a market economy, such as competitiveness, open-mindedness, and adaptability to the requirements of the time. The report concluded that:

> ... economic construction as a central task will stimulate the development of other aspects of ethnic minorities, such as politics, economy and culture,

which in turn will increasingly solidify a new type of socialist ethnic relations and achieve prosperity for each nationality.

(He Jing 1999: 2–3)

The qualities that this document aimed to assign to the ethnic minorities are essentially uniform and allude to the seemingly higher level of development of the Han majority. It neither reflects the diversity among ethnic populations in China nor represents the interests expressed by the ethnic minorities themselves. 'Emancipation of ethnic minorities' minds' was directed at the instillation of a particular kind of identity that would make ethnic minorities conform to the rules of the modernisation project pursued by the Chinese leadership and distance them from their ethnic affiliations.

In 1992, the year the PRC officially embarked on the road of a market economy, Jiang Zemin, in his speech at the CCP Central Conference on ethnic minority work, outlined five aspects of this work that should be stressed in the new period. Again, the economic development of ethnic minorities and ethnic regions was placed at the forefront. The other four aspects of ethnic minority work – the social development and comprehensive progress of minorities, their self-development activities, improvement of the autonomy system for them, and strengthening of ethnic unity – were loosely presented and made directly dependent on the success of economic development (Wang Tiezhi 2001: 5). The prioritisation of economic incentives over cultural and political issues had repercussions for how an ethnic group was sometimes referred to by Chinese scholars. In the framework of a socialist market economy, an ethnic community has often been considered a group with a common ethnic identity based on its 'material relationship and interest' (*wuzi guanxi he liyi*) (Yang Changru 1996: 97).

The economic development-focused interpretation of ethnic relations was one of the factors that shaped a ten-year government initiative called 'Prosperous Frontiers and Wealthy People' (*xing bian fu min*). The initiative started in 2000 and was aimed at assisting 22 ethnic minority groups with populations of less than 100,000 to achieve a better material life (Information Office of China's SC 2005). However, in their blind pursuit of economic development, Chinese government programmes have largely remained insensitive to people's welfare and liveable communities, and to how they are connected to 'scientific' development. The calls of Chinese scholars to incorporate minorities' perspectives on people's well-being into the official concept of development have been largely unheeded. For example, in an attempt to demonstrate the complexity of measuring development, Xiong Jingmin (2002) turns to examples of minority cultures whose traditions include a solicitous attitude toward nature. She poses the question of whether the Naxi Dongba tradition of treating trees as brothers, the Tibetan worshiping of trees, and the Dai tradition of growing trees to be felled for people's livelihood – which are all directed at conservancy and environmental protection – should be regarded as advanced or backward features of their cultures. The official opinion that prevails among the leadership in China is that one of the most serious problems for minorities' development is their 'unhealthy mentality'

(Tian Qunjian 2004: 631),[6] which is largely associated with their traditional (i.e. pre-modern) ways of life, and that economic development is the sole practical solution to the ethnic question (Qing Jue and Jin Binggao 2003). There is little prospect that other determinants of development will be seriously considered in the formulation and implementation of the modernisation project.

But the official argument about the 'unhealthy mentality' of ethnic populations largely ignores the fact that some minorities demonstrate a high level of engagement in business, an activity which is presented by the Chinese state as modern. According to official statistics, in 2000, about 9 per cent of Chinese engaged in business activities. While the rate for the Han (9.52 per cent) is slightly higher than the national average, the Hui, Koreans, Russians and Tatars had far higher rates of engagement in business activities: 13.8 per cent, 17.1 per cent, 19.7 per cent and 16 per cent, respectively (Ma Rong 2003: 33). Ma's explanation for this is the geographical distribution of these minority groups near the state border and their active involvement in the border trade with neighbouring countries. A study by Heberer (2007) demonstrates peculiar entrepreneurial culture and skills among Yi people in south-west China. Furthermore, Naxi and Koreans have historically been praised by the authorities for their higher education enrolment scores than the Han.[7]

In the government's and Party's documents, promoting ethnic minorities' development is presented as a strategic and political aim. As discussed in Chapter 4, official and scholarly publications now link China's overall stability and prosperity to stability and modernisation in the ethnic regions. The means for achieving the goals of ethnic work were formulated at the First National Honorary Conference on Ethnic Unity held by the SC in 1988. Adherence to Marxism and the CCP's teachings on nationalities and patriotism were presented as necessary conditions for satisfactory implementation of the modernisation project (Wang Tiezhi 2001: 9). Equality and unity were deemed two main principles of ethnic work. The political slogan born out of these principles is a revised version of the principle 'the two cannot be separated' (*liang ge li bu kai*) declared in 1957. The principle is now 'three cannot be separated' (*san ge li bu kai*). As one official put it, 'Ethnic minorities cannot be separated from the Han, the Han cannot be separated from ethnic minorities, and ethnic minorities cannot be separated from each other'.[8] In contrast to the initial principle, which was based on simple opposition between the Han and the ethnic minorities, the current principle makes unity and equality among ethnic minorities the third condition of the unity of the country. The introduction of this slogan can be interpreted as an attempt to overcome a dichotomy in the representation of the relationship between the majority and minority groups, and to recognise the diverse conditions of ethnic minority groups in China. However, all ethnic minority groups share a number of discursive preconceptions, as they are all part of the 'ethnic question' and the targets of ethnic work. These preconceptions uniting ethnic groups are set in opposition to the Han majority, and so the dichotomous relationship is not overcome but is further reproduced.

In the official discourse, the ethnic question is presented in exclusively developmental terms, and clashes between ethnic groups and the activities of separatist groups are seen as almost nonexistent or driven by other than ethnic motives. Chinese leaders often praise their ethnic work by pointing to the absence of major ethnic disputes in China. Deng Xiaoping on one occasion contended that 'our ethnic work is right, because it focuses on ethnic equality. We seriously consider ethnic minorities' rights and interests. Our one important characteristic is that we do not have major ethnic disputes' (quoted in He Jing 1999: 3). There is a general and strong conviction expressed across official writings on the ethnic issue in the PRC that the chosen policies are among the most successful in the world (Huang Zuoxiu 2000: 18).

But while it is true that, under the close surveillance of the Chinese army, ethnic unrest in China has never escalated to the level of Nagorny Karabah or East Timor – with the exception of the unrest in Tibet and Xinjiang – ethnic grievances have fed violent clashes.[9] Rather than openly recognise and deal with the diferent levels of ethnic conflict in the PRC, the government prefers to silence and suppress the slightest signs of challenge to its legitimacy. All developments, including ethnic conflicts, that are regarded as possible challenges to the state are dismissed or categorised as a threat to the state's stability. Rather than looking into the causes of the ethnic disturbances, the authorities also see social and ethnic unrest as a problem of underdevelopment, or as an anti-Party or anti-state revolt. In fact, during an interview with an official from the NAC, the official pointed out to me that while class interpretations are not applicable in dealing with the ethnic question, they can still be employed in interpreting such problems as terrorism, as well as acts against the government and the state.[10] While all members of ethnic groups have been characterised as 'working people', those who perpetrate acts against the state or the regime are seen by officials as motivated by class considerations. Another common measure to deal with ethnic disturbances is to violently suppress them and impose marital law in the affected regions, as was demonstrated in the clashes between the Han and Hui in Henan in November 2004. While the scale of these clashes could hardly pose a serious challenge to the authorities, the fact that martial law was imposed demonstrates how sensitive and nervous the authorities are whenever the legitimacy of the Party is at stake.[11]

While China's relaxed one-child policy, certain advantages for enrolment in universities and lower taxes are probably the most attractive incentives for having an ethnic minority identity, the preferential policies are constructed in a way that associates them with the negative aspects of ethnic minority status. This unfavourable association sometimes leads minority individuals who prefer to be part of mainstream society to give up their minority privileges and ascriptions in order to be associated with progress and modernisation.[12] Peculiarly, according to some state regulations, a minority person employed by the state has no privileges at all and faces restrictions similar to the Han.[13] What is more, ethnic minorities who join modern Chinese society and seek a contemporary lifestyle outside of her/his minority home place find that the entitlements of their minority status are often not transferable. Several of my Chinese minority informants who moved from their hometowns in ethnic minority areas to big cities in China's East, like Beijing

144 *The politics of localisation*

and Guangzhou, noted that they were restricted to one child as the one child exception applied only to ethnic minorities living in the minority areas. [14] Some also told me that they preferred to forego minority status entitlements because accepting them would cause them to be looked down upon in their new (modern) living environment. Ethnicity in this discourse then is largely conceived of as being attached to a particular locality. Bearers of an ethnic minority identity are those who represent territorial and cultural spaces assigned to them by the state, and they thus enjoy only a limited form of inclusion. Associating with the qualities of a modern Chinese citizen means eschewing ethnic minority privileges in practice. All that remains is the stamp in one's passport or identity document to designate the ethnic minority group one belongs to.

Essentially, the underlying structure of official rhetoric on the ethnic question has not changed since the socialist era. Then, all miseries in Chinese society were seen as rooted in the class struggle. Today, the ethnic question is seen as rooted in the problems of economic development. According to this logic, balanced economic growth would eliminate the ethnic question. However, it is not clear how cultural differences are relevant to economic explanations of the ethnic question. Can the question be solved solely through economic growth and economic exchange? While political explanations of the ethnic question gave way to cultural considerations with the state's promotion of traditional ethnic cultures, economic concerns take precedence over cultural interests, and the latter are bound to adjust to the former. The official perception of modernisation does not permit the logic of development to serve ethnic minorities' cultures.

The point here is that the interpretation of concepts introduced with the start of the economic and social reforms remains a prerogative of the Party organs and state, and they are revised to fit the political interests of the state rather than reality on the ground. The concepts are interpreted and laid out for the public to convey the political agenda of the country's leadership. Development, mostly economic, is placed at the centre of political rhetoric and is treated as a panacea for almost all problems in Chinese society. The way the developmental rhetoric of the ethnic question is framed reflects and perpetuates the binary opposition between ethnic minorities and the Han majority, with the former judged in need of development and modernisation. It establishes a prescribed course of development that limits ethnic minorities' participation in transformations that should reflect their peculiarities and interests. The ethnic question designates ethnic minorities as carriers of a particular set of attributes that place them in a subordinate position in Chinese society, and in particular geographical parts of the PRC. This is especially tangible in the formulation of the WDP.

The official interpretations and some intermediate effects of the WDP

The initiative to develop the western region of China was proposed by Jiang Zemin during the Ninth NPC in March 1999, and later that year was formulated into the official strategy of the WDP (*xibu dakaifa*).[15] The WDP was conceived by the leadership as a corrective to the regional development strategy undertaken by the central government in the early 1980s.[16] China's shift from self-reliance to an open door policy in the reforms of the 1980s favoured China's coastal areas. Deng Xiaoping's slogan 'let some regions get rich first' laid the ideological basis for the formulation and subsequent implementation of this economic trend. As a developing country, it was argued, China had to concentrate its resources in its more developed coastal region; later the emphasis would shift to the central and western regions, and the diffusion of the coastal development would stimulate the development of the interior. The development of the coastal areas failed to lead to the development of the interior, however. Rather it exacerbated disparities. Thus, the central leadership initiated a new development strategy for the western region.[17] Hu Angang, the leading Chinese economist and director of the China studies division at the Chinese Academy of Science, portrayed the WDP as a centrally-driven effort in which the central government would guarantee the balanced development of the country and tackle the disparities in regional development (Hu Angang 2000). The vital political character of the WDP is evident in the fact that the nominal guiding organ, The SC Leading Group for WDP, was initially presided over by Wen Jiaobao and Zeng Peiyan, two of the top figures in China's ruling establishment, and is comprised of members with the rank of ministers.

Chinese academic and official rhetoric often refers to the WDP as the strategy that the state (the main provider of the common good) follows in representing the people's interests (Chen Yunhui 2000: 205). The goal of the WDP, according to official and academic publications on the issue, is: to make China's west richer; to harmonise the overall development (*xietiao fazhan*) of the country; to provide common wealth (*gongtong fuyu*); and to stabilize the frontiers (*gonggu bianfang*) (Huang Zhu 2000: 23). In other words, theWDP is portrayed as a vitally-important structural adjustment to the country's economy – an effort to address inequalities to economic development through a range of political decisions and strategic projects. One Chinese author bluntly suggests that the WDP aims 'to reduce the difference between China's regions' (*suoxiao dique chabie*), with the project's exogenously-introduced objectives turning into the internal driving force of the transformation (Qian Ning 2003: 92).

In fact, the WDP does not have a single policy line. Nor does any single document detail the WDP's precise plans. Rather, the WDP appears to have an 'aspirational' agenda (Goodman 2004: 319). The two 'circulars' of the SC that outline the general framework of the project for the period from 2001 to 2010 are suffused with 'should' and 'are encouraged' clauses (State Council, Western Region Development Office 2001a, 2001b). The documents are in line with the central government's 'missionary' take on the remote areas of the country and its determination to turn the western region into an 'advanced new West'.[18]

The language of the SC's circulars is rather general and intended to popularise the large-scale infrastructure projects, to attract investments to the region and, to a lesser extent, to promote social engineering and environmental initiatives. Examples include initiatives 'to emancipate the mind, to proliferate knowledge about the market economy', to 'promote material and spiritual civilisation', and 'to reinvigorate our country through science and education and the sustainable development strategy'.

Infrastructure projects have been the most labour- and finance-intensive initiatives of the WDP. In Chinese sources they are called 'key' or 'big' projects. In 2000, the State Development Planning Commission of the PRC approved 'ten major projects' in the West,[19] including the construction of twenty airports in the region; the diversion of natural gas and electricity from the west to the east;[20] the building of eight national highways (to connect the country's major cities), eight inter-provincial highways and local roads between townships and villages in the West; the construction of railway lines (Xian-Nanjing, Qinghai-Tibet); and the development of key water conservancy projects.[21] The government believes that these infrastructure projects are the first step toward successful modernisation. Most of these projects are intended to connect the western and eastern parts of China. Thus main energy recipient of the Three Gorges dam, which relies on the water resources of the West, is China's richest province, Guangdong; the Qinghai-Tibetan railway project is described as a 'symbolic project ... to link Tibet with the rest of China;'[22] and the 3,900-kilometre-long Tarim–Shanghai natural gas pipeline pumps gas from Xinjiang to Shanghai, China's most prosperous city.

A core element in the development of the western provinces is a desire to explore and open up the region's natural resources for the benefit of the rest of the country. While the official language in China celebrates these projects as having 'a bearing on the nation as a whole' (Zeng Peiyang 2003), western scholars have stressed the immediate short-term economic benefits of these infrastructure projects and express concern as to whether they will ever contribute to the integration of the western regions in a coherent nation-state or whether they will have a long-term impact on the general well-being of the local people in China's West (Holbig 2004).

The central government's widely publicised reasons for initiating infrastructure and industry projects in the West were to develop productive forces in the minority region (Guan Guixia 2000: 28) and to provide job opportunities for local people – and officials are quick to showcase achievements in these respects.[23] The labour force in the region, however, increasingly consists of migrant workers from the East at the expense of local employment. Some Chinese scholars see this inflow of workers from the East as a positive development, aguing that 'they will not only increase the level of technology, but will also train local minority specialists', and that they will also bring along an 'advanced' mode of life. Local minority groups, they argue, will enhance their own quality of life after they are exposed to the advanced modes of life of eastern workers (Ma Ping 2001: 38).

The Ministry of Personnel's 'Plan for Human Resource Development in the West in 2000' was designed to attract talented scientists to the West. Working together with the Ministry of Education, the Ministry of Personnel formulated policies to encourage outstanding university students and young teachers to move from the coastal areas to the West (Lai 2002: 456). In the first year after the official launch of the campaign, more than 600,000 Han Chinese moved into Xinjiang Uyghur Autonomous Region.[24] Lim estimates that the majority of people working on the construction sites initiated as part of the WDP are Han migrants from the East. The government justifies the influx of labour by the lack of necessary knowledge among the locals of non-Han descent (Lim 2004). This echoes a more recently expressed conviction of one Chinese official who declared that, on the road to becoming a great power, China should be led by 'an advanced culture and higher-level civilized nationality', implying the leading role of the Han in China's development process (Zheng Bijian 2006).

Tourism has become one of the main industries the government seeks to develop in China's western region, and ten out of twelve provinces included in the WDP declared tourism to be their leading industry (Wei Xiaoan 2001). Described as 'a window to greater openness'(*dui wai kaifang de chuanghu*), tourism was, in fact, one of the touchstones of Deng Xiaoping's modernisation model in the late 1970s and early 1980s. Official publications increasingly present China's ethnic minorities as tourist attractions, yet recent studies on tourism in China argue that the state's active participation in the production of tourist sites and attractions results in a skewed vision of 'exotic and traditional China'(Oakes 1998; Nyíri 2006). A study by Nyíri, for example, points out that the state-produced tourism promotional materials refer to Chinese ethnic minorities 'as people who have never stopped singing and dancing' (Nyíri 2006: 24). This largely uniform and rigid official discourse on modernisation and tourism runs against the recently-documented popularisation of ethnic minority cultures through tourism (Baranovitch 2001; McCarthy 2004; Goodman 2005).

Wilk's phrase 'structures of common difference' may help us understand how diversity is built into the proliferation of tourism (Wilk 1995a). According to Wilk, diversity is a product of the hegemonic structure that regulates the format in which diversity is presented. He argues that 'difference is built upon temporal rhythms, spatial hierarchies, and essentialised age and gender. By making all of these orders appear in some way "natural", global systems of difference suppress and conceal other kinds of variation' (Wilk 1995b: 120). Following Wilk's analogy, it is tempting to suggest that, in the national context of China, diversity is a product of the dominant rhetoric and policies of Chinese officialdom. There is, in fact, something inherently hierarchical and homogenising about how minority difference is articulated and presented in China: in tourism, this difference is celebrated by means of 'exotic' customs, traditions, national dress, folk dance, festivals and so on. These patterns of difference have a uniform character in the way they are organised, presented and celebrated – they are defined according to certain standards and categories formulated by the centre.

Security concerns arising in the 1990s caused the reorientation in the state's development from East to West (Tian 2004: 621). An important incentive for the initiation and realisation of the WDP often emphasised in Chinese official publications is the government's desire to pacify – or 'harmonise and stabilise' (*xietiao, gonggu*) – the state's borders. The WDP's security imperatives are associated primarily with Xinjiang and Tibet, two regions that have been an on-going security concern for the Chinese government. With the collapse of the Soviet Union and the increased number of ethnic conflicts and instability in Central Asia, addressing these security issues has become an urgent concern, with the favoured solution being economic development programmes and extensive infrastructure projects, in tandem with a considerable military presence in the areas.[25] The thinking is that a growing economy will enrich the local inhabitants, and security problems and separatist tensions will decline as a result. As two Chinese scholars metaphorically expressed it, the WDP aims to make the western border a 'steel and iron wall' (*gang qiang tie bi*) to prevent the state's disintegration by forces from outside and inside the country (Yang Faren and Yang Li 2004: 27).

There are numerous environmental, social, cultural and economic damaging effects attributed to the policies of the WDP. One of the human-related problems arising from the infrastructure and construction projects in the West is the requisition of land by the construction companies and state-endorsed developers. Compensation for land requisition in many cases is not paid, which leaves locals without basic means to provide for themselves. One academic report highlights that problem with the construction of the Kunming–Bangkok highway, which goes through mainly ethnic minority areas in Yunnan province (Zhang Xisheng 2001: 9). Similar concerns are expressed about the costs and efects of the numerous dam projects that China is undertaking at the moment.[26] While the Ministry of Land and Resources recognised at least 168,000 cases of illegal land deals in 2003, the actual number of cases violating the rights of peasants could significantly exceed that figure.[27]

The approach taken by the government in its implementation of the WDP is to 'ease the threat to the environment of the Yangtze River brought about by local people'.[28] Since 1998, a ban on forest felling has undermined people's general well-being by significantly reducing their farming land and pressing them to plant grass and trees in the region. The government is quick to place the blame for erosion of the environment on local people without considering the effects of earlier policies, as well as the human costs of current strategies. As a result of earlier developmental experiments, in 2001 in Inner Mongolia the volume of pastureland was 8,280,000 square hectares less than in 1980. The western region is a very fragile area where 80 per cent of China's eroded land and 90 per cent of desertified areas are located (Lai 2002: 445); it has one of the biggest deserts in the world and the world's highest mountain ranges. In such conditions, the already-existing 643 heavy industry enterprises (7 per cent of the country's total), including most of the heavy military industry and the 1,285 medium industry enterprises (8.92 per cent of the country's total), could be too much (Long Yi 2003: 6). Although, rhetorically, environment protection is one of the project's goals, it was secondary to the strategic and economic priorities of the government, at least at the start of the campaign, when the State Environment Protection Agency was excluded from planning and carrying out the WDP (Holbig 2004: 345). At the same time, the chase for hard cash and high economic indicators has contributed more to the deterioration of the environment. In her critical assessment of the WDP, Xiong Jingmin gives an example of disastrous handling of cotton production in Xinjiang (Xiong Jingmin 2002). As part of the new strategy of assisting the western provinces to get rich in the early 2000s, Xinjiang farmers, with governmental approval supported by generous subsidies, were encouraged to produce more raw cotton. However, when the government could not guarantee the purchase of the excessive quantities of the raw material and there was no more incentive to produce large quantities of cotton, the abandoned cotton fields turned into desert.

A study conducted by a team from the Asian Development Bank concluded that minorities are concerned about the availability of jobs, with so many incoming Han migrants, and especially about the reduction in urban employment opportunities for them (Asian Development Bank 2003: 278). In 1999 in Xinjiang, minority people made up only 7.3 per cent of the provincial construction forces.[29] In 2002, out of 2.5 million employees in Xinjiang, only 716,000 were from a minority background. Moreover, the majority of employed minorities were working in the spheres of education, culture, farming and agriculture. Only 24,000 of them were employed in the buoyant construction sector and 4,900 in scientific research[30] Han workers constitute over ninety per cent of the workers at the state-administered construction corps in Xinjiang, the workforce comprised of demobilised PLA soldiers, which control about 48 per cent of Xinjiang (O'Neill 2008). Key industries such as oil exploration in Xinjiang are dominated by the Han. The statistics indicate that among 20,000 oil workers in the Tarim Basin, few jobs were given to minority workers, while in the Taklamakan desert oil exploration project only 253 of 4,000 technical workers are of ethnic minority origins. Academic studies have found that the WDP is more receptive to the nonethnic populations of the region, while minorities feel threatened by the possible migration of Han people from the east where the 'floating' population is estimated to be 100–120 million (Lai 2002: 432; Dillon 2000). Such hostility of the minority populations toward the WDP is somewhat ironic, as this project embodies a clear ethnic character, which is discussed in the next section.

The ethnic character of the WDP

In September–October 1999 the Second Central Conference on Ethnic Work held in Beijing, declared the acceleration of the development of the western region to be a crucial strategic task for the twenty-first century, and an historical opportunity for minorities to develop (Guan Guixia 2000: 28).At the same conference, Jiang Zemin stressed that the accelerated economic development of China's minorities and minority regions was essential to the minority work of the state (quoted in Huang Zhu 2000: 23). Several years prior to this, a poll conducted among regional ethnic affairs officials revealed that the majority of those polled believed that an increasing disparity in development between regions in China might have a negative effect on ethnic relations and could lead to ethnic unrest and conflicts (Sautman 1998: 99). The common interpretation of the WDP's objectives in Chinese writings on the issues emphasises the project's ethnic component, namely:

> ... to liberate and develop the socially productive forces of ethnic minorities areas, decrease the gap in development between the East and the West,

accelerate the development of ethnic minorities and their regions, to implement socialist modernisation and to lay a substantial base for the successful resolution of the current ethnic question.

(Mao Gongning 2001: 31)

China's leaders emphasise the ethnic aspects of the project. In Zhu Rongji's words: 'To implement the strategy of western development is in other words to accelerate the development of ethnic minorities and minority areas' (quoted in Zhou Ping 2002: 49). From the very start, then, the WDP, and not only at a rhetorical level, was presented as a tool that would narrow the development gap between ethnic minorities and China's Han majority group.

Amendments to laws in China are normally driven by alterations in policies, a practice that prioritises governmental policies over legislation. Soon after the WDP was launched, amendments were added to the Law on Regional National Autonomy (LRNA) in 2001. The amended LRNA stipulated the state's obligations to provide assistance to autonomous ethnic minority areas rather than assisting ethnic minorities' areas in their attempt to modernise (Yu Xingzhong 2004). For example, the title of Chapter 6 of the amended LRNA was changed from 'Leadership and Assistance of the State Organs at Higher Levels to 'Responsibilities of the State Organs at Higher Levels'. The formulation of the amended LRNA reflects the spirit of the state's proclaimed agenda of dealing with 'some practical problems in the economic and social development of localities under ethnic autonomy, so as to accelerate the economic and social development in ethnic regions and promote nationality solidarity'.[31] Li Dezhu, head of the State Ethnic Affairs Commission, elucidated the incentive for revising the existing law, pointing out that, in developing the West, the relationship between the interests of the state and of minority groups 'should be correctly handled'.[32]

The revised version of the LRNA further consolidated the primacy of the central government in regulating every aspect of life in autonomous ethnic minority areas, and explicitly linked the WDP strategy with the government position of handling the government's minority policies. Article 6 of the Subsequent Provisions of the SC on the Implementation of LRNA, adopted in 2005, clearly states that 'the state adopts the strategy of Western Development so as to promote the accelerated development of the ethnic autonomous areas. ... '[33] In other words, in a legal sense, the WDP was designed specifically for ethnic minorities and minority areas.

On a policy front, the inclusion in the WDP of the Guangxi Autonomous region, home to China's largest ethnic minority, the Zhuang, shows clearly that the ethnic factor is a defining element of the WDP. The fact that Guangxi is located in southeastern China and that parts of it were included in the coastal development strategy in the 1980s were not obstacles to the decision. In a similar mode, several ethnic minority prefectures of the central provinces, such as the Xianxi Tujia-Miao Autonomous Prefecture of Hunan province, the Enshi Tujia-Miao Autonomous Prefecture of Hubei province and the Yanbian Korean Autonomous Prefecture of Jilin province, were effectively included in the 'western region' (State Council,

The politics of localisation 151

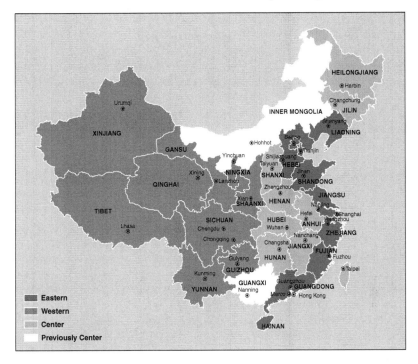

Figure 6.1 Regional divisions of the People's Republic of China
Source: Asian Development Bank (2003: 4). Misspelled provincial names corrected.

Western Region Development Office 2001a). In effect, then, China's 'west' has been extended geographically from the Korean border in the north to the Beibu Gulf near Vietnam in the south, leaving only a narrow belt of provinces in the centre without focused attention from the government.

Soon after the introduction and formulation of the WDP, the government sponsored the publication of a collection of essays on the WDP and the 'ethnic question' by leading scholars on the ethnic issues, complemented by articles from officials dealing with this policy area (Mao and Wang 2000). In the lead article in the collection, Li Dezhu underlines the key aspects of the state-sponsored strategy as speeding the development of economy and culture in ethnic minority regions (Li Dezhu 2000: 2). Referring to the WDP as the key strategic and political tool of the government to address the inequalities in economic developments between the East and West, between different provinces and regions in the West, and within western provinces and regions, Li stipulates that the inequalities in development are the main restriction and barrier to China's achievement of successful resolution of the ethnic question (Li Dezhu 2000: 3). Li cites disparity in economic development as one of the most dire threats to China's unity and stability, which the WDP aims to prevent (Li Dezhu 2000: 6). The success of the WDP, in Li's account, thus rests in part on the successful resolution of the ethnic question, which in turn, is seen in developmental terms. Other scholars support Li's contention that, if the ethnic question is successfully resolved in the West, the whole country's ethnic question will be essentially resolved (Yang Faren and Yang Li 2004: 3). Minorities in this formulation not only take the role of recipients of the government-provided policies, but are also made responsible for the successful realisation of the state's overall modernisation goals.

In his contribution to the volume, Fei Xiaotong, the country's most famous anthropologist and ethnic issues specialist, compares the importance of the WDP to the post-PRC establishment period, when the leaders were preoccupied with ensuring the control and support of the minority populations. In Fei's view, the main objective of minority work during the early years of the PRC was to introduce socialism to minority areas. The WDP, in his interpretation, is the second important step in minority work: a project that allows ethnic minorities to develop their own economies and cultures (Fei Xiaotong 2000: 11). Other contributors to the volume see the WDP as the way to bridge the development gap between the country's western and eastern regions, and speak of the WDP as a unique state-sponsored development opportunity for minorities – one they are urged to firmly seize (*jinjin zhuazhu*) lest conditions deteriorate and economic conflicts (*jingji maodun*) arise with the eastern Han areas (Huang Zhu 2000: 23; Zhou Jian 2000: 195).

Another WDP-related topic that contributors to this volume regard as central, in strikingly similar ways to scholarly work discussed in Chapter 4, is the disparity in the ways of thinking and mentality between people in the West and East (Huang Zhu 2000: 26). Ethnic minorities are encouraged to 'to open up their minds to socialist market economy', and 'not to be afraid of other people getting prosperous, but seek self-development'(*bu pa renjia facai, qiu ziji fazhan*). Liu Wangqing, for example, suggests that, with the economic growth the WDP will guarantee in the minority regions, as well as with the special educational programme to be implemented in the ethnic minority areas, 'the quality of the people will go up and consciousness of minority people will be strengthened' (*suzhi tigao, minzu yishi zengqiang*) (Liu Wangqing 2000: 186). He cites self-respect (*zi zun*) and self-reliance (*zi li*) as two key components of ethnic consciousness (Liu Wangqing 2000: 189). But he also warns of negative aspects of ethnic self-consciousness, and calls for careful promotion of the 'legitimate' (*zhengque*) ones.

Contributor Zhou Jian points out that some aspects of traditional minority culture are not compatible with development, therefore they have to be reformed, as 'without the reform there is no development and no adaptation to modern society' (*bu gai jiu bu fazhan, bu neng shiying xiandaihua shehui*) (Zhou Jian 2000: 197). He cites, for example, the 'traditional mentality' (*chuangtong sixiang*) of ethnic minorities and their inability to adapt to the modern currents of life as the main obstacles to their participation in China's modernisation transformations. Zhou allows only one reservation – for religion and minority traditions – as these, he claims, are essential parts of minority identities. Zhou is not specific, however, about what aspects of minority cultures he would wish to reform and how.

In their study of the relationship between the WDP and the ethnic question, Yang Faren and Yang Li observe that, due to the western region's low level of development, low level of urbanisation and consumption, and high degree of poverty, minority populations 'enjoy the achievements of modern civilisation much less than the provinces in the East' (Yang Faren and Yang Li 2004: 10, 11). They argue that this low level of development is a crucial issue, one that the WDP aims to resolve. Development is here portrayed as a panacea: 'The key to solving all these [minority] problems is in development. Development is a forceful principle' (*jiejue suoyou zhe xie wenti de guanjian quan zai yu fazhan. Fazhan shi ying daoli*) (Yang Faren and Yang Li 2004: 27). Moreover, development, in their view, should be accelerated, as otherwise the gap in development will never be overcome (Yang Faren and Yang Li 2004: 32). What is more, like the contributors to the 2000 volume, Yang and Yang hold ethnic minorities responsible for guaranteeing the overall success of the modernisation project:

> If there is no well-off society among ethnic minorities and in the ethnic minority areas, there is no well-off society countrywide; if there is no economic prosperity and social progress among ethnic minorities and in the minority regions, then there is no prosperity anywhere in the country; if there is no modernisation among ethnic minorities and in the minority areas, then there is no modernisation overall of China.
> (Yang Faren and Yang Li 2004: 28)

Official and scholarly writings on the WDP present ethnic minority areas and China's West as mutually-defining and constituent terms: the West is a region inhabited by minorities, while minorities 'belong to' the West. The discursive characteristics assigned to the one are applied as well to the other. The official discourse thus melds and shapes both representations in the national imaginary. On the one hand, one of the main objectives of the WDP, as formulated by its supporters, is to resolve the ethnic question; on the other hand, resolution of the ethnic question is thought to be one of the guarantors of the project's success (Yuan Jingxia 2002: 22). The next section problematises this supposedly inseparable relationship between the West and ethnic minorities.

How ethnic is China's 'west'?

The main characteristic of China's western region, in view of most observers, is its ethnic character. They reference the following statistics in this regard: all 5 autonomous regions (*zizhiqu*), 27 out of 30 autonomous prefectures (*zizhizhou*) and 83 out of 120 counties (*zizhixian*) are located in western China; and the region is home to 46 out of 55 of China's ethnic minorities. Some talk about 'an invisible line' going through China, partitioning the country along economic, social, climatic and ethnic cleavages (Glantz *et al.* 2001). A different picture of China's ethnic patchwork emerges, however, when other official statistics are considered. To begin with, numerous ethnic minority populations inhabit the east, northeast, and other regions in China. Minorities live in *all* of China's 'developed' coastal provinces: there are 134 ethnic minority townships (*xiang*)[34] in Liaoning,

Table 6.1 Han and minority populations in the western region, 2000

Region	Total population	Han population		Minority population	
Chongqing	30,900,000	28,920,000	93.58%	1,980,000	6.42%
Gansu	25,620,000	23,390,000	91.31%	2,230,000	8.69%
Guangxi	44,890,000	27,680,000	61.66%	17,210,000	38.34%
Guizhou	35,250,000	21,910,000	62.15%	13,340,000	37.85%
Inner Mongolia	23,760,000	18,830,000	79.24%	4,930,000	20.74%
Ningxia	5,620,000	3,680,000	65.47%	1,940,000	34.53%
Qinghai	5,180,000	2,820,000	54.49%	2,360,000	45.51%
Shaanxi	36,050,000	35,870,000	99.51%	180,000	0.49%
Sichuan	83,290,000	79,140,000	95.02%	4,150,000	4.98%
Tibet	2,620,000	160,000	5.93%	2,460,000	94.07%
Xinjiang	19,250,000	7,820,000	40.61%	11,430,000	59.39%
Yunnan	42,880,000	28,550,000	66.59%	14,330,000	33.41%

Source: National Bureau of Statistics of China (2001), table 20.

18 in Zhejiang, 7 in Shandong, 17 in Fujian, 1 in Jiangsu, 6 in Guangdong and 12 on Hainan island (Yang Houdi 2001: 161–232). In fact, there are only two administrative areas in the whole country where there are no registered minority compounds: Shanxi province and the Shanghai municipality.[35] Chinese media reports and academic research reveal that in the 1990s about 24 million ethnic minorities – about a quarter of the entire minority population (according to some sources it is 34 per cent) – did not live in autonomous areas (Lai 2002: 446). [36] At the same time, the population of the majority Han group has been growing in the western provinces since the 1950s when the government started exercising the resettlement of the Han to the western region. Official statistics indicate that the Han population rises twice as quickly as the Uyghur, leaving aside 'floating workers' from the East. [37] Government-produced statistics reveal that even in predominately minority areas the Han nationality dominates. In Yunnan, which is home to twenty-five of China's ethnic minorities and where autonomous areas occupy 70 per cent of the province, the ethnic minorities comprise only one-third of the province's population (Guo Jiaji 2003: 23; see Table 6.1). Therefore, labelling the western region as the 'minority area' does not reflect the actual ethnic distribution in China. What it does instead is brand ethnic minorities with derogatory characteristics associated with life and economic conditions in some parts of the western provinces. This creates an artificial geographical division not only between ethnicities, but also between lifestyles, social conditions, and ultimately between the 'eastern Han part' and the 'western minority region'. By emphasising the ethnic minority character of the western region and by stressing ethnic minorities' 'rootedness' and belonging to the western region, the prevalent discourse localises

The politics of localisation 155

ethnic minorities within a rigidly-defined territorial and social niche, and perpetuates their subjugated position in the Chinese nation – however much the official rhetoric refers to the region as 'liberated'. Such discursive ascriptions in their turn generate a particular range of solutions, such as theWDP, to address the perceived problems.

Related to the aforementioned issue of ascribing western parts of China with ethnic minority characteristics, the official argument that the West is the most underdeveloped area of China and, therefore, needs special treatment from the government is difficult to sustain. China's central provinces, which until recently did not qualify for special help from the central government, [38] had demonstrated no better economic results than some of the western regions when the government launched the WDP (Goodman 2002: 131). Shanxi province, which is officially exclusively Han, had some of the worst economic indicators in the country. Anhui province, which is next to the 'developed' coastal areas, had a deep-seated reputation for being a poor locality and a source of beggars and women fleeing to prosperous neighbouring cities in search of domestic work (Sun Wanning 2001). Generally speaking, the central provinces had a higher GDP than the western region. However, GDP per capita indicated that people living in the western provinces were no worse off than the population of the central region (see Table 6.2). Such a situation leaves one wondering why the central regions were not included in the development project. It also makes one wonder whether economic development was in fact the government's actual objective.

Similarly, Chinese scholars declare that ethnic minority people make up about half of the total population of the poor.[39] Yet, the official rhetoric labels *all* minority regions as poverty-stricken, while the Han areas, many of which have similar or worse indicators of poverty, are never characterised in this manner. In fact, the western region is sometimes referred to as China's 'poverty belt' (Moneyhon 2002). Poverty is often said to have minority characteristics, and the link between the two is reinforced linguistically in expressions such as 'poverty alleviation funds for poverty-striken areas and Ethnic Minority Regions' (State Council, Western Region Development Office 2001a).

Official sources repeatedly stress that economic disparities are unavoidable and very difficult to overcome (Yuan Jingxia 2002: 22). In other words, the development gap is fixed as a general norm. In mixed areas, where both minorities and the majority live together, it is true that the minorities have a much lower income than the Han (Asian Development Bank 2003: 271). But generalisations about and objectifications of ethnic minorities as 'poor populations' not only disempower minorities, they also fail to capture the complexity of the problem of poverty in China. State-published statistics show that some Han-populated regions are as poor as certain minority areas, and not all in minority areas live below the poverty line. For example, a survey conducted by the State Ethnic Affairs Commission in 2004 in 11 provinces of the western region (Tibet was not included in the survey) revealed that most of China's poverty-stricken prefectures are located in the southwestern part of country, with the largest concentration in Sichuan, Guizhou and Yunnan – an area that comprises 62.5 per cent of the 77

Table 6.2 GDP in central and western provinces, 1999 and 2002

Province	GDP 1999		GDP 2002	
	Total (million yuan)	Per capita (yuan)	Total (million yuan)	Per capita (yuan)
Central region				
Anhui	2,908.59	4,707	3,569.10	5,816
Heilongjiang	2,897.41	7,660	3,882.20	10,132
Henan	4,576.10	4,894	6,168.73	6,436
Hubei	3,857.99	6,514	4,975.63	n/a
Hunan	3,326.75	5,105	4,340.94	5,656
Jiangxi	1,962.98	4,661	2,450.48	n/a
Jilin	1,669.56	6,341	2,246.12	8,334
Shanxi	1,506.78	4,727	2,017.54	6,146
Western region				
Chongqing	1,479.71	4,826	1,971.30	6,347
Gansu	931.98	3,668	1,161.43	4,493
Guizhou	911.86	2,475	1,185.04	3,153
Guangxi	1,953.27	4,148	2,455.36	n/a
Inner Mongolia	1,268.20	5,350	1,734.31	7,233
Ningxia	241.49	4,473	329.28	5,804
Qinghai	238.39	4,662	341.11	6,426
Shaanxi	1,487.61	4,101	2,035.96	n/a
Sichuan	3,711.61	4,452	4,875.12	5,808
Tibet	105.61	4,262	161.42	6,093
Xinjiang	1,168.55	6,470	1,598.28	8,382
Yunnan	1,855.74	4,452	2,232.32	n/a

Sources: National Bureau of Statistics of China (2000), table C-09; National Bureau of Statistics of China (2003).

prefectures the government has labelled as the most poverty-stricken (*e kun xian*) (Yuan Yan 2002: 24). This official finding makes the reference to the western region as poor highly problematic. Furthermore, while 257 out of 592 counties included in the state's plan for poverty alleviation were situated in minority areas, the rest were found in the Han-populated regions.[40] In the mid-1990s, Chinese news agencies drew attention to the impressive economic performance of the ethnic minorities in Henan province, where minorities make up only 1.24 per cent of the population but contributed 4 per cent of the provincial GDP.[41]

Official explanations also appeal to naturalist reasoning to explain poverty and the lack of development. See, for example, this explanation: 'Due to natural, historical and societal reasons, ethnic minorities in the project of economic culture development still drag behind developed regions' (Tang Zhixiang 2001: 1). Another study undertaken by Chinese scholars cites 'historical, objective, and concrete reasons' (*lishi de, keguan de, juti de yuanyi*) for the economic development gap between the minority West and predominately Han East (Yang Faren and Yang Li 2004: 15).

Most Chinese writings on development in the western region emphasise its economic and political dependence on the eastern part of the country. In other words, these writings suggest that, in order for the western region to achieve higher development levels, it needs economic assistance from the eastern provinces. This line of thinking is echoed in the formulation of favourable policies in the western region, which significantly differ from the policies implemented toward the East. The western provinces heavily rely on financial subsidies and assistance provided by the centre, while the coastal provinces attract domestic and foreign investments (Dan Ping and Zhang Xiaoxu 1998: 30).[42] Thus, in the early 2000s, government investments accounted for 34.64 per cent of all investments in the western region, while the eastern provinces received only 7.12 per cent of all investments in these regions (Hu Angang and Wen Jun 2003: 112). By contrast, the share of foreign capital in the economy of the western region is insignificant: only 1.24 per cent in 2003, as opposed to 86.2 per cent in the East (Yang Faren and Yang Li 2004: 8). Almost two out of every three enterprises in the western region are state owned (66.2 per cent), while fewer than half are state owned in the East (Tian Qunjian 2004: 629). In other words, the above-mentioned official line of reasoning for western underdevelopment and the framework of development work in the West stress the achievement of economic development indicators through financial investments closely administered by the centre. The development problems of today, however, are in many ways the result of pre-1978 policies. For example, Naughton's study has demonstrated that China's West has suffered more from earlier economic experiments carried out by the government than from the absence of government involvement (Naughton 2004). Nevertheless, the implications of the earlier policies on the economy of the western region remain ignored. Official accounts of the West's 'ethnic character', for instance, fail to address the fact that the majority of the Han population in the minority autonomous areas is made up of urban dwellers, while ethnic minorities cluster in the region's rural expanses.[43]

Though the majority of the small ethnic minority groups live in the mountainous areas of China's vast west, and undeniably require protection and support to maintain their unique lifestyles, traditions and cultures, the crude attachment of the ethnic label to the WDP and the rudimentary classification of China's west as ethnic and the east as Han – whereby the east designates the direction of development and orients the rest of the country towards it – do not capture the diverse experiences of development in China. Such classifications fail to recognise alternative paths of development that are already taking place and contributing in their own ways to China's economic advancement. Studies by Oakes and Litzinger demonstrate how the Miao and Yao minority groups have formulated and expressed their development interests in the spaces opened by the struggles between the Chinese Party-state and transnational capital (Oakes 1999; Litzinger 2002).[44]

158 *The politics of localisation*

If the dominant discussions on development recognised and celebrated these alternative practices as legitimate and desirable, it might help change the current central articulations of development in China. It would resonate with the calls of such prominent Chinese scholars as Wang Hui, who has been highly critical of the dominant official discussions on modernisation and the economic reforms (Wang Hui 2003: 147). Chinese intellectuals have called for more critical analysis as to how internal structures and relationships, such as between the developed east and the underdeveloped west, matter to our understanding of modern China (Wang Hui 2003: 141–87). One of the main challenges for China's modernisation project is to be aware of these internal factors and to overcome the effects of rudimentary classifications of the country's regions on development thinking and the formulation of modernisation strategies. These issues concern how a significant part of China's population – its ethnic minorities – is viewed.

Conclusion

This chapter analyses how ethnic minorities figure in the PRC's post-1978 socio-economic and political policies presented in the language of modernisation and development. The effects of these policies on the status of the ethnic minorities in China's national modernisation project is characterised as *localisation*, a mode of practice and discourse through which the Chinese state limits ethnic minorities' participation in the modernisation project. The Chinese state's localisation of ethnic minorities in the development process distances them from the proliferated mode of modern practices associated with consumerism, competitiveness, science, secularity (*shisu xing*) and openness. These attributes are routinely associated with an idea of the advanced modern culture ascribed to the Han majority. Ethnic minorities are negatively associated with traditional modes of culture marked as being agricultural, religious, autarchic and feudal. This delimitation places ethnic minorities and the Han at opposite ends of the scale measuring the meaning of being modern citizens.

Appadurai argues that in the global context the growing processes that undermine the nation-state's monopolisation of identity forms are beginning to challenge localisation practices of the state (Appadurai 1997: 189). Yet the position of the ethnic minorities in China's modernisation discourse and policies shows that by allocating a very specific place to ethnic minorities and by not recognising their possible deviations from the modernisation path, the Chinese state maintains and strengthens its authority over them. The state's policies towards ethnic minorities aim to curb and subjugate them to the centre through physical (i.e. territorial) attachment to the centre, implementation of the uniform model of economic development, homogenised organisation of diversity and limited preferential treatment. The subordinate status of the ethnic minorities in the Chinese nation-state renders them unable to fully participate in modernisation.

The 'ethnic question', revised since the start of the economic reforms, is largely understood in developmental terms, and targets such problems as poverty, economic stagnation and backward traditions. The notion of development, in turn, is limited to economic progress and serves the political interests of the elite and the Han majority. In general, one could argue that ethnicity in the current formulation of the Party and central government is equated with different aspects of the hampered economic development of particular ethnic groups.

The phrase 'unity in diversity', which the Party uses to describe ethnic minorities, becomes in fact 'uniformity in diversity' when ethnic minorities are considered against the deemed homogeneity of the dominant Han group. On the surface, China's leadership diligently advocates the principle of diversity:

> The richness of the world is a product of its diversity It is this diversity that is at the origin of wealth. It is the roots of prosperity It is also this diversity that made it possible and necessary for countries as well as for the people to interact and co-operate. It does not mean the suppression of difference.
> (Jiang Zemin 1997)

However, such pronouncements are mainly to justify China's political system, which runs on different lines to political systems in the West. The content and meaning of diversity are diminished, while the format the diversity takes is defined by the centre, with the periphery kept from taking any meaningful part in this process. The official development policies essentially juxtapose the ethnic minorities against the dominant Han, localising them in their uniform exoticism and organised difference.

The localised role of ethnic minorities in China's modernisation project contrast starkly with those toward the overseas Chinese. These policies adapt to the transnational and mobile nature of the overseas Chinese, and, indeed, encourage them to be mobile. As we saw in Chapter 5, overseas Chinese have been increasingly encouraged to participate flexibly in China's modernisation. The state's policies towards ethnic minorities and the official language accompanying them, on the other hand, reinforce minorities' subordinate position in the Chinese nation-state and prevent them from engaging in China's transformation on equal terms with other Chinese. The centrally-formulated modernisation strategies neither recognise the peculiarities of ethnic minorities nor account for their diversity.

The form of identity practiced and promoted at the national and, to a certain extent, transnational levels is one that is uniform and intolerant of diversity, and, one is bound to conclude, is of an exclusive ethnic character. The official discourse equates ethnicity and underdevelopment when minorities are concerned, but it does not attribute ethnic characteristics to the dominant group, the Han. The Han thus appear to be beyond any ethnic categorisation. Yet, racial and common ancestry factors are frequently invoked by the leadership in their portrayal of the modernising Chinese nation. As ethnic minorities are not direct descendants of the Yellow Emperor, they are assigned only a limited secondary role in the realisation of China's national modernisation goals.

Conclusion

When I was finishing this manuscript in July–September 2009, issues relating to ethnic minorities and overseas Chinese were brought forcefully to the fore by a series of loosely-related and often coincidental events. As during the events of spring–summer 2008 discussed in the Introduction, the issues associated with our marginal groups – most notably those pertaining to territoriality, ethnicity and citizenship – came again to the forefront in unforeseeable and contingent ways. These powerful events highlight the salience of the analysis undertaken in this book. In the span of just over one year, overseas Chinese and ethnic minorities were brought to worldwide attention twice. By looking at how the conceptual margins of the Chinese nation figure in these events, we can better understand what the Chinese nation is and what it is not, and where it starts and where it ends. In a different way, but one consistent with this book's analysis, these events starkly reveal the ambiguous premises of China's national project which is sustained through the seemingly contradictory discourses and practices of rigid localised and loose de-territorialised identity politics.

In July 2009, violent clashes broke out between the Han and Uyghurs in Urumqi, the capital of China's Xinjiang Autonomous Region. The coverage and interpretation of these events by the Chinese official media followed the patterns of its coverage of the events in Tibetan areas in the previous year. The Chinese government blamed the outbreak of violence in Urumqi, which led to 197 deaths and over 1,500 arrests, on the 'separatist' forces and the Internet, rather than on the PRC's ethnic policies. Commoners from the Han majority in Xinjiang accused Uyghurs of being 'ungrateful' for the development which the region had been enjoying.[1] Despite the problematic nature of the ethnic policies which the unrest in Xinjiang clearly showed, the Chinese leadership insisted that economic development was the main solution to ethnic strife. There were no attempts by the central government to investigate how the implementation of economic development in the minority areas might have caused the friction and violent outbreaks of frustration among the ethnic populations. When President Hu Jintao visited Xinjiang after the violent clashes in late August 2009, he identified economic development as the central task for the region when dealing with ethnic issues.[2] Similarly, a White Paper on Ethnic Policy issued by the central government in September 2009 – only four days before the 60th anniversary of the founding of the PRC – confidently stated, 'The state is convinced that quickening the economic and social development of minority communities and minority areas is the fundamental solution to China's ethnic issues'.³ The Chinese leaders have still not officially recognised that the PRC has ethnic problems which cannot be solved by economic development and modernisation, or indeed that specific development initiatives can exacerbate rather than resolve these problems.

Many Han people in the Xinjiang Autonomous Region were dissatisfied that the government and the Party were not able to protect them from the violent Uyghurs, and became critical of the government's minority policies. They saw the government's policies as too lenient and favourable to the Uyghurs and other minorities.⁴ It is apparent from their accusations that these Han perceive the Chinese government, and even more the Party, as the defender of Han interests rather than representative of all Chinese people, irrespective of their ethnic (or any other) allegiances. Similarly, when further clashes between Uyghurs and Han broke out following mysterious syringe attacks on people in Urumqi in August 2009, many Han protesters demanded the dismissal of the Xinjiang Party secretary on the grounds that he was not able to protect them from the local Uyghurs. From the perspective of the Han, in other words, Uyghurs should be mistrusted and treated as outsiders in their own Autonomous Region, and the Han should be protected from them by the Party.

These events and subsequent ones shed light on the status of Uyghurs and other minorities in the Chinese nation. The violent clashes of the 5 July 2009 in Urumqi were deemed by many in China to have been sparked by a brawl between Uyghur and Han workers at a toy factory in Guangdong. The central government's policies of transferring Uyghur workers, mostly women, to factories in southeast China – which were allegedly aimed at improving mutual understanding and interaction between different nationalities and providing new job opportunities and skills for the Uyghurs – boomeranged in Xinjiang's capital in the form of frustrated hopes, suspicion, mistrust and ultimately violence. The events showed that what had previously been seen by China watchers as a problem confined to ethnic areas concentrated in China's distant west was, in fact, faced in other parts of the country, especially where many migrant workers go for job opportunities. One recent scholarly study estimates that there are around 1.5 million ethnic minorities working at the factories in Guangdong alone (Gladney 2009). While some of the workers had been lured by the promise of better wages and working conditions, many had been coerced into this arrangement by threats of high fines by the state. These state policies played a significant role in the experiences of many ethnic migrant workers. It is therefore short-sighted, as Chapter 6 argued, to see China's ethnic minorities as localised populations, confined to the western part of the country. The so-called 'ethnic question' is not simply a problem of China's west, where many ethnic minorities are concentrated. Equally, the ethnic problems cannot be attributed to ethnic minorities' harsh living conditions and traditional culture, as the official discourse suggests. An analysis of the state's coercive policies of transferring Uyghur workers from predominately Uyghur areas of Xinjiang to the southeastern part of China could help us better understand the deterioration of ethnic relations. ⁵

Another prominent development in Xinjiang is the increased international profile of Rebiya Kadeer, whose role for Uyghurs around the world is now compared to that of the Dalai Lama for Tibetans. A successful businesswoman and mother of eleven children, Kadeer was once celebrated as a symbol of the success of China's ethnic policies and of what ethnic minorities could achieve in China. However, as soon as she openly criticised the Chinese government's treatment of ethnic minorities, in particular Uyghurs, she was imprisoned; later, when she was out on bail for medical treatment, she went into exile in the United States. Upon arriving in the United States in 2005, Kadeer pledged to retain her Chinese citizenship and fight for the human rights of Uyghurs in China. Since then the Chinese state has continued to view Kadeer as a subject of China. After the violent clashes in Xinjiang in July 2009, the Chinese leadership and media implicitly treated Kadeer as a Chinese national – she was called a 'Xinjiang separatist' and a 'Chinese separatist', or simply patronised as 'Rebiya'. From a model Chinese citizen she became a national traitor who subverted China's territorial unity and stability. She is seen as an ungrateful subject of China who betrayed her state and as a traitor seeking to undermine China's territorial unity. Despite her exile and dissident status, in the official representation of Rebiya Kadeer, the Chinese state stresses that she is a subject of the Chinese state. This establishes China's dual relationship with Rebiya Kadeer where she is treated as both being inside and outside of China's sovereignty.

In the case of another Uyghur, the Chinese state has interpreted the issues of citizenship and national affiliation even more loosely. In 2006, Huseyincan Celil, a Canadian national of Chinese Uyghur origins, was arrested in Uzbekistan and handed over to China on the grounds of 'terrorism prevention'. Throughout his trial and subsequent imprisonment, the Chinese government did not recognise his Canadian citizenship, treating him as a Chinese citizen, though according to the Nationality Law, China does not recognise dual citizenship; his Chinese citizenship should have been revoked as soon as he assumed Canadian nationality.

These conflicting ways of dealing with Uyghurs and interpreting their relationship with the PRC reflect the problem of Uyghurs' place in the Chinese nation. Although the case of Uyghurs might appear extreme and unrepresentative of other ethnic minorities in China, it shares common features with them. How to view, define and manage relations with ethnic minorities remains a big question for the Chinese state, especially when the minorities go abroad. The government states that over one million overseas Chinese originate from Xinjiang (Wang Linyan and Long Junying 2009), but it is not clear how many of them are Han, Uyghur or other nationalities. When ethnic minorities stay in China, they are technically subjects of the People's Republic, although many might not have passports and are thus denied the right of free movement. Once they go abroad, their affiliation with the People's Republic is more problematic – most frequently they are seen as traitors, separatists or terrorists who should not be trusted. At the same time, if they do not explicitly renounce their Chinese citizenship, they fall into the Chinese state's formulation of the overseas Chinese. Official Beijing's recently-coined and problematic term 'Chinese ethnic minorities overseas' and the state policies associated with it, as discussed in Chapter 5, show the problems that China encounters in its ethnic relations and the place of ethnic minorities in the Chinese nation. For example, while the Uyghurs' territory, the Xinjiang Autonomous Region, is an inalienable part of the PRC, the position of the Uyghur people is much more ambiguous. At large, the Uyghurs are viewed and treated as problematic subjects of the Chinese nation, who, if they want to be part of China's national modernisation project, have to adjust to the transformations formulated and implemented by the Chinese state. The state's inconsistent applications of the principle of Chinese nationality shows the difficulties of establishing the contours of the Chinese nation even in the legal sense.

But it is not only the Uyghurs who do not sit comfortably within the framework of the officially-defined Chinese nation. While the modernising PRC officially represents itself as a fixed territorial entity whose political boundaries are also the boundaries of a single cultural community, it has been struggling to combine ethnic and territorial elements, continuously fusing and negotiating them. In its search for its own modernisation path, China pursues a nation-building project that shifts the boundaries of the constituencies of the project as it goes along. The official discourse encompasses overseas Chinese as Han while pursuing policies that encourage minorities to change in order to properly join the Chinese nation-state.

The Chinese nation and ethnicity

Part of the problem of meaningfully including ethnic minorities in the conception of the Chinese nation is that many official formulations place significant emphasis on racially-defined ethnic and blood relations as a foundation of the nation. This originally nationalist principle, as discussed in Chapter 1, was recently mentioned at the Eighth National Congress of Returned Overseas Chinese and their Relatives, which took place on 15–17 August 2009, shortly after the unrest in Xinjiang. Commenting on the achievements of the All-China Federation of Returned Overseas Chinese, Wang Zhaoguo, a member of the Political Bureau of the CCP's Central Committee, stressed that 'blood lineage, professional linkage and geographical linkage' served as the bases of the work of the Federation. In other words, blood lineage was stressed as one of the premises on which the government defines who belongs to the returned overseas Chinese and shapes its policies towards this group. 'Blood relations' are also often repackaged as cultural links.[6] This sense of common Chineseness uniting Chinese with their country is often internalised by elite transnational Chinese who find themselves in the advantageous position of benefiting from citizenships of several countries (Liu Hong 2010: 23). Recently, multiple national allegiances of overseas Chinese have been criticised by the PRC's netizens and media in relation to more than twenty actors chosen to be in the Chinese state-commissioned and sponsored film *Founding of the Republic (Jianguo Daye)*, which is linked to the national celebrations of the 60th anniversary of the founding of the PRC.[7] Chinese actors who assumed a nationality of another country were seen by many people in China as not fully patriotic and undeserving of acting in a film glorifying China's revolutionary history. Confronted on this issue by the Chinese media, Wu Junmei, a Chinese actress who has become a US citizen and was selected to play the wife of Chiang Kaishek in the film, defended her choice of US citizenship by stating that 'nationality is just a symbol which does not change the nature of one being Chinese' (Wu Zhong 2009).

In his influential essay on 'Cultural China', briefly mentioned in the Introduction, Tu Weiming, an acclaimed Harvard professor of Chinese origins, echoes Wu Junmei's sentiment. In his analysis of the three symbolic 'universes' of Cultural China, Tu includes overseas Chinese in the second symbolic universe (Tu 1991). He defines Chineseness 'in terms of full participation in the economic, political, and social life of a Chinese community or civilization', which is in line with Sun Yatsen's perspective on the nation and resembles Stalin's and Mao's definitions of a nation, with the exception of their postulation of common territory as a necessary component. Tu argues that common 'ethnicity, language, history, and worldview' constitute the core of Cultural China's second symbolic universe, while constituting most of the first, territorial universe. Tu sees the possibility of overseas Chinese actively participating in the construction of a 'truer' vision of Chineseness. For Tu, overseas Chinese are primary in defining Chineseness. However, it is not clear how China's ethnic minorities feature in Tu's Cultural China. He does not mention them as participants or negotiators of the terms of Cultural China. In other words, Tu, very much like Sun Yatsen and the Chinese revolutionaries of the early twentieth century, considers the Han majority the backbone of Chinese culture.

Importantly, Tu Weiming argues that 'the meaning of being Chinese is basically not a political question' (Tu 1991: 28). This opinion would probably be shared by many people who identify themselves as Han Chinese within and outside China. However, the way the Chinese state utilizes the legal tools of citizenship, nationality and ethnic categorisation – the most basic instruments in constituting the Chinese nation – has real political implications, as they affect the lives of many people inside and outside of China. The status of ethnic minorities in China is strictly designated in line with the procedures of ethnic categorisation discussed in Chapter 2. The rigid character of the regime of ethnicity at the domestic level has recently become evident in the case of He Chuanyang, a high school student from Chongqing whose national exam score, the highest in his province, was annulled after it was discovered that his father had changed Chuanyang's nationality status from Han to the Tujia minority in order to qualify for twenty additional exam points (Li 2009). At the same time, the rigidity of the Chinese law does not prevent many overseas Chinese from taking advantage of a foreign citizenship without revoking their Chinese citizenship, and from benefiting from favourable treatments made available to them by the Chinese state, as discussed in Chapter 5. While this grey area in Chinese law has been intensively debated by many overseas Chinese (who lobbied the Chinese government to amend the Nationality Law to create a legal foundation for dual citizenship), the decision of the government was that 'the conditions for the dual nationality law have not matured' sufficiently (Liu Hong 2010: 22). Unlike many other states which changed their legislation in favour of dual citizenship, China operates within the single citizenship framework and does not show signs of wanting to change it. Rather, China is quite successful at by-passing its own territorial limitations in conceiving citizenship and in liaising with the Han overseas Chinese on the assumption of their patriotic and ethnic allegiances to China. The consolidation of a single transnational patriotic front around the centre in Beijing makes this arrangement more than an exercise conducive to China's economic prominence. It takes the form of an ethnic-ideological formation affecting the way the Chinese nation is shaped. The ambiguity of the term 'Chinese nation' and the flexibility and rigidity used in designating who belongs to it, and to what nationality within it, shows the contingent premises of the Chinese nation.

The narrow and broad senses of the Chinese nation, and the ambiguity at the heart of the term *zhonghua minzu*, which as we have seen has been used by Chinese governments in definitive terms since the early twentieth century, reveals a conceptual problem which China's leadership has not resolved. The PRC continues to experiment with both the notions of its imperial past and the legal norms of the modern international system. The term *minzu* (nation or nationality) is very illustrative. Whenever it is used in the context of the PRC, ethnic minorities and ethnic minority areas immediately come to mind. While the official interpretation would be that *minzu* is a short version of the concept *shaoshu minzu*, the minority connotations of *minzu* are so imbedded in the subconsciousness of Chinese that it is very unlikely that they would use it when they talk about the Han nationality in the context of the Chinese state. This liberates the Han majority from the associations that burden 55 other officially-recognised ethnic groups in China. It is likely that, from the point of view of the official Chinese, the Han majority group is not viewed as an ethnic conglomeration – as it was at the end of the nineteenth century when Sun Yatsen, in an attempt to consolidate the Chinese nation, introduced the principle of nationalism (*minzu zhuyi*) as part of his *Three Principles of the People*. Notably, the most acclaimed Chinese anthropologist, Fei Xiaotong, talked about two different levels of understanding *minzu* (1988: 167). In Fei's interpretation, at one level this concept encompasses all people living within the territorial boundaries of the PRC, and refers to *zhonghua minzu*. At another level, it refers to *shaoshu minzu*, or ethnic minorities. Importantly, the Han nationality is left out of Fei's interpretation. In other words, the Han Chinese, of which overseas Chinese are often deemed to be part, are not ascribed ethnic attributes and could be seen as post-*minzu* – that is, post-ethnic – and modern, in contrast to other ethnic minorities. At the same time, racially-invoked Han ethnicity with emphasis on common blood and ancestry is reinvented and utilised by the Chinese state, and embraced by many overseas Chinese, such as Wu Junmei, as a category uniting China with overseas Chinese. Thus, ethnicity is produced as a notion that combines opposite, conflicting characteristics. Used in different contexts for different audiences, it can connote either backwardness or development, traditionalism or modernity, sedentarism or mobility, and localised or de-territorialised identities.

The unifying principles of China's national modernisation project, as discussed in Chapter 3, tell us what Chinese leaders would like China and the Chinese

166 *Conclusion*

people to be. China's official scholarly attempts to produce China's own modernisation theory are incapacitated by the conviction in the validity of 'scientific' interpretations of human development. While these attempts cannot effectively foretell China's development, they unmistakably point to China's aspirations to be a developed and internationally respected nation. This drive to convince itself and the world that China's development model is distinct and deserving, and the way Chinese scholars think about China's development process and that of the world demonstrate an almost fatal inability to escape the legacies of Western imperialism. Far from overcoming these legacies, Chinese officials and scholars adopt and recreate them through generating new relations of inequality and domination within and outside China.

In the process of working towards national modernisation goals, Chinese leaders keep experimenting with legal, policy-oriented, and conceptual aspects of Chinese nationhood. The ways these experiments are implemented at the conceptual margins of the Chinese nation highlight its problematic nature. The constitutive elements of the Chinese nation can be understood through processes involving the extremes of modern/traditional, barbarian/civilised, marginal/core, and inside/outside. The Chinese nation is produced somewhere in-between, at the meeting points, often coincidental ones, of these dialogical processes. Overseas Chinese and ethnic minorities – groups which Chinese governments have aspired to bring into line with its nation-building attempts – reflect this incongruity at the heart of the Chinese national project.

The Chinese nation and territoriality

Many scholars discuss the coming of a borderless world of diasporic networks, or the further eruption of ethnic conflicts and their significance for the idea of a nation-state. This book, however, demonstrates how the phenomenon of transnationalism does not conflict with the nation-state. In China, it shapes the nation-state, including the way it formulates its national identity. China's national identity is constructed through the state's transnational initiatives to invoke a common modernising identity and its denial of alternative development paths to the ethnic minority populations within the PRC. Examining the intersection of territorial and conceptual discourses shows how the politics of official identity is played out and how identity strategies transform the Chinese nation without necessarily eroding it. Our analysis demonstrates that, although marginal groups are clearly, albeit problematically, defined through official categorisation and institutional policies, it is not clear what constitutes the core of the Chinese nation. The 'core' thus is best understood through the analysis of its relationships with its conceptual margins.

By looking at how China has been historically preoccupied with certain population groups across its national borders, and how it produced particular representations of these groups, this book demonstrates that territory is both a salient and an ambivalent feature in the construction of the Chinese nation. The flexible use of territoriality as an attribute of the Chinese nation can be shown by briefly summarising the official use of *minzu*. When the *minzu* concept was first popularised, at the time when the Chinese national idea was fuelled by the modernisation drive and the resistance to the imperialist ambitions of Western powers and Japan, it was not used in a territorially-binding way. On the contrary, as discussed in Chapter 1, stress was placed on the common racial origins of Chinese worldwide. Following the establishment of the PRC, the CCP's utilisation of the term *minzu* shifted to the domestic level and was directed at the formulation of policies towards China's minority nationalities through the class interpretation of the nationality question (Chapter 3). Territorial boundaries were a guarantee of the survival of the communist regime within the PRC, but did not limit the regime to the restricted territory.

The framework of the post-socialist modernisation project in China suggests that the values promoted as part of the project include overseas Chinese who are not part of China's territory. At the same time, the state-led national modernisation project limits the participation of the diverse populations within the territory of China who do not subscribe to the uniform values promoted by the project. In particular, Chapter 3 shows how the very concept of modernisation as used in China's official discourse precludes accounting for diversity in Chinese society, and creates the Chinese nation through a series of hierarchical relations at subnational and transnational levels. The analysis of the state discourses and policies toward ethnic minorities and overseas Chinese demonstrates the Chinese leadership's attempt to create a unified modernising Chinese identity across its territorial borders. In this attempt, overseas Chinese are produced as progressive and patriotic members of the Chinese nation who actively participate in the national modernisation project, while ethnic minorities are symbolically and geographically localised to a secondary role within China. These politics of de-territorialisation and localisation are two sides of one national project aimed at refining the power of the Chinese state.

Despite their marginal positions, overseas Chinese and ethnic minorities have been at the crux of important political events in distant and recent Chinese history. It remains to be seen whether the issues pertaining to overseas Chinese and ethnic minorities will continue to be at the forefront of future Chinese politics. The analysis presented in this book suggests that these marginal groups are crucial for understanding the nature of the Chinese nation. This is because, when brought together, these groups and their relationships to the Chinese nation highlight the issues at the heart of China's identity politics and the legitimacy of the Communist Party. These issues relate to the questions of who comprises the Chinese nation and who it represents. As China's role in the world grows, these questions are likely to become more prominent. The changing statuses of overseas Chinese, ethnic minorities and other marginal groups in China further reveal how China's leaders interpret China's national identity, deal with difference, and accommodate the changes engulfing China and the world.

Notes

Introduction

1 See, for example, the report by Shaila Dewan 'Chinese Students in US Fight View of Their Home', *New York Times*, 29 April 2008.
2 Chang Ping, a deputy editor-in-chief of the Southern Metropolis Daily, wrote in his blog 'if we use nationalism as the weapon to resist the westerners, then how can we persuade the ethnic minorities to abandon their nationalism and join the mainstream nation-building?' Many forums on the China.com labelled Chang Ping a traitor. See, for example www.danwei.org/internet/southern_metropolis_chang_ping.php.
3 In his early reform period speeches, Deng Xiaoping called for a dialogue and a more active collaboration between mainland and overseas Chinese, as well as encouraging overseas Chinese communities to contribute to the nation-state economic modernisation. He also appealed to their patriotic feelings, saying that 'they also want to see China grow strong and prosperous'(Deng Xiaoping 1986). In a later speech criticising Western-imposed economic sanctions after the Tiananmen tragedy, Deng Xiaoping (1990) refers to both mainland and overseas Chinese with the motto to 'bestir our selves' in order 'to revitalize the Chinese nation'.
4 Speech by Hu Jintao to the 17th National Congress, 15 October 2007, www.china elections.net/newsinfo.asp?newsid = 12146 (accessed 25 September 2009).
5 There are no Chinese popular organisations for ethnic minorities.
6 This methodological tool is suggested by Foucault, who calls for taking the analysis of the technologies of power outside the workings of institutions, to concentrate on the analysis of function and de-centre the object of analysis (madness, delinquency, nation etc. are not treated as a ready-made objects) (Foucault 2007: 1 17–18).

1 Overseas Chinese and ethnic minorities in imperial and Republican China

1 Hostetler presents a fuller account of this argument in her 2001 monograph (Hostetler 2001).
2 Perdue (2005a) presents a rich account of the official historical narratives of the Zhungah Mongols created by the Qing with the help of the Jesuits. Numerous ethnographic atlases and maps were produced to categorise nationalities inhabiting the territory of the Empire, assigning them with particular histories, identities and cultures.
3 Crossley (1990: 8) points to the evidence that in the late Qing period the intermingled idea of ethnic and racial distinction was embraced, and shaped the ethnic composition of the Empire.

4   The Chinese term *minzu* derives and was developed from Western, Japanese and Soviet interpretations of the idea of nationhood, simultaneously fusing and differing from them. There is no direct translation of the concepts of nation and nationality into Chinese, and there is no English equivalent for the Chinese concept *minzu*. *Minzu*, a key term, is used in Chinese interchangeably for 'nation', 'nationality' and 'ethnic group'.

5   The relation between the two has come through significant transformations. The modern understanding of *ti–yong* is similar to that between value and instrument. For more on the development of *ti–yong* connotations, see Tong Shijun (2000: Chapter 4) and Hughes (2009).

6   Hao Chang (1971) notes that in his post-exile writings, Liang clearly refers to *qun* as a nation-state rather than as both the national and world community, the trend which dominated in his pre-exile writings. He later recognised the impracticality of the ideal of a universal community. Liang's view of nationalism was of popular character where state was the property of the public *guomin*, unlike the earlier imperial notion of *guojia*, where it essentially was regarded as the property of the dynastic family or revolutionaries' blurring of blood, race and political boundaries of the nation-state.

7   Sun Yatsen's three principles of people are nationalism, democracy and people's livelihood. For more on Sun Yatsen's principles, see Sun Yatsen (1932), D'Elia (1974) and Chen (1995).

8   It was the first domestic law that dealt with overseas Chinese affairs. It followed the *jus sanguinis* principle in defining Chinese as anyone, regardless of the locality, born to a father who was Chinese at the time of its birth or to a Chinese mother if the father's identity was indeterminate or unknown (McNair 1933: 122).

9   *Zhong* is often used together with *zu* (tribe, clan, lineage). Dikötter (1992: 70–71) gives the following explanations of *zhong*: '*Zhong* was the central element of a complex terminology, it meant "seed", "breed", or "biological species", and was used in association with *lei*, "type", "category", in *zhonglei* at discursive level of race as type'.

10 The myth of blood was sealed by elevating the figure of the Yellow Emperor to a national symbol. The Yellow Emperor (*Huangdi*) was a mythical figure thought to have reigned from 2697 to 2597 BC. He was hailed as the first ancestor (*shizu*) of the Han race, and his portrait served as the frontispiece in many nationalist publications.

11 Sun Yatsen writes in his *Three Principles of People*: 'The Chinese people have shown the great loyalty to family and clan with the result in China there have been familyism and clan-ism but no real nationalism. Foreign observers say that the Chinese are like a sheet of loose sand. ... The unity of the Chinese people had stopped short at the clan and has not extended to the nation. ... China, since the Ch'in and Han dynasties, has been developing a single state out of a single race, while foreign countries have developed many states from one race and have included many nationalities within one state. ... The Chinese race totals four hundred million people, for the most part, the Chinese people are of Han or Chinese race with common blood, common language, common religion, and common customs – a single, pure race' (Sun Yatsen 1932: 2, 5).

12 In addition to common blood as the first and most important characteristic of the race/nation, Sun Yatsen, among others, mentions a common lifestyle (livelihood), language, religion, customs and habits. Although he recognises (1932: 12) that there are several races numbering in total no more than a million people of 'alien' races within the territory of China, such as Mongolians, Manchus, Tibetans and Turks, later in the book, he notes that at least two of them (Mongols and Manchus) were absorbed by the Han, thus 'becoming

fully Chinese', i.e. Han (ibid.: 31).   Thus, he continues, 'although China has been twice subjected politically, the race has not been seriously injured' (ibid.).

13 According to Sun Yatsen (1932: 8) a group of people united by the force of nature is a race, and a group developed by human forces is a state. He further equates race and nationality in opposition to state.

14 Harrison (2000: 100–101) gives a detailed historical account of different flags which were considered to be adopted as a national symbol during the period of Republican China, and describes the political tensions and debates alongside which the five-colour flag was recognised as a national one. Sun Yatsen famously opposed this decision and called for the adoption of the Shining Sun flag as the national.

15 Although the First CCP Congress took place in 1921, it did not issue any declarations; therefore, CCP documentary history begins in 1922, when two public statements, the First Manifesto on the Current Situation and the Manifesto of the Second Congress were issued (Brandt *et al.* 1959).

16 In 1934–35 The Chinese communists covered a 6,000-mile trek across China from southwest to northwest to escape the threat of annihilation by GMD forces, which took them through some of the most heavily populated minority areas. During this time, it became imperative that communists gained the support of the minorities in their struggle against GMD.

17 There is no single opinion on this issue. While Chang Chih-I (in Moseley 1966) notes that self-determination for minorities continued to be emphasised by the party until at least 1946, Connor (1984: 84) notes that 'this emphasis is not reflected in known party declarations made after the mid-1930s'.

18 Stalin (1954: 339) makes a clear distinction between the right of self-determination and the right of national autonomy. He states that 'cultural-national autonomy presupposes the integrity of the multi-national state, whereas self-determination goes outside the framework of this integrity, and that self-determination endows a nation with complete rights, whereas national autonomy endows it only with "cultural rights"'.

2 Overseas Chinese and minority nationalities in socialist nation-building

1 For the classic study advancing this argument, see Fairbank (1968).

2 This is not to say that other criteria of Stalin's, such as common territory, language and livelihood, fitted well to China's situation. On the contrary, as Dreyer points out (1976: 143–46), they were lacking in most cases.

3 Heberer (1989: 12) introduces the term 'nationality-state' for a state where 'all nationalities are normally equal and do not question the integrity of the state'.

4 The Manifesto of the Second National Congress lists 'unification of China proper (including Manchuria) into a genuine democratic republic' and 'the achievement of a genuine democratic republic by the liberation of Mongolia, Tibet, and Xinjiang into a free federation' among seven primary CCP objectives (Manifesto 1959: 64).

5 For more on social transformation in minority regions, see Fei Xiaotong (1981a, 1981b).

6 This institution was later renamed the Central University for Nationalities.

7 In 1952 the General Programme for the Implementation of Nationality Regional Autonomy of the Chinese People's Republic was adopted. It classified minority areas into three levels: regional, district and county.

8 In Fei Xiaotong's interpretation, an identification project was necessary in order to guarantee equal representation of the ethnic minorities' interests.
9 At the time of the PRC's creation in 1949, there were eleven written languages of ethnic minorities used regularly, and seven used sporadically (Heberer 1989: 16).
10 A survey carried out in the 1950s revealed that out of every one hundred overseas Chinese who remitted money to China, 38 were manual labourers, 18 were shop proprietors, 14 were store employees, 10 were hawkers, 9 were store managers and 1 had other positions (Lu Yusun 1956: 57–58).
11 Of the thirty overseas Chinese positions, five were allotted to Malaya, four each to Indonesia and Thailand, two each to Indo-China and the Americas, and one each to Burma, Philippines, North Borneo, Mongolia/Korea, Japan, India/Pakistan, Europe, Africa and Oceania. Four were left unidentified (Fitzgerald 1972: 19).
12 In 1946 a CIA report on Chinese Minorities in Southeast Asia warned of the potential utilisation of the Chinese communities in the Southeast Asian countries as the 'fifth column' (Central Intelligence Group 1946).
13 A special task of enrolling more overseas Chinese students into schools in mainland China was carried out by agents sent for this purpose to the overseas Chinese schools as students by the All-China Student's Union (Lu Yusun 1956: 50)
14 The Five Principles of Peaceful Coexistence were formulated by the Chinese government in 1954. These principles were: mutual respect for territorial integrity and sovereignty; mutual nonaggression; noninterference in each other's internal affairs; equality and mutual benefit; and peaceful coexistence. At the Bandung Conference in 1955, the PRC together with other Asian and African countries formulated the Ten Principles on the basis of the Five Principles.
15 As revealed by Chang Paomin (1980: 290), although most of the Chinese in Southeast Asia belonged to the working class, they (especially in Malaysia and Singapore) were supportive of noncommunist or anti-communist parties.

3 Post-socialist modernisation and China's national outlook

1 Worship of Western values was intrinsic in the 1980s criticism of Chinese traditional culture and was epitomised in the TV series *River Elegy*. Public debate on the need of Westernisation resurfaced in the late 2000s with the publication of the books *The Ugly Chinese* by Bai Yang and *Chinese History Revisited* by Xiao Jiansheng. All three works were banned in the PRC. A number of the Chinese intellectuals, referred to as liberals by the scholars of Chinese intellectual thought, have called for embracement of Western values and institutions (Fewsmith 2001; Zhang Xudong 2002; Davies 2007).
2 *Xinhua*, 26 June 2005.
3 See 'Building harmonious society crucial for China's progress: Hu', *People's Daily Online*, 27 June 2005, http://english.peopledaily .com.cn/200506/27/eng20050627_192495.html.
4 *People's Daily Online*, 1 March 2004.
5 For the full text of the White Paper on China's Peaceful Development Road, see *People's Daily Online*, 22 December , 2005, www .china.org.cn/english/2005/Dec/152669.htm.
6 'Central Committee's Foreign Affairs Meeting Held in Beijing; Hu Jintao and Wen Jiabao Made Keynote Speeches', *People's Daily*, 24 August 2006.

7 *People's Daily Online*, 15 February 2007.
8 See 'The Report on the National Conference on United Front Theoretical Work' (1989) and 'The United Front is Still the Magic Weapon' (1989).
9 'Speech by Hu Jingtao to the 17th National Congress', *Shanghai Daily*, 25 October 2007.
10 Woodside (1998) has made a well-observed comment on the perception of post-modernism by Chinese scholars, which seems to be appropriate in our case: 'Postmodernist complaints about the deficiencies of "foundational" theories of this kind are still confined largely to a Western academic intelligentsia; they may even seem – to Asian intellectuals who misunderstand them – to be a veiled effort to deny Asians to the empowerment of modernity'.
11 Callahan (2008) discusses a similar trend in Chinese social sciences where the production of distinctly Chinese notions is regarded as a manifestation of China's growing soft power.
12 The 'five stresses' are the stress on decorum, courtesy, hygiene, discipline and morals, and the 'four beauties' are to do with the improvement of mind, language, behaviour and environment (Chang Ching-li 1983: 23).
13 For a discussion on the influences of the new discourse on harmonious society on China's policies, see Zheng and Tok (2007)..
14 The themes of China Modernisation Reports curiously mirror the priority policy orientations of Chinese leadership. The topic for the 2009 Report is Cultural Modernisation; 2007 – Ecological Modernisation; 2006 – Societal Modernisation; 2005 – Economic Modernisation; 2004 – Regional Modernisation; 2003 – Modernisation Theory, Orientations and Prospects.
15 See Greenhalgh and Winckler (2005) for more on the centrality of science in contemporary China.

4 Ethnic minorities and overseas Chinese in the post-socialist modernisation discourse

1 According to the official Chinese statistics, in 2007 there were 2.9 million ethnic minority officials serving at the local levels of administration (regions, prefectures and counties). See 'China has nearly three million cadres from ethnic minorities', *People's Daily Online*, 24 February 2007, http://english.people.com.cn/200702/24/eng20070224_352120.html. However, the proportion of ethnic minorities in Party organs at the local level is much lower than the proportion in administration. Party secretaries in the PRC's autonomous regions are commonly Han Chinese.
2 In the co-authored book, Ma Rong and Zhou Xin (1999) argue for the need to dilute ethnic identities of minorities in China and strengthen their identification with the Chinese state.
3 The Chinese BBC discussion thread is available at https://meme2028.appspot.com/news.bbc.co.uk/chinese/simp/hi/newsid_5360000/newsid_5366500/5366548.stm (accessed 20 June 2007).
4 According to Zhuang Guotu (2001: 380), overseas Chinese invested around 2.277 billion US$ in south China in the period from 1979 to 2000. See Chapter 5 for a more detailed discussion of overseas Chinese investments in China.
5 Actually used FDI is a statistical indicator used in China's annual statistical reports to denote foreign capital utilised by all units and departments, including the Sino-foreign joint ventures, Sino-foreign cooperative enterprises, ventures exclusively with foreign

investment, foreign-funded stock companies, Sino-foreign cooperative development projects and other corporate enterprises (including the enterprises funded by entrepreneurs from Hong Kong, Macao and Taiwan).
6 The Chinese-Thai president of a TV station in Thailand similarly views China as 'a reliable backing for overseas Chinese'. See 'Mighty China is a strong backing for overseas Chinese', *People's Daily Online*, 1 October 2009, http://english.people.com.cn/90001/90776/90785/6775898.html.
7 The other three traditions are the tradition of hard work and self-sacrifice, the tradition of getting on well with others, and the tradition of unity and mutual help (FBIS, 22 June 2001).
8 FBIS, 22 June 2001.
9 See, for example, 'Overseas Chinese donate to help fight snow havoc', *People's Daily Online*, 7 February 2008, http://english.people.com.cn/90001/90776/6351934.html (accessed 20 September 2009), and 'Chinese living abroad donate 160 million *yuan* to quake-hit regions', *People's Daily Online*, 16 May 2008, http://english.people.com.cn/90001/90776/6412727.html (accessed 20 September 2009).
10 Chinese spies have been identified as the single greatest risk to the American technology sector by a congressional advisory panel (*Times* online, 15 November 2007, www.timesonline.co.uk/tol/news/world/article2878525.ece, accessed 25 September 2009).
11 'US arrests four "Chinese spies"', *BBC News Online*, 11 February 2008, http://news.bbc.co.uk/2/hi/americas/7239829.stm (accessed 25 September 2009).
12 FBIS, 29 September 1999.
13 'My Chinese Heart' (*wo de Zhongguo xin*) is a popular song among overseas Chinese, www.youtube.com/watch?v = kaEOfSxi6jI&feature = related (accessed 25 September 2007).

My Chinese Heart

My dreams revolve around the rivers and mountains
    I have not been in touch with my home country for many years
    But no matter what, nothing can change
    My Chinese heart
Wearing a western suit
    My heart remains a Chinese heart
    Early in my days my ancestors had already
    Imprinted me with a Chinese mark
Yangtze River, Great Wall
    Yellow Mountain, Yellow River
    Weighs heavily in my heart
    No matter what, no matter where
    My heart is the same
The blood that flows in my heart
    Is filled with sounds from the Chinese nation
    Even if I was born in a foreign country, it still doesn't change,
    I still have a Chinese heart
Yangtze River, Great Wall
    Yellow Mountain, Yellow River
    Weighs heavily in my heart
    No matter what, no matter where
    My heart is still the same

174 *Notes*

14 The Chinese government often invites overseas Chinese to take part in the ceremonies to honour the Yellow Emperor, who is commonly seen as the 'ancestor of all Chinese'. Recently, joint ceremonies between the Chinese and Taiwanese played an important role in the rapprochement between the PRC and Taiwan. Notably, ethnic minorities so far have not taken part in these ceremonies. See '10,000 Chinese pay homage to Yellow Emperor', *People's Daily Online*, 5 April 2009, http://english.people.com.cn/90001/90776/90882/6630061.html (accessed 20 September 2009).
15 FBIS, Xinhua news, 1 August 2001.
16 'Senior official urges overseas Chinese youth to contribute to China's rejuvenation', *People's Daily Online*, 22 April 2007, http://english.people.com.cn/200704/22/eng20070422_368633.html (accessed 20 September 2007).
17 'The Chinese Embassy Holds National Day Reception for Overseas Chinese to Celebrate the 59th Anniversary of the Founding of the People's Republic of China', 24 October 2008, http://uk.chineseembassy.org/eng/sghd/t519449.htm (accessed 20 September 2009).

5 Transnationalising Chineseness: 'overseas Chinese work' in the reform period

1 The conference participants emphasised the need for re-establishing the overseas connections, for the rehabilitation of the victims of the 'Gang of Four' activities, for the protection of the overseas Chinese remittances, and for the relaxation of the entry/exit regulations for overseas Chinese and Chinese nationals with overseas connections. They urged the adoption of provisions which would facilitate the return of the overseas Chinese to the motherland for settlement; encouraged investment; underlined the importance of the favourable conditions for overseas Chinese students to attend schools on the mainland; and encouraged the overseas Chinese to choose the nationality of their country of residence and to abide by the law of their host country (Wang Chun 1980:16–18).
2 *Constitution of the PRC*, Section 2, Article 50 states: 'The People's Republic of China protects the legitimate rights and interests of Chinese nationals residing abroad and protects the lawful rights and interests of returned overseas Chinese and of the family members of Chinese nationals residing abroad'.
3 Initially this body was set up in 1949 after the establishment of the PRC and was called The Overseas Chinese Affairs Commission (*Huaqiao shiwu weiyuanhui*). It preserved the same title after it was re-established in 1974 until 1978 when it was re-named as the OCAO.
4 *Xinhua*, FBIS, 29 December 2001.
5 Qian Qichen quoted in *Xinhua*, FBIS, 19 January 1999.
6 'Chairman Lin Jun Delivers Report on the Work of the All-China Federation of Returned Overseas Chinese and Their Relatives to the Eighth National Congress of the Federation' ('*Zhongguo Qiaolian zhuxi Lin Jun xiang ba ci quanguo guiqiao qiaojuan daibiao dahui quanti daibiao zuo gongzuo baogao*', 15 July 2009, www.bjdch.gov.cn/n1569/n4897217/n4897272/8062332.html (accessed 25 September 2009).
7 'Top leaders attend congress of returned overseas Chinese', *People's Daily Online*, 14 July 2009, http://english.people.com.cn/90001/90776/90785/6700026.html (accessed 25 September 2009).
8 The party was initially established in San Francisco in 1925 to promote the interests and rights of overseas Chinese, to improve their status and image. In 1931 Zhigongdang'

central office was moved to Hong Kong. After establishment of the PRC, the party's centre moved from Hong Kong to Guangzhou. Since 1953 Zhigongdang is based in Beijing. There were 18,000 party members in 2001, and 17 provincial and 2 municipal offices across the country. In 1997, 540 Zhigongdang members were representatives in local and national People's Congresses, and 1,598 were representatives in the CPPCC at different levels (Lu Meiyuan and Quan Haosheng 2001: 280).

9 Between the 10th and the 11th NPCs Zhigongdang conducted 200 training sessions attended by 6,000 people (Lu Meiyuan and Quan Haosheng 2001: 283).

10 The local authorities, with the Central authorities' blessing, play an active role in the transformation of the overseas Chinese' imaginary cultural homeland of *qiaoxiang* into reality. Tourism and publications catering for the overseas Chinese audience proved to be especially successful. In 1999 China attracted 108,141 overseas Chinese tourists, but hopes that this rate will rise significantly with the help of specially-favourable policies directed at satisfying overseas Chinese interests (Mao Yong 2001: 8).

11 Compensation to employees is an indicator used by the IMF in calculation of migrant remittances. In contrast to Workers' remittances, which refer to cash transfers from migrants to resident households in the countries of origin, compensation to employees refers to the wages, salaries and other remuneration paid to individuals who work in a country other than where they legally reside (Migration Policy Institute 2003).

12 This strategy was also called 'to lure phoenix' policy (*yin feng*) (Wu Kaijun 2003: 18).

13 *Xinhua*, FBIS, 21 January 1999.

14 Interview with an official from the All-China's Federation of Returned Overseas Chinese, August 2003.

15 Quoted in *Xinhua*, FBIS, 28 February 2003.

16 More specifically, they constitute 40–50 per cent of all Chinese in the USA, 70–80 per cent in Canada, 80 per cent in Japan, 70 per cent in Australia, and 80 per cent in Western Europe (Zhuang Guotu 2001: 361).

17 'Haiwai huaqiao huaren chaoguo 3500 wan: you shuiyuan de defang jiu you huaren' (The number of overseas Chinese exceeds 35 million: wherever there is water there are Chinese), *Huanqiu Wang*, 26 February 2008, http://huaren.huanqiu.com/news/2008-02/65262.html (accessed 20 September 2009).

18 The Law was adopted at the 13th Meeting of the Standing Committee of the Sixth NPC, promulgated by Order No. 32 of the President of the PRC on 22 November 1985, and effective as of 1 February 1986. The law permitted departing from the country and granting passports if an invitation letter and sponsorship from abroad are provided (Xiang Biao 2003:26).

19 '370,000 students return to China after studying abroad over last 30 years', *People's Daily Online*, 4 January 2009, http://english.people.com.cn/90001/90776/90882/6566748.html (accessed 20 September 2009).

20 Returned Overseas Students Industry Parks (*huiguo liuxuesheng chanye yuanqu*) is a key initiative of the Chinese government to attract Chinese students abroad to return to China. In 2003 there were more than 60 such parks nationwide which employed more than 2,000 returned students (Wu Kaijun 2003: 14–15). They enjoy significant benefits from the government. For example, the industry park in Shenzhen annually receives RMB 300 mln (US$3.8 million) in investment funds from the provincial government (Xiang Biao 2003: 30).

21 *Xinhua*, FBIS, 5 December 2003.

22 *Xinhua*, FBIS, 28 December 2003.

176 *Notes*

23 Wen Jiaobao quoted in *Zhongguo Xinwen She*, FBIS 20 July 1996.
24 *Xinhua*, FBIS 29 September 1999.
25 *Xinhua*, FBIS, 22 December 2001.
26 *Xinhua*, FBIS, 22 December 2002.
27 *Xinhua*, FBIS, 8 February 2002.
28 *Xinhua*, FBIS, 1 August 2001.
29 *Beijing Zhongguo Xinwen She*, FBIS, 16 January 2002.
30 *Zhongguo Xinwen She*, FBIS, 8 October 2003.
31 'Cao Yanling: A Heroine as the Leader of Overseas Chinese', All China Women's Federation, 5 March 2007, www .womenofchina.cn/Profiles/Officials/14595.jsp (accessed 25 September 2007).
32 *Zhongguo Xinwen She*, FBIS, 3 November 2003.
33 The series brought success to the television station that had been in existence for less than a year, and which had been the first to buy the rights to broadcast the documentary outside China. Besides broadcasting the documentary in prime time every night, the station also rebroadcast the documentary in the morning and at noon the following day The Phoenix Television station broadcasts to more than 30 countries and regions in Asia.
34 *Zhongguo tongxun she*, FBIS, 20 January 1997.
35 '"Media and Image of China" discussed at Weiming Lecture Hall', Peking University, 29 September , 2009, http://english.pku.edu.cn/News_Events/News/Focus/2454.htm (accessed 10 October 2009).
36 'Chinese Entrepreneurs Buy Overseas TV Channels', *CMM Intelligence* 13(13), July 23 2009, www.cmmintelligence.com/?q = node/7486 (accessed 10 October 2009).
37 'Ambassador Fu Ying attending the evening party hosted by the Chinese community in the UK to celebrate the 60th anniversary of the PRC', 29 September 2009, www . chinese-embassy.org.uk/eng/sghd/t623802.htm (accessed 10 October 2009).
38 *Beijing Zhongguo Xinwen She*, FBIS, 29 December 2001.
39 *Beijing Zhongguo Xinwen She*, FBIS, 29 December 2001.
40 *Xinhua*, FBIS, 26 July 2002.
41 'Overseas Chinese in Mexico make donations for the construction of the 2008 Beijing Olympic stadium', *Xinhua News Online*, 4 April 2006, http://news.xinhuanet.com/sports/2006-04/02/content_4375940.htm (accessed 25 September 2007).
42 'Beijing Olympics' profit exceeds 1 billion yuan', Consulate-General of the People' s Republic of China in Chicago, 19 June 2009, www .chinaconsulatechicago.org/eng/wh/t568562.htm (accessed 25 September 2009).
43 According to Zhuang Guotu (2000: 3) in Southeast Asia, the original historical destination for overseas Chinese migrants, the environment for Chinese settlement is not favourable: in Indonesia overseas Chinese are not recognised as a minority group; in Malaysia the government maintains the regime of natural assimilation. Apart from Singapore, other Southeast Asian states restrict settlement of highly-skilled IT professionals from Mainland China in their countries.
44 Hungarian Association leader quoted in Nyíri (1999a: 253).
45 Interview with an official from the ACFROC, August 2003.
46 *People's Daily*, FBIS, 22 December 2000.
47 Vice-premier Qian Qichen, FBIS, 6 January 2001.
48 *Xinhua*, FBIS, 20 June 2001.
49 *Hong Kong Wen Wei Po*, FBIS, 2 April 2003.
50 Quoted in *Hong Kong Wen Wei Po*, FBIS, 2 April 2003.
51 *Hong Kong Wen Wei Po*, FBIS, 2 April 2003.
52 *Xinhua*, FBIS, 8 May 2000.

53 *Xinhua*, FBIS, 9 August 2002.
54 *Xinhua*, FBIS, 9 April 2003.
55 *Beijing Zhongguo Xinwen She*, FBIS, 11 February 2001.
56 *Beijing Zhongguo Xinwen She*, FBIS, 2 February 2001.
57 Interview with the a scholar at the Research Centre for Overseas Chinese, Institute of Ethnology, Chinese Academy of Social Sciences, August 2003.
58 Gladney (2004: 239) reports that about 25 organisations and websites worldwide with representatives inAmsterdam, Munich, Istanbul, Melbourne, NewYork andWashington DC popularise the case for independent 'Eastern Turkestan'.

6 The politics of localisation: ethnic minorities in post-socialist modernisation

1 The White Paper on National and Regional Autonomy 2005 affirms that by 2003 there had been 513 minority art performance troupes set up, 122 radio broadcasting organisations working in 15 ethnic minority languages, 4,787 titles of books in ethnic minority languages had been published, and seven regular traditional ethnic minority sports competitions had been conducted (*White Paper on Regional Autonomy for Ethnic Minorities in China* 2005. www .chinadaily.com.cn/english/doc/2005-02/28/content_ 420337.htm (accessed 5 September 2009).
2 A plethora of inspiring studies offer a critical perspective on the PRC's practices towards ethnic minorities. To name just a few: Harrell 1995a; Brown 1996; Mackerras 1996; Safran 1998; Gladney 2004.
3 Wang Hongman (2000) gives a comprehensive overview of the PRC's ethnic minority policies in the reform period.
4 The last recognised ethnic group was identified in 1979 which is Jinuo. MaYin (1989) argues that it was recognised because it was compatible with the Marxist evolutionary explanations of primitive ethnic minorities, progressing from matriarchal to patriarchal society. While most of the identification was completed in the 1970s, there are fifteen more groups considered for minority status. The 1990 census revealed that there were 749,341 ethnically 'unidentified' people. In 2000 the number of ethnically 'unidentified' people dropped to 734,438 (Table 2-1, Tabulation on the 2000 Population Census of the People's Republic of China: 299).
5 'Ethnic question' and 'nationality question' can be used interchangeably, as both notions of a nationality and an ethnic group are encompassed by the Chinese term *minzu*. However, in the pre-reform period the translation of the Chinese term *minzu wenti* was dependent on a Stalinist formulation of the 'nationality question'. In the post-Mao period, the official discourse has been increasingly distancing itself from the pre-reform reliance on the political terminology of the era of Soviet influence. Behind these nuances lies one of the most daring modernisation undertakings across the world, which attunes the vocabulary to the government-driven nature of the projects and Western concepts. However, a number of scholars (Chen Kejin 2003;Wu Xiaohua 2003) voiced the opinion that *minzu* cannot be replaced by the Western term of 'ethnic group' because this does not reflect the 'scientific' (positivist) and political character of *minzu*, but it indicates a subjective social grouping based on a common cultural sentiment or interest.
6 One of the recent official documents on China's ethnic policies reads: 'the ethnic minorities are encouraged to adopt new , scientific, civilized and healthy customs in daily life ... ' (Information Office of China's SC 2005).
7 See Gao (2008) for the discussion on how Chinese Koreans negotiate the social label of 'model minority' attached to them.

8 Interview with an official from the Nationalities Affairs Commission, August 2003.
9 Pang (1998) provides an analysis of one account of unrecognised ethnic conflicts in China, namely clashes between Utsat and Han on Hainan island. It is worth pointing out the apparent similarity in the context leading to one of the 1994 ethnic conflicts reported by Pang and the clashes between Han and Hui communities in Henan in November 2004. In both cases the incidents were triggered by casual traffic accidents in which representatives of two opposing communities were involved. Pang suggests that, due to the authorities' inability and negligence in dealing with ethnic conflicts, they are 'routinised' and turn from occasional and individual into group experiences (Pang 1998 152–54). In 1990 there were a series of insurgents against Chinese rule in Xinjiang. March 2008 and July 2009 were marked by a series of violent unrests in China's Tibetan areas and Xinjiang.
10 Interview with an official from the Nationalities Affairs Commission, August 2003.
11 *New York Times* (2 November 2004) estimated the number of involved in the clashes at about 500.
12 This assertion is based on several informal interviews with representatives of minority nationalities who study at 'key universities' in Beijing and would like to pursue further careers in the capital. Gao's research among Chinese Koreans in Northeast China found that some of the interviewed Koreans viewed the minority preferential policies with 'profound uncertainty' and felt that they did not need them as they did well without them (Gao 2008: 61).
13 Asian Development Bank 2003: 279.
14 In contrast, Chinese studying or working abroad would not be punished in any way if they re-enter the PRC for living and employment with more than one child.
15 Across the English-speaking world, the following translations of the name of the project are common: 'opening up west', 'great leap west', 'western development'. With regard to the use of the Chinese name of the project, some Chinese scholars expressed certain concerns. Yang Tingshuo (quoted in Zhang Haiyang 2001, note 1) points to the assimilationist and discriminatory connotations of the 'kaifa' term. He notes that the meaning of the word implies the imposition of the Han values onto the minority cultures, which are being 'opened up' (ibid.).
16 There is an abundant body of literature on Chinese regional development in the period of reform and opening up. Among the most influential studies are Goodman and Segal (1994), Yehua (2000), Zweig (2002) and Naughton and Yang (2004).
17 In 2003, similar regional development policies were initiated for the North-Eastern and Central provinces. Lai (2007) provides an examination of these developments.
18 One of the opening paragraphs of the Circular of the SC on Policies and Measures Pertaining to the Development of the Western Region reads as follows: 'The Development of the Western Region is a large-scale, systemic campaign as well as a formidable historic mission'.
19 In 2003, China's investments in infrastructure projects constituted 55.2 per cent of its overall investment in the region. According to *Xinhua* news agency, a total of about US$102.4 billion has been invested in over 60 large infrastructure projects in the region from 2000 to 2005. Over this period, the government invested about US$55.42 billion and allocated about US$60.24 billion as transfer payment or special subsidies for the development of the western region (*Xinhua* in FBIS, 5 February 2005).
20 The Western region is home to about 80 per cent of the nation's hydropower supply and 58 per cent of China's natural gas reserve (Lai 2002: 445). The state initiative to 'open up' the region's mineral resource has taken three dimensions: transmission of gas from west

to east (*xi qi dong shu*); transmission of electricity from west to east (*xi dian dong song*); and transmission of coal from west to east (*xi mei dong yuan*) (Ma Ping 2001: 38).

21 *Xinhua* in FBIS, 5 February 2005.
22 *People's Daily*, 20 October 2004.
23 *China Daily*, 11 December 2002.
24 East Turkistan Information Centre 2001.
25 Recent reports point to the transfer of up to 40,000 troops to Xinjiang (Japan Economic newswire quoted in Moneyhon 2002).
26 In 2004, China was working on 88 dams and at least 36 more were planned (BBC News online, 21 June 2004).
27 *China Reform Monitor* 563, 14 October 2004.
28 See *People's Daily*'s report, no date, www.china.org.cn/english/travel/49672.htm#.
29 Xinjiang Statistical Yearbook 2002.
30 Xinjiang Provincial Yearbook 2003.
31 *Xinhua*, 28 February 2001 quoted in Tibet Information Network 13 March 2001.
32 Quoted in *Xinhua*, FBIS 19 May 2000.
33 See Order of the SC No. 435 'Several Provisions of the State Council on the Implementation of the Law of the People' s Government of China on Regional Autonomy by Ethnic Minorities', May 19 May 2005, http://eng.nmgnews.com.cn/system/2008/09/26/010116628.shtml (accessed 29 September 2007).
34 According to the SC regulations, minority autonomous townships could be set up in the areas where the nationality which is granted autonomous status constitutes not less than 30 per cent of the population in the community. There are more than 1,200 ethnic minority townships in China at present, most of which were established since the 1980s (Guo Xiolin 2004: footnote 17, 194).
35 While there are no officially-recognised ethnic minorities in Shanghai, the city hosts a substantial community of unrecognised Subei people (Honig 1992).
36 *Xinhua* in FBIS, 6 November, 1997.
37 'The great leap West: China', *The Economist* 372(8390), 28 August 2004: 38.
38 See Lai 2007 for discussion on the recently initiated policies toward the central region.
39 Zhang Jianxin 2000: 10; Wu Shimin 2006, 4 attributes 47.7 per cent of ethnic minorities to the total number of China' s poor in 2005.
40 In 1994 the state adopted a seven-year priority poverty alleviation programme (Information Office of the SC of the PRC 1999).
41 *Xinhua* 5 June 1997, FBIS.
42 The case of Shanghai is an exception as its development in the mid-1990s was char - acterised by direct involvement and support from the centre (Goodman 2002: 145).
43 Xinjiang is one of the typical examples of this situation, where the Han live in the industrialised and urbanised north of the province, while ethnic minorities populate the rural south.
44 See also Goodman (2005) for a similar line of analysis based on research conducted among the Salar in Qinghai.

Conclusion

1 The Associated Press quoted the following statement from a Han man, Liu Qiang, in Urumqi: 'We have been good to them. We take good care of them. But the Uyghurs are stupid. They think we have more money than they do because we're unfair to them'. Associated Press, July 7, 2009 (http://china.usc.edu/ShowArticle.aspx?articleID = 1536&AspxAutoDetectCookieSupport = 1).

2 'Chinese President tells Xinjiang leaders work for unity', *Xinhua*, 25 August 2009, http://news.xinhuanet.com/english/2009-08/25/content_11943502.htm, accessed 3 September 2009.
3 Information Office of the SC of the People's Republic of China, White Paper on Ethnic Policy: 'China's Ethnic Policy and Common Prosperity and Development of All Ethnic Groups', 27 September 2009, www.chinadaily.com.cn/china/2009-09/27/content_8743072.htm, accessed 29 September 2009.
4 'In the aftermath of the Shaoguan brawl, Guangdong party secretary Wang Yang visited and consoled the injured Uyghur workers, but allegedly ignored the injured Han workers. This angered the Han workers and increased their suspicion of the government's policy. … Even as ethnic groups, such as the Uyghurs, complain they are being exploited or discriminated by the Han, many Han accuse the government of doing the same. In the end, as China's economy advances, political and economic equality between Han and non-Han is being undermined.' Jian Junbo, 'Ghost of Marx haunts China's riots', *Asia Times Online*, July 8, 2009, www.atimes.com/atimes/China/KG08Ad02.html.
5 For more on the state's policy of transferring Uyghur women to eastern China, see the report by Uyghur Human Rights Project, 8 February 2008, 'Deception, Pressure, and Threats: The Transfer of Young Uyghur Women to Eastern China', www.uhrp.org/articles/762/1/Deception-Pressure-and-Threats-The-Transfer-of-Young-Uyghur-Women-to-Eastern-China-/index.html).
6 Duara (2009: 3–5) notes that it is hard to distinguish Chinese 'culturalism' from 'ethnic or national identification'.
7 Subsequently, the issue of the foreign nationality of actors in the film was hotly debated on the Internet in China, and the 'List of Foreign Actors in *Founding of the Republic*' was circulated, http://piaozu.com/html/20098/3848.htm (accessed 28 October 2009).

Bibliography

Agnew, J. (1998) *Geopolitics: Re-visioning World Politics*, London: Routledge.
Aierken Aihemaiti (1999a) 'Shaoshu minzu zai dangdai zhongguo de gongzuo' (The role of ethnic minorities in the present day China), *Journal of the Xinjiang Pedagogical Institute: Social Sciences Edition*, 1: 26–30.
—— (1999b) 'Shaoshu minzu xiandaihua yu chuangtong wenhua de tiaosh(Modernisation of ethnic minorities and the adjustment of traditional cultures),*Xinjiang Zhigong Daxue Xuebao* (Journal of Xinjiang Employee University), 7(1): 1–7.
Anagnost, A. (1997) *National Past-Times: Narrative, Reprsentation, and Power in Modern China*, Durham, NC: Duke University Press.
—— (2004) 'The corporeal politics of quality (Suzhi)', *Public Culture*, 16(2): 189–208.
—— (2008) 'From "class" to "social strata": Grasping the social totality in reform-era China', *Third World Quarterly*, 29(3): 497–519.
Anderson, B. (1991) *Imagined Communities: Reflections on the Origin and Spread of Nationalism*, London: Verso.
Appadurai, A. (1997) *Modernity at Large: Cultural Dimensions of Globalisation*, Minneapolis: University of Minnesota Press.
Armstrong, J.D. (1977) *Revolutionary Diplomacy: Chinese Foreign Policy and the United Front Doctrine*, Berkley: University of California Press.
Asian Development Bank (2003) *The 2020 Project: Policy Support in the People's Republic of China*, Manila: Asian Development Bank, www.adb.org/Documents/Reports/2020_Project/default.asp#contents (accessed 20 September 2009).
Bailey, P. (2006) 'Recruitment of Workers for Britain and France' in L. Pan (ed.) *The Encyclopaedia of the Overseas Chinese*, 2nd edn, Singapore: Editions Didier Millet, pp. 64–65.
Barabantseva, E. (2008) 'From the language of class to the rhetoric of development: discourses of "nationality" and "ethnicity" in China', *Journal of Contemporary China*, 17(56): 565–589.
Baranovitch, N. (2001) 'Between alterity and identity: new voices of minority people in China', *Modern China*, 27(3): 359–401.
Basch, L., Glick-Schiller, N. and Blanc-Szanton, C. (1994)*Nations Unbound: Transnational Projects, Postcolonial Predicaments, and Deterritorialised Nation-States*, Langhorne, PA: Gordon & Breach.
Bell, D. (2000) *East Meets West: Human Rights and Democracy in East Asia*, Princeton: Princeton University Press.
Bell, D. and Hahm, C. (eds) (2003) *Confucianism for the Modern World*, Cambridge: Cambridge University Press.

Bibliography

Ben-Ami, S. (ed.) (2000) *Ethnic Challenges to the Modern Nation State*, London: Macmillan.
Benton, G. and Gomez, E.T . (2008) *The Chinese in Britain, 1800–Present: Economy, Transnationalism, Identity*, Houndmills: Palgrave Macmillan.
Billig, M. (1995) *Banal Nationalism*, London: Sage.
Blum, S.D. and Jensen, L.M. (eds) (2002) *China off Center: Mapping the Margins of the Middle Kingdom*, Honolulu: University of Hawaii Press.
Brandt, C., Schwartz, B. and Fairbank, J. (1959) *A Documentary History of Chinese Communism*, London: George Allen and Unwin Ltd.
Brown, M. (ed.) (1996) *Negotiating Ethnicities in China and Taiwan*, Berkley: University of California Press.
—— (2002) 'Local government agency: manipulating Tujia identity', *Modern China*, 28(3): 362–95.
Calhoun, C. (1997) *Nationalism*, Buckingham: Open University Press.
Callahan, W.A. (2006) *Cultural Governance and Resistance in Pacific Asia*, London: Routledge.
—— (2008) 'Chinese visions of world order: post-hegemonic or a new-hegemony?', *The International Studies Review*, 10 (4): 749–61.
—— (2009) *China: The Pessoptimist Nation*, Oxford: Oxford University Press.
Central Intelligence Group (1946)*Chinese Minorities in Southeast Asia*, ORE-7, December 2, United States Central Intelligence Agency, Freedom of Information Act Reading Room, www.cia.gov.
Chang Ching-li (1983) 'Promotion of Socialist Spiritual Civilization on the Chinese Mainland', *Issues and Studies*, August: 23–40.
Chang Paomin (1980) *China, Vietnam and the Overseas Chinese*, Berkeley: Center for Chinese Studies.
Chen, Leslie (1995) 'On Sun Yat-sen's three principles of the people', paper presented to the 1995 ASPAC Conference of the Association for Asian Studies, Pacific University, *Selected Paper Series*, Pacific University, Forest Grove, Oregon, www . chen-jiongming.com/English/material/paper/chen_paper2.htm, (accessed 20 September 2007).
Chen Fei (2002) 'Xiandaihua shiye zhong de huaqiao huaren yu Zhongguo de guanxi' (Overseas Chinese relations with China in the context of modernisation),*Ba gui qiaoshi* (Bagui Journal of Overseas Chinese History), 3: 42–45.
Chen Kejin (2003) 'Lishi shang Zhongguo he Zhonghua minzu de xingcheng yu fazhan wenti shilun milüe' (Commentary on the historical form and development of China and the Chinese nation), *Yunnan shehui kexue* (Yunnan Social Sciences), 4: 65–69.
Chen Lijuan (2004) 'Huaqiao huaren – Zhongguo minzu zhuyi' (Overseas Chinese and Chinese nationalism), *Dushu*, 5: 13–22.
Chen Yunhui (2000) 'Xibu dakaifa de zhuti xing ji minzu xing: Liyi guanxi yu shehui wending' (The essential character of the Western Development Project and minority character: interest relations and social stability) in G. Mao and T. Wang (eds) *Xibu Dakaifa yu Woguo Minzu Wenti* (The Western Development Project and Our Country's Ethnic Question), Beijing: Central University for Nationalities Press.
Chen Yunyun (2009) 'Lun huaqiaohuaren zai zhongguo gaige kaifang jincheng zhong de zhoangyao zuoyong' (Analysis of overseas Chinese' important contributions to China's reform and opening-up), *Shehui Jianshe* (Society Construction): 34–36.
Chen Zhihong (1997) 'Huaren jingji yu gaige kaifang' (Overseas Chinese Economy and Reform and Opening-up), *Waixiang jingji* (External Economy), 2–3: 44–46.

Bibliography 183

Cheng Xi (1999) 'Gaige kaifang yilai zhongguo zhengfu xuanpai liuxuesheng de zhengce yang' (The evolution of the Chinese government's policies on selecting and sending students studying sbroad in the period of reform and opening-up), *Huaqiao huaren shi yanjiu* (Overseas Chinese History Studies), 1: 37–44.

Chiang Kaishek (1947) *China's Destiny and Chinese Economic Theory*, London: Dennis Dobson Ltd.

China Modernisation Net (no date) www.modernization.com.cn/theory.htm (accessed 27 September 2009).

China Modernisation Report (*Zhongguo xiandaihua baogao*) (2002) Zhongguo kexueyuan zhongguo xiandaihua yanjiu zhongxin (Centre for Modernisation Research of the Chinese Academy of Sciences), Beijing: Beijing University Press.

Chong Erkang (1999) 'Dangdai haiwai huaren shulüe' (Commentary on the contemporary overseas Chinese), *Nankai xuebao* (Nankai Journal), 5: 149–60.

Chow Kaiwing (1997) 'Imagining boundaries of blood: Zhang Binglin and the invention of the Han "race" in Modern China' in F. Dikotter (ed.) *The Construction of Racial Identities in China and Japan*, London: Hurst, pp. 34–52.

Christiansen, F. (1993) 'Zhang Jian's Bianfa Pingyu – a Place for Gradual Reform in Late Imperial and Early Republican China?' in K.W. Radtke and T. Saich (eds) *China's Modernisation*, Stuttgart: Franz Steiner Verlag, pp. 39–57.

—— (2003) *Chinatown, Europe: An Exploration of Overseas Chinese Identity in the 1990s*. London: RoutledgeCurzon.

Common Programme of the Chinese People's Political Consultative Conference 1949 (1962) in A.P. Blaustein (ed.) *Fundamental Legal Documents of Communist China*, South Hackensack, NJ: Fred B. Rothman and Co., pp. 34–53.

Connor, W. (1984) *The National Question in Marxist-Leninist Theory and Strategy*, Princeton, New Jersey: Princeton University Press.

Constitution of the Communist Party of China (2002) amended and adopted at the 16th National Congress of the CCP on 14 November, www.china.org.cn/english/features/49109.htm (accessed 20 September 2007).

Constitution of the People's Republic of China (1982) adopted 4 December, http://english.people.com.cn/constitution/constitution.html (accessed 25 September 2009).

Constitution of the Soviet Republic (1931) in *Documents from Communist China*, http://sourcebook.fsc.edu/history/communistchina.html (accessed 20 September 2007).

Cressey, G.B. (1955) 'The 1953 census of China', *The Far Eastern Quarterly*, 14 (3): 388.

Crossley, P. (1990) 'Thinking about ethnicity in early Modern China', *Late Imperial China*, 11(1): 1–35.

Crossley, P.K., Siu, H.F. and Sutton, D.S. (eds) (2006) *Empire at the Margins: Culture, Ethnicity, and Frontier in Early Modern China*, Berkley and Los Angeles: University of California Press.

Dan Ping and Zhang Xiaoxu (1998) 'Guojia dui zhongxi bu shaoshu minzu diqu fuchi guzhengce yanjiu' (Research on the state's policies of assistance towards Western Region's ethnic minorities), *Minzu wenti yanjiiu* (Ethnic Issues Research), 5: 28–31.

Davies, G. (2007) *Worrying about China: the Language of Chinese Critical Inquiry*, Harvard: Harvard University Press.

D'Elia, P.M. (1974) *The Triple Demisms of Sun Yatsen*, New York: AMS Press.

Deng Xiaoping (1979) 'The United Front and the Tasks of the Chinese People's Political Consultative Conference in the New Period' in *Selected Works of Deng Xiaoping*, Vol. 2, http://english.peopledaily.com.cn/dengxp/ (accessed 20 September 2009).

—— (1986) 'For the Great Unity of the Entire Chinese Nation' in *Selected Works of Deng Xiaoping*, Vol. 3, http://english.peopledaily .com.cn/dengxp/ (accessed 20 September 2009).

—— (1990) 'We are working to revitalize the Chinese Nation' in *Selected Works of Deng Xiaoping*, Vol. 3, http://english.peopledaily .com.cn/dengxp/ (accessed 20 September 2009).

Dikötter, F. (1992) *The Discourse of Race in Modern China*, London: Hurst and Company.

—— (1997) 'Racial discourse in China' in F. Dikotter (ed.) *The Construction of Racial Identities in China and Japan: Historical and Contemporary Perspectives*, London: Hurst and Co., pp. 12–33.

Dillon, M. (2000) 'China goes West: laudable development? ethnic provocation?', www . uyghuramerican.org/layout/set/print/content/view/full/200 (accessed 25 September 2007).

Ding Zhigang and Han Zuozhen (2003) 'Wo guo xibei shaoshuminzu xiandaihua jincheng zhong de zhengzhi wenhua chuangxing' (Political culture transformation among northwest ethnic groups in the process of modernization), *Xibei Shi Daxue Bao* (Journal of Northwest Normal University), 40(6): 120–24.

Dirlik, A. (2002) 'Modernity as history: post-revolutionary China, globalisation, and the question of modernity', *Social History*, 27(1): 16–39.

Doty, R.L. (1996) *Imperial Encounters: The Politics of Representation in North-South Relations*, Minneapolis: University of Minnesota Press.

Douw, L. (2000) 'Diasporas and transnational institution-building: some research question' in C. Huang, G. Zhuang and K. Tanaka (eds) *New Studies on Chinese Overseas and China*, Leiden: International Institute for Asian Studies, pp. 5–29.

Dreyer, J.T. (1975) 'Go West young Hhan: the hsia-fang movement to China' s minority areas', *Pacific Affairs*, 48 (3): 353–69.

—— (1976) *China's Forty Millions: Minority Nationalities and national Integration in the PRC*, Cambridge, Massachusetts: Harvard University Press.

—— (2000) *China's Political System: Modernisation and Tradition*, 3d Edition, London: Allyn and Bacon.

Duara, P. (1999) 'T ransnationalism in the era of nation-states: China, 1900–1945' in B. Meyer and P. Geschiere (eds) *Globalisation and Identity: Dialectics of Flow and Closure*, Oxford: Blackwells, pp. 46–69.

—— (2003) 'Nationalism and transnationalism in the globalisation of China', *China Report: Journal of East Asian Studies*, 39(1): 1–14.

—— (2005) 'The legacy of empire and nations in EastAsia' in P. Nyíri and J. Breindenbach (eds) *China Inside Out: Contemporary Chinese Nationalism and Transnationalism*, Budapest: Central European University Press, http://cio.ceu.hu/courses/CIO/modules/Modul03Duara/pd_index.html (accessed 25 September 2007).

—— (2009) *The Global and Regional in China's Nation-Formation*, London: Routledge.

Eisenstadt, S.N. (1999) 'Multiple modernities in an age of globalisation', *Canadian Journal of Sociology*, 24(2): 283–95.

—— (2000) 'Multiple modernities', *Daedalus*, 129(1): 1–29.

Elegant, R. (1959) *The Dragon's Seed: Peking and the Overseas Chinese*, New York: St. Martin's Press.

Elliott, M.C. (2001) *The Manchu Way: The Eight Banners and the Ethnic Identity in Late Imperial China*, Stanford: Stanford University Press.

Escobar, A. (1995) *Encountering Development: The Making and Unmaking of the Third World*, Princeton: Princeton University Press.

Fairbank, J.K. (ed.) (1968) *The Chinese World Order: Traditional China's Foreign Relations*, Cambridge, MA: Harvard University Press.

Fang Xiongpu (1997) 'Haiwai qiaotuan de fazhan yanbian jiqi xiangguan zhengce' (The Evolution of the overseas Chinese associations and related policies), *Huaqiao huaren lishi yanjiu* (Overseas Chinese Histories Studies), 1: 8–11.

Featherstone, M. and Lash, S. (1995) 'Globalisation, modernity and the spatialization of Social Theory: an introduction' in M. Featherstone, S. Lash and R. Robertson (eds) *Global Modernities*, London: Sage, pp. 1–24.

Fei Xiaotong (1981a) 'Modernisation and national minorities in China' in *Toward a People's Anthropology*, pp. 78–92, Beijing: New World Press.

—— (1981b) 'Social Transformation' in *Toward a People's Anthropology*, Beijing: New World Press, pp. 36–59.

—— (1988) 'Plurality and unity in the configuration of the Chinese people', *The Tanner Lectures on Human Values* delivered at The Chinese University of Hong Kong, November 15 and 17, www .tannerlectures.utah.edu/lectures/fei90.pdf (accessed 20 September 2007).

—— (2000) 'Zhi "xingbian fumin xingdong" lingdao xiaozu de yi feng xin' (A letter of the leadership group of 'Prosperous borders, rich nation initiative') in G. Mao and T. Wang (eds) *Xibu Dakaifa yu Woguo Minzu Wenti* (The Western Development Project and our Country's Ethnic Question), Beijing: Central University for Nationalities Press, pp. 9–12.

Feng Ertang (1999) 'Dangdai haiwai huaren milüe' (Contemporary overseas Chinese strategy), *Nankai xuebao* (Nankai Journal), 5: 149–60.

Fewsmith, J. (2001) *China since Tiananmen: Politics of Transition*, Cambridge: Cambridge University Press.

Fitzgerald, J. (1996) 'The nationless state: the search for a nation in modern Chinese nationalism' in J. Unger (ed.) *Chinese Nationalism*, New York: Sharpe, pp. 56–85.

Fitzgerald, S. (1972) *China and the Overseas Chinese: A Study of Peking's Changing Policy 1949–1970*, Cambridge: Cambridge University Press.

Fogden, S. (2003) 'Writing insecurity: the PRC's push to modernise China and the politics of Uighur identity', *Issues and Studies*, 39(3): 33–74.

Ford, P. (2009) 'Beijing launching a "Chinese CNN" to burnish image abroad', *Christian Science Monitor*, 5 February 2009. www .csmonitor.com/2009/0205/p01s01-woap.html (accessed 25 September 2009).

Foucault, M. (2002) 'Subject and power ' in J. Faubion (ed.) *Power, Essential Works of Foucault 1954–1984*, London: Penguin, pp. 326–48.

—— (2007) *Security, Territory, Population: Lectures at the College de France, 1977–78*, translated by G. Burchell, Basingstoke, UK: Palgrave Macmillan.

Gao, F. (2008) 'What it means to be a "model minority": voices of ethnic Koreans in Northeast China', *Asian Ethnicity*, 9(1): 55–67.

General Programme of the CPR for the Implementation of Regional Autonomy for Nationalities (1962) in A.P. Blaustein (ed.) *Fundamental Legal Documents of Communist China*, South Hackensack, NJ; Fred B. Rothman and Co., pp. 180–92.

Gladney, D.C. (1994) 'Salman Rushdie in China: religion, ethnicity, and state definition in the People's Republic' in C. Keyes, K. Kendall and H. Hardacre (eds) *Asian Visions of Authority: Religion and the Modern States of East and Southeast Asia*, Honolulu: University of Hawaii Press, pp. 255–78.

—— (1995) 'Economy and ethnicity: the revitalization of a muslim minority in Southeastern China' in A. Walder (ed.) *The Waning of the Communist State: Economic Origins of*

Political Decline in China and Hungary, Berkley: University of California Press, pp. 242–66.
—— (1996) *Muslim Chinese: Ethnic Nationalism in the People's Republic*, Cambridge, MA: Harvard University Press.
—— (2004) *Dislocating China: Reflections on Muslims, Minorities, and Other Subaltern Subjects*, London: Hurst and Company.
—— (2009) 'An ethnic struggle in China goes global', *YaleGlobal Online*, 9 July, http://yaleglobal.yale.edu/content/ethnic-struggle-goes-global (accessed 28 August 2009).
Glantz, M., Ye, Q. and Ge, Q. (2001) 'China' s Western region development strategy and the urgent need to address creeping environmental problems', *Aridlands Newsletter* 49, May–June, http://ag.arizona.edu/OALS/ALN/aln49/glantz.html (accessed 25 September 2007).
Glick Schiller, N., Basch, L. and Blanc-Szanton, C. (1992) 'Transnationalism: a new analytic framework for understanding migration', *Annals of the New York Academy of Sciences*, 645: 1–24.
Godley, M.R. (1981) *The Mandarin-Capitalists from Nanyang: Overseas Chinese Enterprise in the Modernization of China 1893–1911*, Cambridge: Cambridge University Press.
Goodman, D.S.G. (2002) 'The politics of the West: equality, nation-building and colonisation', *Provincial China*, 7(2): 127–50.
—— (2004) 'The campaign to "Open up the West": national, provincial-level and local perspectives', *The China Quarterly*, 178: 317–34.
—— (2005) 'Exiled by definition: the Salar and economic activism in Northwest China', *Asian Studies Review*, 29(4): 325–43.
Goodman, D. and Segal, G. (eds) (1994) *China Deconstructs: Politics, Trade and Regionalism*, London: Routledge.
Greenhalgh, S. and Winckler, E.A. (2005) *Governing China's Population: From Leninist to Neoliberal Biopolitics*, Stanford, CA: Stanford University Press.
Grosby, S. (1995) 'Territoriality: the transcendental, primordial feature of modern societies', *Nations and Nationalism*, 1(2): 143–62.
Grunfeld, T. (1985) 'In Search of Equality: Relations Between China' s Ethnic Minorities and the Majority Han', *The Bulletin of Concerned Asian Scholars*, 17(1): 54–67.
Guan Guixia (2000) 'Lun xibu kaifa yu minzu gongzuo' (Discussing the Western Development Project and ethnic work), *Pandeng* (Ascent), 107(4): 27–32.
Guarnizo, L.E. and Smith, M.P (eds) (1998) *Transnationalism from Below*, New Brunswick, NJ: Transaction Publishers.
Guibernau, M. (1996) *Nationalisms: the Nation-state and Nationalism in the Twentieth Century*, London: Polity Press.
Guo Jiaji (2003) 'Zhongguo de minzu zhengce: chengjiu yu tiaozhan'(China's ethnic policies: achievements and challenges), *Minzu wenti yanjiu* (Ethnic Issues Research), 1: 22–25.
Guo Xiolin (2004) 'Marking out boundaries: politics of ethnic identity in Southwest China', in F. Christiansen and U. Hedetoft (eds) *The Politics of Multiple Belonging: Ethnicity and Nationalism in Europe and East Asia*, pp. 185–204, Aldershot: Ashgate.
Hamashita, T. (2008) *China, East Asia and the Global Economy: Regional and Historical Perspectives*, London and New York: Routledge.
Han Ziliang (2007a) 'Cong ren de xiandaihua kan shaoshu minzu xiandaihua' (Ethnic minorities modernisation from the perspective of humanistic modernization),*Journal of Yili Prefecture Communist Party Institute* (Zhonggong Yili Zhou Wei Dangxiao Xuebao), 2: 74–77.

—— (2007b) 'Qianyi shaoshu minzu xiandaihua' (The discussion of ethnic minorities' modernisation), *Zhonggong Wulumuqi Shi Wei Dang Xiao Xuebao* (Journal of the Urumqi Municipal Committee Party School), 1(3): 36–39.
Hao Chang (1971) *Liang Ch'i-ch'ao and Intellectual Transition in China, 1890–1907*, Cambridge, MA: Harvard University Press
Harrell, S. (ed.) (1995a) *Cultural Encounters on China's Ethnic Frontiers*, University of Washington Press.
—— (1995b) 'Civilizing projects and the reaction to them' in S. Harrell (ed.) *Cultural Encounters on China's Ethnic Frontiers*, pp. 3–36, Universtiy of Washington Press.
—— (1999) 'The role of periphery in Chinese nationalism' in S.-M. Huang and C.-K. Hsu (eds) *Imagining China: Regional Division and National Unity*, Taipei: Academia Sinica Press, pp. 133–60.
Harrison, H. (2000) *The Making of the Republican Citizen: Political Ceremonies and Symbols in China, 1911–1929*, Oxford: Oxford University Press.
Hart, T.G. (1985) 'China's Modernization in Comparative Perspective',*Issues and Studies*, September: 35–68.
Harvey, D. (1989) *The Condition of Postmodernity. An Enquiry into the Origins of Cultural Change*, Cambridge, MA: Basil Blackwell.
—— (2005) *A Brief History of Neoliberalism*, Oxford: Oxford University Press.
Hastings, A. (1997) *The Construction of Nationhood: Ethnicity, Religion and Nationalism*, Cambridge: Cambridge University Press.
He Chuanqi (1999) *Di Er Ge Xiandaihua: Renlei Wenming Jincheng de Jushi* (The Second Modernisation: Condition in Human Civilisational Course), Beijing: Gaoji jiaoyu chubanshe.
—— (2003) *Dongfang Fuxing: Xiandaihua de San Tiao Daolu* (Asian Renaissance: Three Roads to Modernisation), Beijing: Commercial Press.
He Chuanqi *et al.* (2007) *China Modernisation Report Outlook (2001–2007)*, Beijing: Beijing University Press.
He Jiasheng (1997) 'Huaren ziben dui zhongguo xiandaihua jianshe de zuoyong'(The role of overseas Chinese capital in China's modernisation), *Jinan xuebao: zhexue shehui kexue* (Journal of Jinan University: Philosophy and Social Sciences Edition), 19(1): 22–33.
He Jing (1999) 'Deng Xiaoping dui xin shiqi minzu gongzuo de gongxian'(Deng Xiaoping's contribution to ethnic work in the new period), *Qian yan* (Front Line), 8: 2–4.
He Xingliang (1996) 'Shichang jingji yu zhonguo shaoshu miznu' (Market economy and China's ethnic minorities), *Sixiang zhanxian* (Ideological Front), 6: 72–78.
He Zhonghua (1996) 'Xiandaihua guannian yu xifang wenhua chuantong'(The concept of modernisation and Western cultural traditions), *Shandong Daxue Bao* (Journal of Shangdong University), 1(102): 70–77.
Heberer, T. (1989) *China and Its National Minorities: Autonomy or Assimilation*, Armonk: Sharpe, Inc.
—— (2007) *Doing Business in Rural China: Liangshan's New Ethnic Entrepreneurs*, Seattle: University of Washington Press.
Henderson, J. (2008) 'China and global development: toward a Global-Asian Era?'. *Contemporary Politics*, 14(4): 375–92.
Holbig, H. (2004) 'The emergence of the campaign to open up the West: ideological formation, central decision-making and the role of the provinces', *The China Quarterly*, 335–57.
Honig, E. (1992) *Creating Chinese Ethnicity: Subei People in Shanghai, 1850–1980*, New Haven, CT: Yale University Press.

Hostetler, L. (2000) 'Qing connections to the early modern world: ethnography and cartography in eighteenth-century China', *Modern Asian Studies*, 34, No. 3: 623–62.
—— (2001) *Qing Colonial Enterprise: Ethnography and Cartography in Early Modern China*, Chicago: University of Chicago Press.
Houston, S. and Wright, R. (2003) 'Making and Re-making Tibetan Diasporic Identities', *Social and Cultural Geography*, 4(2): 217–232.
Hsia, T.-T. and Haun, K.A. (1976) *Pekin's Policy towards the Dual Nationality of the Overseas Chinese: a Survey of its Development*, Washington: Library of Congress.
Hu Angang (2000) 'On China Reforms and Go-West Policy', interview with *Asian Affairs*, www.asian-affairs.com/China/huangang.html (accessed 25 September 2007).
Hu Angang and Wen Jun (2003) 'Zhongguo minzu diqu xiandaihua zhuigan: xiaoying, tezheng, chengyin jiqi houguo' (On the pursuit of modernisation in China's ethnic minorities areas: reasons, effect, characteristics, and consequences), *Guangxi minzu xueyuan xuebao* (Journal of Guangxi Institute of Ethnic Minorities), 1: 107–14.
Huang Zhu (2000) 'Xibu dakaifa yu minzu wenti' (The Western Development Project and the ethnic question) in G. Mao and T. Wang (eds) *Xibu Dakaifa yu Woguo Minzu Wenti* (The Western Development Project and our Country's Ethnic Question), Beijing: Central University for Nationalities Press, pp. 21–26.
Huang Zuoxiu (2000) 'Minzu gongzuo, ni zou hao!' (Ethnic work, you are going well!), *Minzu gongzuo* (Ethnic Work), 11: 18.
Hughes, C. (2009) 'The enduring function of the "substance-essence" ("*ti-yong*") dichotomy in Chinese nationalism' in W.A. Callahan and E. Barabantseva (eds), *Soft Power, Norms and Foreign Policy*, unpublished book manuscript.
Humphrey, C. (no date) 'Cosmopolitanism and kozmopolitzm in the political imaginary of Soviet citizens', www.innerasiaresearch.org/KOZMOPOLIT.pdf (accessed 25 September 2007).
Huntington, S. (1996) *The Clash of Civilizations and the Remaking of World Order*, New York: Simon & Schuster.
Information Office of China's SC (2005) 'White Paper on Regional Autonomy for Ethnic Minorities in China', http://www.chinadaily.com.cn/english/doc/2005-02/28/content_420337.htm (accessed 25 September 2007).
Information Office of the SC of the PRC (1999) *White Paper on National Minorities Policy and Its Practice in China Ethnic Minorities*, http://www.china.org.cn/e-white/4/index.htm (accessed 25 September 2007).
Jiang Zemin (1992) 'Speed up the reform: opening up and the modernization construction in order to win greater victories in the project of socialism with Chinese characteristics', *People's Daily*, 21 October.
—— (1997) 'The Right to Diversity', interview with *Asian Affairs*. www.asian-affairs.com/China/jiang/html (accessed 25 September 2007).
Jin Binggao (1988) 'When does the word "minority nationality" appear in our country?', *Bulletin of the History of the Tibet Communist Party 1* (No. 19 of the General Series), 5 January: 45.
—— (1999) 'Zhongguo minzu lilun fazhan er shi nian' (Development of the PRC's ethnic theory in the last twenty years) in Zhang Dongliang (ed.) *Zhongguo Minzu Wu Shi Nian Lilun yu Shixian* (Fifty Years of Theory and Practice in China's Ethnic Work), Beijing: Central University for Nationalities Press, pp. 88–105.
—— (2002) 'Wo guo shaoshu minzu gainian de lishi kaocha' (Inquiry into our country's concept of minority nationalities), *Zhongguo Minzu Bao* (China Nationalities' Newspaper), 1(1): 3.

Joppke, C. (1998) 'Immigration challenges the nation-state' in C. Joppke (ed.) *Challenge to the Nation-State: Immigration in Western Europe and the United States*, New York: Oxford University Press, pp. 5–46.

Kahn, J.S. (1998) 'Southeast Asian identities: Introduction' in J.S. Kahn (ed.) *Southeast Asian Identities: Culture and the Politics of Representation in Indonesia, Malaysia, Singapore, and Thailand*, London: I.B. Tauris Publishers, pp. 1–27.

Kaiser, R.J. (2004) 'Homeland making and the territorialisation of national identity' in D. Conversi (ed.) *Ethnonationalism in the Contemporary World: Walker Connor and the Study of Nationalism*, London: Routledge, pp. 229–47.

Karl, R.E. (2002) *Staging the World: Chinese Nationalism at the Turn of the Twentieth Century*, Durham, NC: Duke University Press.

Kim, S. and Dittmer, L. (1993) 'Whither China's quest for national identity?' in L. Dittmer and S.S. Kim (eds) *China's Quest for National Identity*, Ithaca: Cornell University Press, pp. 237–90.

King, A.Y.G. (2002) 'The Emergence of Alternative Modernity in East Asia' in D. Sachsenmaier, J. Riedel and S.N. Eisenstadt (eds) *Reflections on Multiple Modernities: European, Chinese and Other Interpretations*, Leiden: Brill, pp. 140–52.

Lai, H. (2007) 'Developing central China: a new regional programme', *China: an International Journal*, 5(1): 109–28.

Lai, H.H. (2002) 'China's Western Development Program: its rationale, implementation, and prospects', *Modern China*, 28(4): 432–66.

Landsberger, S. (1993) 'Chinese visual propaganda during the "four modernisations" (1978–88)' in K.W. Radtke and T. Saich (eds) *China's Modernisation*, Stuttgart: Franz Steiner Verlag, pp. 177–94.

Larry, D. (ed.) (2007) *The Chinese State at the Borders*, Vancouver: University of British Columbia Press.

Law of The People's Republic Of China On Regional National Autonomy (1984) http://en.ec.com.cn/pubnews/2004_04_13/200862/1008415.jsp (accessed 25 September 2007).

Le Shui (1997) 'Haiwai huaren de zhongzu benzhi nan yi gaibian' (The ethnic nature of overseas Chinese is difficult to change), *Bagui Qiaoshi Bagui* (Journal of Overseas Chinese History), 1 (33): 13–16.

Leibold, J. (2007) *Reconfiguring Chinese Nationalism: How the Qing Frontier and Its Indigenes Became Chinese*, New York: Palgrave Macmillan.

—— (2008) 'Whose people's games? ethnic identity and the 2008 Beijing Olympics', *China Beat*, www.thechinabeat.org/?p = 299 (accessed 20 September 2008).

Levenson, J.R. (1971) *Revolution and Cosmopolitanism: the Western Stage and Chinese Stages*, Berkley: University of California Press.

Lewis, N.A. (2008) 'Spy cases raise concern on China's intentions', *New York Times*, 10 July.

Li, R. (2009) 'Another blow to credibility of exam system: Top student cheated on ethnicity', *South China Morning Post*, July 1, p. 5.

Li Anshan (2002) 'A survey of studies on ethnic minorities huaqiao-huaren in the People's Republic of China (1980–2000)' in Shen Yuanfang and P. Edwards (eds) *Beyond China: Migrating Identities*, Canberra: Australian National University Press, pp. 90–103.

Li Dezhu (2000) 'Xibu dakaifa yu wo guo minzu wenti' (The Western Development Project and our country's ethnic question) in G. Mao and T. Wang (eds) *Xibu Dakaifa yu Woguo Minzu Wenti* (The Western Development Project and our Country's Ethnic Question), Beijing: Central University for Nationalities Press, pp. 1–8.

Li Qiuxiang (2002) 'Min zu gaige: shaoshu minzu jinkuai xiandaihua de biyouzhilu' (Reforming ethnic minorities: the only way to speed up modernisation of ethnic minorities),

Neimenggu Daxue Xuebao (Renwen shehui kexue ban) (Journal of Inner Mongolia University (Humanities and Social Sciences)), 34(2): 108–12.

Lien Kuan (1978) 'History of Overseas Chinese and Their Glorious Tradition', *Peking Review*, 21: 15.

Lim, L. (2004) 'China's Drive to Transform Tibet', *BBC News online*, 6 September, http://news.bbc.co.uk/2/hi/asia-pacific/3625588.stm (accessed 27 September 2007).

Lin Jinzhi, Li Guoliang *et al.* (1993) *Huaqiao huaren zhonguo geming he jianshe (huaqiao huaren yanjiu congshu)* (Overseas Chinese in China's Revolutionary Construction (Overseas Chinese Research Series)), Fujian: Renmin Chubanshe.

Lin Xiaodong (2000) 'Shilun huaqiao huaren gang ao tongbao dui zuguo dalu de touzi jiqi falü baohu' (On the investment of overseas Chinese in Mainland China and its legal protection), *Huaqiao huaren lishi yanjiu* (Overseas Chinese History Studies), 2: 28–33.

Litzinger, R. (2002) 'Theorizing postsocialism: reflections on the politics of marginality in contemporary China',. *The South Atlantic Quarterly*, 101 (1): 22–55.

Liu, A. (1996) *Mass Politics in the People's Republic: State and Society in Contemporary China*, Boulder: Westview Press.

Liu, L. (2006) *The Clash of Empires: the Invention of China in Modern Worldmaking*, Cambridge, MA: Harvard University Press.

Liu Hong (1998) 'Old linkages, new networks: the globalisation of overseas Chinese voluntary associations and its implications', *China Quarterly*, 155: 582–609.

—— (2005) 'New migrants and the revival of overseas Chinese nationalism', *Journal of Contemporary China*, 14(43): 291–316.

—— (2010) 'Overseas Chinese and a rising China: the limits of a diplomatic "Diaspora Option"' in Y. Zheng (ed.) *China and International Relations: Chinese Views and the Contribution of Wang Gungwu*, London: Routledge.

Liu Quan and Dong Yinghua (2003) 'Zuguo dalu yu Taiwan xiyin haiwai huaren rencai cuoshi zhi bijiao' (A comparative study of measures to attract talents of overseas Chinese between the mainland China and Taiwan), *Huaqiao huaren lishi yanjiu* (Overseas Chinese History Studies), 1: 16–23.

Liu Wangqin (2000) 'Guanyu xibu dakaifa zhong de minzu guanxi wenti' (The question of ethnic relations in the Western Development Project) in G. Mao and T. Wang (eds) *Xibu Dakaifa yu Woguo Minzu Wenti* (The Western Development Project and our Country's Ethnic Question), Beijing: Central University for Nationalities Press, pp. 182–90.

Long Yi (2003) ' *Quanmian jianshe xiaokang shehui yu jiakuai minzu qu fazhan*' (Comprehensive construction of moderately developed society and speeding-up of the development in minority areas), *Minzu Wenti Yanjiu* (Ethnic Issues Research), 7: 2–10.

Louie, A. (2004) *Chineseness Across Borders: Renegotiating Chinese Identities in China and the United States*, Durham, NC: Duke University Press

Lu Meiyuan and Quan Haosheng (eds) (2001) *Guiqiao Qiaojuan Gaishu* (Returned Overseas Chinese and Overseas Chinese Relatives), Beijing: Zhongguo huaqiao chubanshe.

Lu Yusun (1956) *Programs of Communist China for Overseas Chinese*, Hong Kong: The Union Research Institute.

Luo Rongqu (1997) *Xiandaihua Xinlun Xupian – Dongya yu Zhonghua de Xiandaihua Jincheng* (New Modernisation Theory: East Asian and Chinese Modernisation Process), Beijing: Beijing daxue chubanshe.

Luova, O. (2006) 'Mobilizing yransnational ethnic linkages for economic development: the case of Yanbian Korean autonomous prefecture', *China Information*, XX(I): 33–67.

Ma Ping (2001) 'Xibu dakaifa dui dangdi minzu wenti guanxi de yingxiang ji duice' (The impact of the Western Development Project on the local ethnic relations), *Minzu Wenti Yanjiu* (Ethnic Issues Research), 5: 37–42.

Ma Rong (2003) 'Zhongguo ge zuqun zhijian de jiegou xing chayi' (Structural differences among China's ethnic minorities), *Minzu Wenti Yanjiu* (Minority Issues Research), 10: 27–38.

—— (2006) 'Ethnic relations in contemporary China', *Policy and Society*, 25(1): 85–108.

—— (2007) 'A new perspective in guiding ethnic relations in the twenty-first century: "de-politicization" of ethnicity in China', *Asian Ethnicity*, 8(3): 199–217.

Ma Rong and Zhou Xin (1999) *Zhonghua Minzu Ningjuli Xingcheng yu Fazhan* (The formation and development of the cohesion of the Chinese nation), Beijing: Beijing University Press.

Ma Shipin (1996) 'Shaoshu minzu xiandaihua yu chuantong de tiaoshi'(Ethnic minorities' modernisation and adjustment of traditional culture), *Journal of Guangdong Institute for Nationalities: Social Sciences Edition*, 38(3): 1–3.

Ma Yin (ed.) (1989) *China's Minority Nationalities*, Beijing: People's Publishing Society.

McCarthy, S.K. (2004) 'Gods of wealth, temples of prosperity: party-state participation in the minority cultural revival', *China: an International Journal*, 2(1): 28–52.

—— (2009) *Communist Multiculturalism: Ethnic Revival in Southwest China*, Seattle: University of Washington Press.

Mackerras, C. (1996) *China's Minority Cultures: Identities and Integration Since 1912*, New York: St. Martin's Press.

McNair, H. (1933) *The Chinese Abroad*, Shanghai: Commercial Press.

Manifesto of the Second National Congress of the CCP (July 1922) (1959) in C. Brandt, B. Schwartz and J. Fairbank (eds) *A Documentary History of Chinese Communism*, London: George Allen and Unwin Ltd., pp. 63–65.

Mao Gongning (2001) 'Guanyu xibu dakaifa zhong ruogan zhongda wenti de sikao' (On several important issues in the Western Development Project), *Minzu Wenti Yanjiu* (Ethnic Issues Research), 5: 30–36.

Mao Gongning and Wang Tiezhi (eds) (2000) 'Xibu dakaifa yu woguo minzu wenti' (The Western Development Project and our country's ethnic question), Beijing: Central University for Nationalities Press.

Mao Yong (2001) 'Dui wo guo fazhan dongnanya huaren huaqiao xungen lüyou de sikao' (The Analysis of the Benefits of the Overseas Chinese' 'Look for Roots' Tourism for the Country's Development), *Dongnanya* (South-East Asia), 2: 8–12.

Mao Zedong (1945) 'On Coalition Government', political report made to the Seventh National Congress of the Communist Party of China, April 24, *Selected Works of Mao Tse-tung*, www.marxists.org/reference/archive/mao/selected-works/volume-3/mswv3_25.htm (accessed 24 September 2007).

—— (1947) 'The Present Situation and Our Tasks', December 25, *Selected Works of Mao Tse-tung*, http://www.marxists.org/reference/archive/mao/selected-works/volume-4/mswv4_24.htm (accessed 24 September 2007).

—— (1949) 'Long live the great unity of the Chinese People', declaration of the First Plenary Session of the Chinese Peoples' Political Consultative Conference, 30 September *Selected Works of Mao Tse-tung*, www.marxists.org/reference/archive/mao/selected-works/volume-5/mswv5_02.htm (accessed 24 September 2007).

—— (1957) 'On the Correct Handling of ContradictionsAmong the People', speech delivered at the Eleventh Session (Enlarged) of the Supreme State Conference, *Selected*

Works of Mao Tse-tung, www .marxists.org/reference/archive/mao/selected-works/volume-5/mswv5_58.htm (accessed 24 September 2007).
Marshall, T.H. (1992) 'Citizenship and social class' (1950) in T.H. Marshall and T. Bottomore, *Citizenship and Social Class*, London: Pluto Press, pp. 3–51.
Maybury-Lewis, D. (1997) *Indigenous Peoples, Ethnic Groups, and the State*, Boston: Allyn and Bacon.
Meyer, B. and Geschiere, P . (eds) (1999) *Globalization and Identity: Dialectics of Flow and Closure*, London: Blackwell.
Migration Policy Institute (2003) 'Migration information source: fresh thought, authoritative data, global reach', www.migrationinformation.org/USfocus/print.cfm?ID = 137, 1 June (accessed 25 September 2007).
Mittelman, J.H. (ed.) (1996) *Globalization: Critical Reflections*, Boulder: Lynne Rienner Publishers.
Moneyhon, M. (2002) 'Controlling Xinjiang: autonomy on China's "new frontier"', *Asia-Pacific Law and Policy Journal*, 3(1): 120–52.
Moseley, G. (1965) 'China's fresh approach to the national minority question', *The China Quarterly*, 24: 15–27.
—— (1966) *The Party and the National Question in China*, Cambridge, MA: MIT Press.
National Bureau of Statistics of China (2000) *China Statistical Yearbook*, Beijing: China Statistics Press.
—— (2001) *China Statistical Yearbook*, Beijing: China Statistics Press
—— (2003) *China Statistical Yearbook*, Beijing: China Statistics Press.
Naughton, B.J. (2004) 'The Western Development Program' in B. Naughton and D.L. Yang (eds) *Holding China Together: Diversity and National Integration in the Post-Deng Era*, Cambridge: Cambridge University Press, pp. 253–95.
Naughton, B. and Yang, D. (eds) (2004) *Holding China Together: Diversity and National Integration in the post-Deng Era*, Cambridge: Cambridge University Press.
Norbu, D. (2001) *China's Tibet Policy*, Richmond: Curzon.
Nyíri, P. (1999a) 'Chinese or ganisations in Hungary 1989–96: a case study in PRC-oriented community politics overseas' in F . Pieke and N. Mallee (eds) *Internal and International Migration: Chinese Perspectives*, Richmond: Curzon, pp. 251–79.
—— (1999b) *New Chinese Migrants in Europe: The Case of the Community in Hungary*, Aldershot: Ashgate.
—— (2001) 'Expatriating is patriotic? The discourse on "new migrants" in the People' s Republic of China and identity construction among recent migrants from the PRC', *Journal of Ethnic and Migration Studies*, 27(4): 635–53.
—— (2002) 'From class enemies to patriots: overseas Chinese and emigration policy and discourse in the People's Republic of China' in P. Nyíri and I. Saveliev (eds)*Globalising Chinese Migration: Trends in Europe and Asia*, Aldershot: Ashgate, pp. 208–41.
—— (2006) 'The yellow man' s burden: Chinese migrants on a civilizing mission', *The China Journal* 56, July: 83–106.
Oakes, T. (1998) *Tourism and Modernity in China*, London and New York: Routledge.
—— (1999) 'Bathing in a far village: globalization, transnational capital, and the cultural politics of modernity in China', *Positions: east asia cultures critique*, 7 (2): 307–42.
Ong, A. (1996) 'Cultural citizenship as subject making: immigrants negotiate racial and cultural boundaries in the United States', *Current Anthropology*, 35: 737–62.
—— (1997) 'Chinese modernities: narratives of nation and of capitalism' in A. Ong and D. Nonini (eds) *Ungrounded Empires: The Cultural Politics of Modern Chinese Transnationalism*, London: Routledge, pp. 171–97.

—— (1999) *Flexible Citizenship: the Cultural Logics of Transnationality*, Durham, NC: Duke University Press.
Ong, A. and Nonini, D. (eds) (1997) *Ungrounded Empires: The Cultural Politics of Modern Chinese Transnationalism*, London: Routledge.
O'Neill, M. (2008) 'The conqueror of China's wild West'. *Asia Sentinel*, 13 April, www.asiasentinel.com/index.php?option = com_content&task = view&id = 1 148&Itemid = 31 (accessed 20 September 2008).
Pang, K.-F. (1998) 'Unforgiven and remembered: the impact of ethnic conflicts in everyday Muslim-Han social relations on Hainan island' in W. Safran (ed.) *Nationalism and Ethnoregional Identities in China*, London: Frank Class Publishers, pp. 143–16.
Perdue, P.C. (2005a) *China Marches West: The Qing Conquest of Central Eurasia*, Cambridge, MA: Harvard University Press.
—— (2005b) 'Where do incorrect political ideas come from?Writing the history of the Qing empire and the Chinese nation' in J.A. Fogel (ed.) *The Teleology of the Modern Nation-State: Japan and China*, Philadelphia: University of Pennsylvania Press, pp. 174–99.
Potter, P.B. (2007) 'Theoretical and conceptual perspectives on the periphery in contemporary China' in D. Larry (ed.) *The Chinese State at the Borders*, Vancouver: University of British Columbia Press, pp. 240–70.
Purcell, A. (1965) *The Chinese in Southeast Asia*, London: Oxford University Press.
Pye, L. (1985) *Asian Power and Politics*, Massachusetts: Cambridge.
Qian Ning (2003) 'Shui she xibu fazhan de zhuti: lun shaoshu minzu zai xibu fazhan zhong de diwei yu zuoyong' (Who are the subjects in the Western Development: on the role of ethnic minorities), *Guizhou Minzu Xueyuan Bao* (Journal of Guizhou Institute for Ethnic Minorities), 6 (82): 92–97.
Qing Jue and Jin Binggao (2003) 'Zhongguo gongchandang di san dai lingdao jiben guanyu shaoshu minzu he minzu diqu jingji fazhan de lilun yu zhengce'(The CCP Third Generation Leadership's Theory and Policies of Regional National Autonomy), *Heilongjiang Minzu Sikan* (Heilongjiang National Series), 3: 19–25.
Qiu Liben (2004) 'Cong guoji qiaohui xindongxiang kan woguo qiaohui zhengce' (Assessing China's remittances policies from the perspective of the international remittances), *Huaqiao Huaren Lishi Yanjiu* (Overseas Chinese History Studies), 6: 8–20.
Radtke, K.W. (1993) 'Troubled Identity' in K.W. Radtke and T. Saich (eds) *China's Modernisation*, Stuttgart: Franz Steiner Verlag, pp.13–37.
'The Report on the National Conference on the United Front Theoretical Work' (1989) *Issues and Studies*, 25(6): 136–44.
Rossabi, M. (ed.) (2004) *Governing China's Multiethnic Frontiers*, Seattle: University of Washington Press.
Rostow, W.W. (1960) *The Stages of Economic Growth: A Non-Communist Manifesto*, Cambridge: Cambridge University Press.
Ruan Xihu (2008) 'Ethnicity: minzu yihuo zuqun?'(Ethnicity: nationality or ethnic group?), *Huaqiao Huaren Lishi Yanjiu* (Overseas Chinese History Studies), 2, June: 32–36.
Safran, W. (ed.) (1998) *Nationalism and Ethnoregional Identities in China*, London: Frank Class Publications.
Sautman, B. (1998) 'Preferential policies for ethnic minorities in China: the case of Xinjiang' in W. Safran (ed.) *Nationalism and Ethnoregional Identities in China*, London: Frank Class Publishers, pp. 86–113.
—— (2009) 'Scaling back ethnic minority rights? The new debate about China's ethnic policies', paper presented at the British Inter-University China Centre conference on the Global Politics of China, University of Manchester, 27–28 November.

Bibliography

Schein, L. (1997) 'Gender and internal orientalism in China', *Modern China*, 23(10): 69–98.

—— (2000) *Minority Rules: The Miao and the Feminine in China's Cultural Politics*, Durham, NC: Duke University Press

Schoenhals, M. (1994) '"Non-people" in the People's Republic of China: a chronicle of terminological ambiguity', Working Paper, Indiana University, www.indiana.edu/~easc/resources/working_paper (accessed 25 September 2007).

Shambaugh, D. (1993) 'Introduction: the emergence of "Greater China"', *The China Quarterly*, 136: 653–59.

Shapiro, M. (2004) *Methods and Nations: Cultural Governance and the Indigenous Subject*, London: Routledge.

Shih, C. (2002) *Negotiating Ethnicity in China: Citizenship as a Response to the State*, London: Routledge.

—— (2007) *Autonomy, Ethnicity, and Poverty in Southwestern China: The State Turned Upside Down*, New York: Palgrave Macmillan.

Shin, L.K. (2006) *The Making of the Chinese State: Ethnicity and Expansion on the Ming Borderlands*, Cambridge: Cambridge University Press.

Sie Hok Tzwan (1997) 'The ethnic Chinese minorities: on attitudes to survival' in G. Zhuang (ed.) *Ethnic Chinese at the Turn of the Centuries*, Fuzhou: Fujian People's Publishing House, pp. 80–99.

Siu, L. (2001) 'Diasporic cultural citizenship: Chineseness and belonging in Central America and Panama', *Social Text*, 69, 19(4): 7–28.

Solinger, D.J. (1999) *Contesting Citizenship in Urban China: Peasant Migrants, the State, and the Logic of the Market*, Berkeley: University of California Press.

Songben Zhencheng (2003) *Zhongguo Minzu Zhengce Zhi Yanjiu* (China's Minority Policies and Research), Beijing: Minzu chubanshe.

Soysal, Y.N. (1994) *Limits of Citizenship: Migrants and Postnational Membership in Europe*, Chicago: The University of Chicago.

Stalin, J.V. (1954) 'Marxism and the national question' in J.V. Stalin, *Works*, Moscow: Foreign Languages Publishing House.

State Council, Western Region Development Office (2001a) *The Circular of the State Council's General Office on the Distribution of 'Suggestions on the Implementation of Policies and Measures Pertaining to the Development of the Western Regions'*, 29 September, www.chinawest.gov.cn/english/asp/start.asp?id=c (accessed 25 September 2007).

—— (2001b) *The Circular of the State Council on Policies and Measure Pertaining to the Development of the Western Region*, 1 January, http://english.enorth.com.cn/system/2001/05/30/000002026.shtml (accessed 25 September 2007).

Sun Wanning (2001) 'Discourses of poverty: weakness, potential and provincial identity in Anhui' in J. Fitzgerald (ed.) *Rethinking China's Provinces*, London: Routledge, pp. 153–78.

—— (2002) *Leaving China: Media, Migration, and Translational Imagination*, Lanham: Rowman and Littlefield Publishers.

Sun Yatsen (1932) *San Min Chu I: The Three Principles of the People*, Shanghai: The Commercial Press Limited.

Tan Tianxing (1994) 'Huaqiao huaren yu zhongguo shehui jingji fazhan' (Overseas Chinese and development of China's socialist economy), *Bagui qiaoshi* (Bagui Journal of Overseas Chinese History), 4(24): 29–34.

Tang Zhixiang (2001) 'Guanyu jiaqiang xin shiqi minzu gongzuo de ji ge wenti' (Several issues on strengthening ethnic work in the new era) in Tian L. and Yang C. (eds) *Minzu*

Yanjiu Lun Wenji (Collection of Essays on Nationalities' Research), Beijing: Minzu chubanshe, pp. 1–10.

Tapp, N. (2003) 'Exiles and Reunion: nostalgia among overseas Hmong (Miao)' in C. Stafford (ed.) *Living with Separation in China: Anthropological Accounts*, London: RoutledgeCurzon, pp. 155–75.

Thunø, M. (2001) 'Reaching out and incorporating Chinese overseas: the trans-territorial scope of the PRC by the end of the 20th century', *The China Quarterly*, 168: 910–29.

Tian Qunjian (2004) 'China develops its West: motivation, strategy, and prospect', *Journal of Contemporary China*, 13(41): 611–36.

Tong Shijun (2000) *The Dialectics of Modernisation: Habermas and the Chinese Discourse of Modernisation*, Sydney: Wild Peony Pty Ltd.

Toops, S.W. (2004) 'The demography of Xinjiang' in S.F. Starr (ed.) *Xinjiang: China's Muslim Borderland*, Armonk: M.E. Sharpe, pp. 241–63.

Tu, W.-M. (1991) 'Cultural China: the periphery as the center', *Daedalus*, 120(2): 1–32.

'The United Front is Still the Magic Weapon' (1989) *Issues and Studies,* 25(7): 137–43.

Van Slyke, L.P. (1970) 'The United Front in China', *Journal of Contemporary History*, 5(3): 119–35.

Vertovec, S. and Cohen, R. (1999) 'Introduction' in S. Vertovec and R. Cohen (eds) *Migration, Diasporas and Transnationalism*, Cheltenham and Northampton: An Elgar Reference Collection, pp. xiii–xxviii.

Wakeman, F. (2002) 'Chinese modernity' in D. Sachsenmaier, J. Riedel and S.N. Eisenstadt (eds) *Reflections on Multiple Modernities: European, Chinese and Other Interpretations*, Leiden: Brill, pp. 153–64.

Wang, L. and Long, J. (2009) 'Overseas Chinese urged to "spread the truth about Xinjiang riot"', *China Daily*, 15 July, www.chinadaily.com.cn/china/2009xinjiangriot/2009-07/15/content_8428818.htm (accessed 28 August 2009).

Wang Chun (1980) *Chinese Communist United Front and Economic Plunder of Overseas Chinese*, Taipei: World Anti-Communist League.

Wang Gongan (ed.) (1999) *Huaqiao Huaren yu Guogong Guanxi* (Overseas Chinese and their Relations with the State), Wuhan: Wuhan chubanshe.

Wang Gungwu (1989) 'Patterns of Chinese migration in historical perspective' in R.J. May and W.J. O'Malley (eds) *Observing Change in Asia: Essays in Honour of J.A. Mackie*, Nathurst, NSW: Crawford House Press, pp. 33–48.

—— (1991a) *The Chineseness of China: Selected Essays*, Hong Kong: Oxford University Press.

—— (1991b) *China and the Chinese Overseas: Selected Essays*, Singapore: Times Academic Press.

—— (2000) *The Chinese Overseas: From Earthbound China to the Quest for Autonomy*, Cambridge, MA: Harvard University Press.

Wang Hongman (2000) *Xin Zhongguo Minzu Zhengce Gailun* (Introduction to New China's Policy towards Minority Nationalities), Beijing: Zhongyang minzu daxue chubanshe.

Wang Hui (2003) 'Contemporary Chinese thought and the question of modernity' in T. Huters (ed.) *China's New Order*, Cambridge, MA: Harvard University Press, pp. 141–87.

Wang Lei (1983) 'The definition of "nation" and the formation of the Han nationality', *Social Sciences in China*, 2: 167–88.

Wang Lian (no date) 'Xibu shaoshu minzu diqü yimin yu guowai qiaowu gongzuo yanjiu: yi Xinjiang wei lie' (Research on migrants from the western ethnic minority regions and the overseas Chinese work: Xinjiang as an example), www.sis.pku.edu.cn/wanglian/yj/hrhq/xjqw/xjqw.htm (accessed 27 September 2007).

Wang Tiezhi (2001) 'Shehui zhuyi jianshe xinshi minzu gangling he zhengce' (Ethnic necessities and policies in the new period of socialist construction), *Minzu Wenti Yanjiu* (Ethnic Issues Research), 1: 4–13.

Wei Xiaoan (2001) *Muji Zhongguo Lüyou* (Witnessing China's Tourism), Shijiazhuang: Hebei Jiaoyu Chubanshe.

Wilk, R. (1995a) 'Learning to be local in Belize: global systems of common difference' in D. Miller (ed.) *Worlds Apart: Modernity through the Prism of the Local*, London: Routledge, pp. 110–33.

—— (1995b) 'The local and the global in the political economy of beauty: from Miss Belize to Miss World', *Review of International Political Economy*, 2(1): 117–34.

Woodside, A. (1998) 'Territorial order and collective-identity tensions in confucian Asia: China, Vietnam, Korea (Early Modernities)', *Daedalus*, 127(3): 191(30).

—— (2007) 'The Centre and the borderlands in Chinese political theory' in D. Larry (ed.) *The Chinese State at the Borders*, Vancouver: University of British Columbia Press, pp. 11–28.

Wu, D.Y. (1991) 'The construction of Chinese and non-Chinese identities', *Daedalus*, 120 (2): 159–79.

Wu Hongqin (1996) 'Haiwai huaren de minzu rentong yu guojia guannian bianxi' (The concept of state and analysis of overseas Chinese national and self-identity), *Huaqiao Huaren Lishi Yanjiu* (Overseas Chinese History Studies), 1: 1–6.

Wu Kaijun (2003) 'Gaige kaifang yilai yinjin haiwai huaqiao huaren ziyuan de fenxi' (Analysis of the work to attract overseas Chinese resources since the start of the reform), *Qiaowu Gongzuo Yanjiu* (Overseas Chinese Work Research), 2: 18–20.

Wu Qianjin (2000) 'Huaqiao huaren huazu wenti zai zhongguo dui wai guanxi zhong de chijiu xing' (The persistent character of the overseas Chinese question in China's foreign relations), *Guoji Guancha* (International Observer), 5: 25–28.

Wu Shimin (2006) 'Renzhen guanche luoshi zhongyang jingji gongzuo huiyi jingshen jiakui minzu diqu jingji fazhan' (Earnest implementation of the spirit of the central conference on economic work will accelerate economic development of minority regions) in Z. Ge (ed.) *Zhongguo Shaoshu Minzu Diqu Fazhan Baogao* (The Report on China Minority Areas' Development 2005), Beijing: Minzu chubanshe, pp. 1–13.

Wu Xiaohua (2003) 'Lun minzu yu zuqun de jieding' (The definitions of *minzu* and *zuqun* concepts)'. *Guangxi Minzu Yanjiu* (Ethnic Research in Guangxi), 1: 12–16.

Wu Zhong (2009) 'China's birthday movie has many seeing red', *Asia Times Online*, 26 August 2009, www.atimes.com/atimes/China/KH26Ad01.html (accessed 3 September 2009).

Xiang Biao (2003) 'Emigration from China: a sending country perspective', *International Migration*, 41(3): 21–48.

Xiang Dayou (1993) 'Shilun shaoshu minzu huaqiao huaren wenti: xianzhuang yu lishi de fenxi' (The discussion of the issue of ethnic minorities overseas Chinese: current situation and historical analysis), *Bagui qiaoshi* (Bagui Journal of the Overseas Chinese History), 3: 1–8.

Xiong Jingmin (2002) 'Xibu kaifa de wenhua ziyuan yu fazhan moshi' (Cultural sources of the Western Development Project and developmental model), *Dushu*, 3: 127–30.

Xu Zhaoling (1996) 'Zhonghua wenhua de chuanbo yu haiwai huaren' (Overseas Chinese and transmittion of Chinese culture), *Dongnanya Yanjiu* (South-East Asian Research), 1: 24–27.

Yan Hairong (2003) 'Neoliberal governmentality and neohumanism: or ganising suzhi/ value flow through labor recruitment', *Cultural Anthropology*, 18(4): 493–523.
Yang Changru (1996) 'Xian jieduan zhongguo minzu wenti xianshi' (A brief introduction into China's ethnic question of the contemporary period), *Guizhou Minzu Yanjiu* (Guizhou Ethnic Research), 7: 97–101.
Yang Faren and Yang Li (2004) *Xibu Dakaifa yu Minzu Wenti* (The Western Development Project and the Minority Question), Beijing: People's Press.
Yang Houdi (ed.) (2001) *Zhongguo de Minzu Xiang* (China's Ethnic Villages), Beijing: Minzu chubanshe.
Yang Jingchu (1989) 'Zhongguo xiandaihua jianshe zhong hanzu he shaoshu minzu guanxi de ji ge wenti' (Several questions in the Han-minority relations in China's modernisation construction), *Minzu yanjiu* (Ethnic Research), 5: 17–24.
Yang Qingyu (2004) 'Yunnan shaoshu minzu xiandaihua fazhan de teshu xing' (On the peculiarities of the process of modernization of the minority nationalities in Yunnan), *Yunnan Minzu Daxue Xuebao* (Journal of Yunnan Nationalities University), 21(5): 100–103.
Yashin, M. (2000) 'Introducing step mothertongue' in M. Yashin (ed.) *Step-Mothertongue: from Nationalism to Multiculturalism: Literatures of Cyprus, Greece and Turkey*, London: Midlesex University Press, pp. 1–21.
Yehua, D.W. (2000) *Regional Development in China: States, Globalization and Inequality*, London: Routledge.
Yen, C.-H. (1976) *The 1911 Revolution and the overseas Chinese with Special Reference to Singapore and Malaya*, Kuala Lumpur: Oxford University Press.
—— (1981) 'Ch'ing changing images of the overseas Chinese (1644–1912)', *Modern Asian Studies*, 15:2: 261–85.
Yu Xingzhong (2004) 'From State Leadership to state Responsibility: Comments on the New PRC Law on Regional Autonomy of Ethnic Minorities', Working Paper, Chinese University of Hong, http://www .cuhk.edu.hk/gpa/xzyu/work1.htm (accessed 25 September 2007).
Yuan Jingxia (2002) 'Xianyi xibu dakaifa zhong de minzu wenti' (National question in the Western Development), *Qinghai minzu yanjiu* (Ethnic Research in Qinghai), 13(3): 21–23.
Yuan Yan (2002) 'Shaoshu minzu te kun qingkuang wenjuan diaocha fensi baogao' (The report of the survey analysis of the situation with extreme poverty among ethnic minorities) in Z. Ge (ed.) *Zhongguo Shaoshu Minzu Diqu Fazhan Baogao* (The Report on China Minority Areas' Development 2005), Beijing: Minzu chubanshe, pp. 22–30.
Zarrow, P. (1994) 'Review essay: nationalism and alienation in modern China', *Bulletin of Concerned Asian Scholars*, 26(1–2), January–June: 93–110.
Zeng Peiyang (2003) 'Report on the implementation of the 2002 plan for national economic and social development and on the 2003 draft plan for national economic and social development', *Xinhua News Agency*, 20 March, http://news.xinhuanet.com/english/2003-03/20/content_789895.htm (accessed 25 September 2007).
Zeng Yuming (1993) 'Gaige kaifang yu minzu diqu de xiandaihua'(Reforms and modernisation of the minority regions), *Z hongnan Minzu Xueyuan Xxuebao* (Journal of South-Central Minorities Institute: Philosophy Edition), 3(1–5): 48–52.
Zeng Yunhua (2008) 'Huaqiaohuaren yu Zhongguo de haiwai liyu' (Overseas Chinese and China's interests abroad), *Bagui Qiaokan* (Overseas Chinese Journal of Bagui), 4: 43–47.
Zhang Chonggen, Na Ren Aoerqi and Sun Zhaowen (1996) *Zhonguo Minzu Gongzuo Fang Tanlu* (Dialogues on Minority Work), Beijing: Jingguan jiaoyu chubanshe.

Zhang Haiyang (2001) 'Zhongguo de xibu kaifa yu gaige shenhua' (China's Western Development and deepeining of the reforms) in Zhao Shiling (ed.)*Yazhou Baogao* (Asia Report), Changchun: Changchun chubanshe, pp. 252–65.

Zhang Jianxin (2000) 'Xibu dakaifa yu minzu fazhan' (Western Development Project and ethnic development), *Minzu yanjiu (Ethnic Research)*, 5: 8–11.

Zhang Weiwei (1996) *Ideology and Economic Reform under Deng Xiaoping: 1978–1993*, London: Kegan Paul International.

—— (2005) 'Overseas Chinese and the concept of "Greater China"', *Refugee Survey Quarterly*, 24(4): 65–73.

Zhang Xisheng (2001) 'Shilun xibu kaifa guocheng zhong shaoshu minzu quanyi de baozhang wenti' (Protection of ethnic minorities' rights and interests in Western Development), *Miznu wenti yanjiu* (Ethnic Issues Research), 4: 7–10.

Zhang Xudong (2002) (ed.) *Whither China? Intellectual Politics in Contemporary China*, Durham, NC: Duke University Press.

Zhang Xuehui and Jiang Zuodong (1997) 'Huaqiao huaren zai zhongwai guanxi zhong de gongzuo zai ti yanjiu' (Analysis of the role of the overseas Chinese in Chinese foreign relations), *Bagui Qiao Shi* (Bagui Journal of Overseas Chinese History), 2(34): 18–22.

Zhang Zhizuo (2003) 'Cong chuantong de zhongguo xibei minzu guanxi kan xibei diqu de xiandaihua' (Modernisation of the north-western regions from the perspective of the traditional ethnic relations in China's north-west), *Qinghai Minzu Yanjiu* (Ethnic Research in Qinghai), 14(1): 4–8.

Zhang Zhongliang (2003) *Xiandaihua Xin Lun. Yi Dang de San Dai Lingdao Jiti Shehui Zhuyi Lilun Yanjiu* (New Modernisation Theory: Analysis of the Party Leadership Third Generation's Socialism Theory), Changsha: Hunan Renmin Chubanshe.

Zhao Gang (2006) 'Reinventing China: imperial Qing ideology and the rise of modern Chinese National Identity in the early twentieth century', *Modern China*, 32(3): 3–30.

Zhao Heman (1994) 'Huaqiao huaren jingji yu zhongguo dui wai kaifang' (Overseas Chinese economy and China's opening-up), *Bagui Qiaoshi* (Bagui Journal of Overseas Chinese History), 1 (21): 8–12.

—— (2004) 'Shaoshu minzu huaqiao huaren yanjiu zhong de ruogan wenti'(On important issues in the study of ethnic minorities huaqiao-huaren), *Huaqiao Huaren Lishi Yanjiu* (Overseas Chinese History Studies), 3: 10–22.

Zhao Hongying (2000) 'Jin yi er shi nian lai zhongguo dalu xinyimin ruogan wenti de sikao' (On the new migrants from mainland China over the past two decades), *Huaqiao Huaren Lishi Yanjiu* (Overseas Chinese History Research), 4: 7–16

Zhejiang Province Overseas Chinese Office (2002) 'Jiaru WTO dui qiaowu jingji keji gongzuo de yingxiang' (The impact of China's accession to WTO on economic and technological aspects of the overseas Chinese work), *Qiaowu gongzuo yanjiu* (Overseas Chinese Work Research), 1: 8–9.

Zheng, Yongnian and Sow Keat Tok (2007) '"Harmonious society" and "harmonious world": China's policy discourse under Hu Jingtao', *China Policy Institute Briefing Series* Issue 26, October . www.nottingham.ac.uk/cpi/documents/briefings/briefing-26-harmonious-society-and-harmonious-world.pdf (accessed 20 August 2008).

Zheng Bijian (2006) 'China's peaceful development and Chinese civilized revival', *People's Daily Online*, 10 April, http://english.people.com.cn/200604/10/eng20060410_257308.html (accessed 20 August 2009).

Zheng Yongting (2005) *Rende Xiandaihua Lilun yu Shijian* (Theory and Practice of Humanistic Modernisation), Beijing: Renmin Chubanshe.

Zhou Chuanbin (2004) 'Lun zhongguo tese de minzu gainian' (The characteristics of the Chinese *minzu* concept), *Minzu Wenti Yanjiu* (Ethnic Issues Research), 3: 2–13.

Zhou Enlai (1973) 'Report to the tenth national congress of the Communist Party of China' delivered on August 24 and adopted on August 28, 1973, *The Tenth National Congress Of The Communist Party Of China (Documents)*, Beijing: Foreign languages press, www.etext.org/Politics/MIM/classics/mao/cpc/10cong.html (accessed 28 September 2007).

Zhou Jian (2000) 'Lun xibu dakaifa dui minzu guanxi de yingxiang'(The discussion of the Western Development Project's influence on ethnic relations) in G. Mao and T. Wang (eds) *Xibu Dakaifa yu Woguo Minzu Wenti* (The Western Development Project and Our Country's Ethnic Question), Beijing: Central University for Nationalities Press, pp. 191–201.

Zhou Longe and Long Xiangyang (2002) 'Guanyu "huaqiao huaren yu guoji guanxi" de sikao' (Analysis of the 'overseas Chinese and international relations'), *Xiandai Guoji Guanxi* (Contemporary International Relations), 6: 42–46.

Zhou Lüe (2002) 'Cultural identity of the overseas Chinese in the context of globalisation' in Hao Shiyuan (ed.) *Haiwai Huaren Yanjiu Lunji* (Selected Papers on Overseas Chinese), Beijing: Zhongguo shehui kexue chubanshe, pp. 337–47.

Zhou Ping (2002) 'Wo guo shaoshu minzu diqu kaifa guocheng zhong de ji ge zhengzhi wenti' (Some political issues in the process of developing our country's ethnic areas), *Minzu Wenti Yanjiu* (Ethnic Issues Research), 6: 49–55.

Zhu Huiling (1998) 'Gaige kaifang yilai haiwai huaqiao zai zhongguo da yinjin waizi zhijie touzi huodong zhong diwei yu zuoyong' (The status and role of the overseas Chinese investments in the direct foreign investment activities in mainland China since the start of the reform and opening-up), *Huaqiao Huaren Lishi Yanjiu* (Overseas Chinese History Studies), 4: 14–18.

Zhuang Guotu (1997) 'Dui jin 20 nian lai huaren guoji yimin huodong de sikao' (Analysis of the activities of the Chinese immigrants in the last 20 years), *Huaqiao Huaren Lishi Yanjiu* (Overseas Chinese History Research) 2: 1–6.

—— (2000) '1978 nian yilai zhongguo zhengfu dui huaqiao huaren taidu he zhengce de bianhua' (Post-1978 Chinese government's attitude and policies towards the overseas Chinese), *Nanyang wenti yanjiu* (Southeast Asia Issues Research), 3: 2–13.

—— (2001) *Huaqiao Huaren yu Zhongguo de Guanxi* (Overseas Chinese' Relations with China), Shenzhen: Guangdong gaoji jiayu chubanshe.

—— (2006) 'China's policies towards overseas Chinese'in L. Pan (ed.)*The Encyclopaedia of the Overseas Chinese*, 2nd edn, Singapore: Editions Didier Millet, pp. 98–103.

Zweig, D. (2002) *Internationalizing China: Domestic Interests and Global Linkages*, Ithaca: Cornell University Press.

—— (2006) 'Learning to compete: China's efforts to encourage a "reverse brain drain"' in C. Kuptsch and E.F. Pang (eds) *Competing for Global Talent*, Paris: International Labour Organisation, pp. 187–213.

Index

Bandung Conference 58
borders 3; *see also* boundary agreement with Russia 22
boundary 2, 5–6, 19–20, 34; of the nationstate 8–9; *see also* borders

Chiang Kaishek 30, 32, 35
China Modernisation Report 70–1, 83–6
Chinese empire 19, 21–2, 34; celestial order of 11; *see also Tianxia*
Chinese identity 3, 10, 109, 128–9; and *tiyong* 26
Chinese nation 2, 27, 33, 68, 109, 165; and blood relations 163–4; character of 7–10, 93; ethnic minorities in 94, 106–7; future of 4, 6; membership in 12; and *minzu* 30–1; and modernisation 86–7; overseas Chinese in 106–7, 124; and the people 44; and territoriality 166–7
citizenship 6, 9, 108, 116, 162; and class 11, 67; dual 29, 117, 164–5; flexible 109, 120, 123–4; minority 51; and population quality 79
class 6, 37, 52, 62; and cosmopolitanism 45; and the people 40, 43; and race 41; struggle 39
Confucianism 11, 20, 80; and migration 22–3
Cultural China 3, 164
Cultural Revolution 58–61, 139

Deng Xiaoping 67–8, 140; development strategy 66, 145, 147; on ethnic work 89, 140, 143; on overseas Chinese 100, 102, 105; TV series 127
discourse 4, 7, 13, 89; on ethnic minorities 81, 92, 96–7; hierarchical 106–7; on modernisation 69, 81, 86–7, 97;
non-territorial 27; on overseas Chinese 100–5
domestic cosmopolitanism 15, 41, 45–6, 51–2

ethnic diversity 93–4; and the Chinese nation-state 29–30; during Ming and Qing 19–21; and modernisation 93, 99; and 'structures of common difference' 147; and 'unity in diversity' 159; and Yangtze River Model 77
ethnic internationalism 15, 41, 46–7, 56
ethnic minorities 2–3, 9–10, 34; business 142; the CCP on 35–6; conceptualisation of 18–19; de-politicisation of 95–6; and domestic cosmopolitanism 45–6; during the Republican period 34; in modernisation discourse 81, 94, 99; online discussions on 98–9; overseas 134–6, 162; representations of 88–9, 93, 154–5; status of 161, 164; and tourism 147; in the United Front 39–40, 43, 68; in WDP 152–3
ethnic question 138, 140, 142, 161; rhetoric on 144; and WDP 151–3
ethnic work 16, 48, 140, 141, 143; *see also* nationality work
ethnicity 4, 34, 163, 165; and class 62; during the Qing 22

Fei Xiaotong 152, 165
Foucault 7

globalisation 7–8, 108
Greater China 3, 104

haiwai huaren 11; *see also* overseas Chinese

Index

the Han 29, 31, 141, 161; Chiang Kaishek on 32; in *China Modernisation Report* 78; migration 59, 146–7, 154; and *minzu* 48–50; in modernisation discourse 91, 93, 99; as the national core 38, 96; and overseas Chinese 103–4, 133; in WDP 157
harmonious society 66, 78, 82, 88
Hu Jintao 12, 66, 82; on the Chinese nation 68; on Xinjiang riots 160
huaqiao 24, 55, 117; *see also* overseas Chinese

jus sanguinis 11, 14, 55, 58; and the Nationality Law 29

Liang Qichao 26–7, 28
localisation 16, 109, 139, 158

Mao Zedong 12, 39; on nation-building 36, 50; on overseas Chinese and minority nationalities 40; on the people 44, 53
margins 1; conceptual 3–4, 160; territorial 3–4; *see also* periphery
migration 18, 114, 124, 136; Han 59, 146–7, 154; and Opium Wars 23–4; prejudices against 22
minority identification project 10, 51, 53
minority nationalities 10, 35, 40, 53; *see also* ethnic minorities
minzu 14, 47, 49–50, 167; Fei Xiaotong on 165; nationalist discourses on 30–1; and the people 44–5; and republican flag 32
minzu gongzuo see ethnic work
modernisation 2; Chinese theory of 71–3; Deng Xiaoping on 89; and ethnic minorities 53–3, 73, 91, 94; humanistic 78, 79; international 82–3; and knowledge civilisation 80; and national discourse 88; and nationalism 4–5, 25–6; and nation-making 64, 74, 87; non-revolutionary 66–7, 69; overseas Chinese in 111; and scientific language 85; and Westernisation 65–6
modernity 4, 69; and sovereignty 12; Western visions of 26
multiculturalism 93, 124–5, 129–30; China's 138

nation-state 2, 6–9; and globalisation 108; and national territory 22, 34
national autonomy 36, 51, 59; law 150

national question 34, 43, 48; the CCP on 35, 41, 50–1; and WDP 90
nationalism 4–5; de-territorialised 118, 137; nationalists and communists on 34; Sun Yatsen on 28; and transnationalism 136; types of 6
Nationality Law 29, 40, 116–17, 164
nationality work 53, 54, 139; *see also* ethnic work
New Chinese Migrants 118–19; programmes for 120; the role of 121–2

overseas Chinese 1–3, 8, 10–11, 34, 117; the CCP on 37, 54–5, 57; conceptualisation of 18–19; during the late Qing 23–5; and ethnic internationalism 46–7; FDI 116; and foreign trade 22; law 112, 114; media 27, 127–8; and modern China 27–8; and the Olympics 129; organisations 125–6; and patriotism 101–3, 110; as a political force 104–5, 130–1; remittances 114–15; representations of 81, 88–9, 100–01; students 1–2; in the United Front 39–40, 42, 68; work 16, 42, 108–9, 111, 113

periphery 3; *see also* margins
population quality 78, 79

race 31, 33, 34, 38; and the Chinese nation 47; and class 41; 'yellow' 28, 30
Rebiya Kadeer 162

Second Modernisation Theory 71; and national geo-body 75–6
self-determination 35–6, 43
shaoshu minzu 10, 35, 48–9, 95; *see also* ethnic minorities
sovereignty 2, 11, 58; and modernity 12; territorial 7, and transnational links 29
spiritual civilisation 78–9
Sun Yatsen 27, 28–9, 34, 165; on *minzu* 30–1, 32

Taiwan 105, 119, 122, 131–2
territoriality 4, 9–10, 137; beyond 5–7; and the Chinese nation 166–7; during the Qing Empire 22; and modernisation 87; and overseas Chinese 29
ti-yong 26–7
Tianxia 11; and cosmopolitanism 46
Tibet 1–2, 105, 107; and diaspora 134–5

United Front 12, 14, 35, 37, 39; of modernisation 67–8, 111; and overseas Chinese 39–40, 42, 54–5, 57, 105; and the people 45; as a revolutionary struggle 41–2

Western Development Project 16, 90, 144–5; effects of 148–9; and infrastructure projects 146; and security concerns 147–8; and tourism 147

Xinjiang 59, 149, 160, 162–3

Yangtze River Model 75–6; and national development 77
Yangwu movement 26
Yellow Emperor 28, 30–1, 104, 159

Zheng He 22

A library at your fingertips!

eBooks are electronic versions of printed books. You can store them on your PC/laptop or browse them online.

They have advantages for anyone needing rapid access to a wide variety of published, copyright information.

eBooks can help your research by enabling you to bookmark chapters, annotate text and use instant searches to find specific words or phrases. Several eBook files would fit on even a small laptop or PDA.

NEW: Save money by eSubscribing: cheap, online access to any eBook for as long as you need it.

Annual subscription packages

We now offer special low-cost bulk subscriptions to packages of eBooks in certain subject areas. These are available to libraries or to individuals.

For more information please contact webmaster.ebooks@tandf.co.uk

We're continually developing the eBook concept, so keep up to date by visiting the website.

www.eBookstore.tandf.co.uk